THE MUSIC OF BRUCE SPRINGSTEEN AND THE E STREET BAND

By the same author

NON-FICTION

The Comédie-Française
from Molière to Éric Ruf

Rameau

The Rise and Fall of the
Royal Shakespeare Company

The Company

FICTION

Élodie Duquette

THE MUSIC OF BRUCE SPRINGSTEEN AND THE E STREET BAND

SIMON TROWBRIDGE

ENGLANCE *PRESS*

First published by
Englance Press, Oxford, in 2022

Paperback edition, 2022

ISBN 978-1-7392053-0-0

Copyright © 2022 by Simon Trowbridge

All rights reserved. No part of this book may be reproduced, copied, adapted, displayed, stored, distributed or transmitted in any form.

Frontispiece:
The E Street Band at Wembley Arena, London, 29 May 1981.
Clarence Clemons, Bruce Springsteen, Garry Tallent and Steve Van Zandt.
Photograph by David Corio (Michael Ochs Archives/Getty Images).

To Dinah

So in America when the sun goes down and I sit on the old broken-down river pier watching the long, long skies over New Jersey and sense all that raw land that rolls in one unbelievable huge bulge over to the West Coast, and all that road going, and all the people dreaming in the immensity of it…

        Jack Kerouac, *On the Road*

CONTENTS

Preface		16
One: Growing Up		**20**
1	Some Formative Influences	20
2	Guitars	23
Two: Origins of the E Street Band		**26**
1	Asbury Park	26
2	Steel Mill	28
3	Transition	30
4	'Play Me Something'	33
Three: The Studio on Route 303		**36**
1	Recording Sessions 1972	36
2	Greetings from Asbury Park, New Jersey	38
3	The Greetings Tour	41
Four: A Place Called E Street		**44**
1	Recording Sessions 1973	44
2	The Wild, the Innocent and the E Street Shuffle	45
3	The Wild, the Innocent Tour	50
Five: Last Chance		**54**
1	Recording Sessions 1974-75	54
2	Born to Run	63
3	The Born to Run Tour	67

Six: Trouble in the Heartland — 74

1. Recording Sessions 1977-78 — 74
2. Darkness on the Edge of Town — 78
3. The Darkness Tour — 84

Seven: Come Together — 87

1. Recording Sessions 1979-80 — 87
2. The River — 90
3. The River Tour — 99

Eight: Reasons to Believe — 105

1. Recording Sessions 1982-84 — 105
2. Nebraska — 110
3. Born in the USA — 114
4. The Born in the USA Tour — 120

Nine: Doubts — 126

1. Recording Sessions 1987 — 126
2. Tunnel of Love — 127
3. The 1988 Tours — 130

Ten: Hiatus — 134

1. A New Band — 134
2. Greatest Hits — 135
3. The Ghost of Tom Joad — 136

Eleven: Wait for Me — 139

1. Tracks — 139
2. The Reunion Tour — 140

Twelve: Dream of Life — 144

1. Recording Sessions 2002 — 144
2. The Rising — 145
3. The Rising Tour — 151

Thirteen: Devil's Arcade — 154

1. Devils and Dust and The Seeger Sessions — 154
2. Recording Sessions 2007 — 155
3. Magic — 156

4	The Magic Tour		159
5	Working on a Dream		161
6	Working on a Dream Tour		163

Fourteen: Darkness and Light — 165

1	Wrecking Ball and High Hopes		165
2	The River Redux		170

Fifteen: Ghosts — 172

1	Confessions		172
2	Recording Sessions 2019		172
3	Letter to You		174

Appendices — 179

1	Keys		181
2	Chronology 1942-1985		186
3	Evolution of the E Street Band		192
4	E Street Band Recording History		194
5	E Street Discography		197
6	Official Concert Recordings		203
7	E Street Band Tours		206
8	E Street Band Concerts in Europe		209

Index — 221

THE E STREET BAND

Roy Bittan
Clarence Clemons
Danny Federici
Nils Lofgren
Patti Scialfa
Bruce Springsteen
Garry Tallent
Steve Van Zandt
Max Weinberg

Associate members

Jake Clemons
Charles Giordano
Soozie Tyrell

Former members

Ernest Carter
Suki Lahav
Vini Lopez
David Sancious

The E Street Band at the Joe Louis Arena in Detroit, Michigan, July 1984.
L-R: Clemons, Springsteen, Weinberg, Scialfa, Tallent, Lofgren, Bittan, [Federici out of shot].
Photograph by David Gahr (Getty Images).

PREFACE

I was thirteen years old and sitting beside my father as he drove our old yellow Volvo over the Hammersmith flyover and down into west London. One of the huge roadside advertising hoardings stood out from the rest: movie screen wide, it displayed the cover of the *Born to Run* album and proclaimed 'Finally London is Ready for Bruce Springsteen and the E Street Band'.

'Who the hell is Bruce Springsteen?' my dad asked.

Rock music was meant to be my one area of expertise, but I didn't know. I looked to my right and, between the blur of rushing cars, saw the same slogan glowing in red neon across the front of the Hammersmith Odeon. Whoever Springsteen and the big saxophonist were, they weren't playing Wembley Arena or Earls Court. (Somewhere inside the venue, Springsteen was tearing down as many of the posters as he could find.)

At that time, I loved the Beatles, the Who and Bob Dylan, and liked the Rolling Stones, Led Zeppelin and Pink Floyd. Dylan was an exception, because I was generally indifferent to solo artists. For that reason, I was not particularly interested in David Bowie or Van Morrison. I didn't think any more about Springsteen, and forgot he existed, until, three years later, in the summer of 1978, I was on holiday with my family, staying at a little hotel in the Cumbrian hills. Once a week, between 1972 and 1979, the BBC's classical music channel, Radio 3, gave over a half-hour slot to the music critic and jazz specialist Derek Jewell who called his show *Sounds Interesting*. Jewell reviewed the important new rock and pop releases with the same level of seriousness that his colleagues at the station spoke about classical music. I'd brought a little transistor radio with me so that I could listen to Jewell's programme – I expected him to review Dylan's new album, *Street Legal*. Imagine my frustration when he started to talk about a new release by someone called Bruce Springsteen, with *Street Legal* relegated to a few minutes at the end of the programme. Jewell played 'Racing in the Street', so I pictured the singer as a solo artist sitting at a piano (I didn't immediately make the connection with the Hammersmith billboard).

Cut to Birmingham in December 1980. Birmingham's miles of grey asphalt, concrete underpasses, blackened brick houses and desolate clumps of bare trees, were covered by thick snow, greyish white but turning to orange slush beneath the overhead streetlamps. John Lennon had just been murdered in New York, the most traumatic event of my young life, an event that ended my childhood with a single blow.

The night after Lennon's murder, amid all the programmes about him, one of the television channels, almost certainly BBC2, and possibly during a repeat of an episode of *The Old Grey Whistle Test*, showed the film clip of Springsteen and the E Street Band playing 'Rosalita' in concert. Sitting around a black and white TV set with my college friends in the small kitchen of our flat, that one clip – the exuberance of the music, the energy of the performance and the youthful life-affirming power it contained – provided a brief distraction on such a dark night. Suddenly I knew who Springsteen was.

For weeks, when I thought about John Lennon, Springsteen and the E Street Band performing 'Rosalita' would come into my mind as a kind of antidote. Six months later, on 8 June 1981, I saw Springsteen and the band close out their European tour at the National Exhibition Centre on the outskirts of Birmingham. The things I remember of that show, forty years later, are the way the songs made me feel (I was hearing them for the first time and didn't even know their names), the volume and clarity of the sound, Springsteen's charisma and madcap energy, the colour of Clarence Clemons's suits (red and white, if you're interested), the elegant shape of Springsteen's Telecaster guitar, Miami Steve's hat, the theatricality and yet simplicity of the lighting, the length of the concert (the band came back on for one last encore as spectators were leaving the auditorium), and, most of all, the fact that I was watching a band.

Like most of the great groups, the E Street Band was the product of a particular place and time – the New Jersey Shore during the late 1960s and early 1970s. Asbury Park at that time was a seaside resort that had seen better days. Its buildings, boardwalk and funfair rides were slowly rotting and rusting in the sun and wind, and many of its businesses were closed and boarded up. Pleasant enough during the day when the beach was packed, it was a fairground of cheap pleasures and incipient danger at night. Outside of the holiday season when the boardwalk was bare, it could be a melancholy place, but also poetic in the way coastal towns are when they are empty under grey skies. Its young had to negotiate racial tension and their anxiety over being drafted to Vietnam.

However, this narrow strip of land between the sea and the conservative hinterland of New Jersey offered its own modest version of the freedoms enjoyed on the other side of the country in Los Angeles. Its local music scene, so close and yet so far from the skyline of New York, was a haven for young misfits with guitars who were looking for somewhere to play. The world of Asbury Park left an indelible mark on Springsteen's writing, and its bar band style of music would be the starting point of the E Street Band's journey. The founding members of the E Street Band were bound by the ties of a shared history, and Springsteen remained committed to the band after he had been signed by Columbia as a solo artist. His greatest and most resonant music was written for these musicians and recorded with them.

This book is about the recordings Springsteen made as the leader of the E Street Band and the accompanying tours. I've included for analysis the solo recording *Nebraska* because it formed part of the *Born in the USA* sessions and the songs were recorded by the band if not used, and *Tunnel of Love* because band members contributed to most of the tracks and the band toured the record.

PART I
1949-1972

ONE: GROWING UP

I   SOME FORMATIVE INFLUENCES

Bruce Springsteen was born in Long Branch, New Jersey, in September 1949 and grew up in Freehold, a town in central Jersey some eighteen miles inland from Asbury Park and the Jersey Shore. His father, Douglas, was a factory worker (when he wasn't driving a bus or unemployed) who drank heavily and who suffered, undiagnosed, from severe depression. His mother, Adele, was a loyal, if long-suffering, wife and a dedicated, loving parent. Born in Brooklyn, New York, in 1925, she came from an Italian family. Her father had emigrated to the US from Vico Equense (Naples). Douglas was of Irish descent on his mother's side and Dutch on his father's side. Springsteen is a toponym meaning 'steppingstone'. The first Europeans to colonise the area, in the early 17th century, were from the Netherlands. When the British took control, Freehold was a small settlement surrounded by farmland. Freehold was a place of little significance between the War of Independence – when it was a Loyalist stronghold and the site of the Battle of Monmouth – and Springsteen's birth.

The neighbourhood in which the Springsteens lived, close to the town centre, was typical of small-town America, its straight streets lined by small detached white timber houses, many with porches. As revealed by Springsteen in some of the most powerful pages of his autobiography, *Born to Run*, published in 2016, the dominant person in his life as a young child was his paternal grandmother: she took possessive ownership of the boy and gave him the licence to behave how he wanted, day and night. When Springsteen was born, his parents were living with his grandparents in Randolph Street, beside the Saint Rose of Lima church. When Douglas and Adele moved into their own house around the corner in Institute Street, Springsteen would run away to stay with his grandparents in a house that had become crumbling and sordid. When grandmother died and the boy was returned, it was too late: the father's disconnection with his son was deeply rooted.

Springsteen grew up with his sister Virginia in a working-class community, overwhelmingly Catholic, made forbidding and insular by shared hardships. Young, withdrawn, rebellious Springsteen was instructed, singled out and disciplined by nuns at the neighbourhood's catholic school, Saint Rose of Lima, an experience that provided vivid imagery for many of his early songs. In Freehold, in the 1950s and 60s, you were meant to conform: typically, if you were working-class, you didn't go to university or leave the state (unless you were drafted to Vietnam). Typically, you went from school to work in one of the factories, making rugs, coffee or Scotch tape.

Listening to Springsteen's albums, with his autobiography as a guide, it becomes clear that his own early life experience, psychology and personal obsessions informed the work to a very large degree. In his first albums, Springsteen wrote about the place where he was born and grew up, in the 1950s and 1960s. Working-class life as lived in New York's unfashionable underbelly, a place where rural flatlands, oil refineries and small-town suburbia co-existed and where any straight highway became a metaphor for escape despite the allure, at least in summer, of a coastline of rundown pleasure resorts, with their clubs, funfairs in dusty fields and beaches filled on the weekends with New York girls, provided a backdrop for many of the songs. The young Springsteen realised that his home region was unusual, singular, largely unknown and therefore worth writing about. It provided him with strong visual metaphors and vivid characters, and, in early songs such as 'Spirit in the Night' and 'Fourth of July, Asbury Park', he performed the trick of transforming this mundane world into something strange, romantic and transformative. While rooted in New Jersey, the young Springsteen was also influenced by New York, a place of escape and the subject of 'It's Hard to Be a Saint in the City' and 'New York City Serenade', but he quickly came to portray his local environment – and the wider eastern United States – more realistically. The countryside and reservoir in the sombre, evocative ballad 'The River' are located not far from Freehold, and in the lyrics Springsteen tells the story of his sister and brother-in-law.

Another theme, connected, concerns Springsteen's troubled relationship with his father, a man whose bitterness and anger had become inoperable by the time Springsteen could talk. In writing songs such as 'Independence Day', 'My Father's House' and 'Walk Like a Man', Springsteen seemed to be trying to come to terms with his own experiences. 'It was a real classic little town I grew up in,' Springsteen told *Rolling Stone*'s Fred Schruers in 1981. 'Everything was looked at as a threat, kids were looked at as a nuisance and a threat. And when you're a kid, your parents become fixtures, like a sofa in the living room, and you take for granted what they do.'

They never had enough money. Douglas Springsteen drove a used car that would not go into reverse: his son had to get out and push it. This is funny, sad and a metaphor. The failures of his own life meant that he was scornful of his son's hopes and ambitions. He was introverted, dejected and violent. It is a terrible burden for a child to bear, loving his father but also fearing him. As Springsteen grew up, he saw aspects of his father – introspection, the loner instinct, a tendency for depression – in himself, a realisation that terrified him. Music was his only way out. He knew it, which was perhaps why his need to succeed was so intense.

The influence of childhood and growing up on Springsteen's imagination, was profound. For years, deep into his thirties, he would drive back to the neighbourhood where he grew up. Despite, or perhaps because of, this childhood psychosis, his ties to his home region are unbreakable. I can't think of another contemporary creative artist who examines his upbringing in both his work and public utterances as obsessively as Springsteen: and Springsteen was doing this from a very early age, on the stage between songs and in interviews.

A third major theme is the great political and social issue of Springsteen's adolescence and early manhood – the Vietnam War and its impact on the ordinary people and communities that suffered the consequences of choices made by the political class. Springsteen was eleven when President Kennedy escalated American involvement in the war by sending to Vietnam thousands of military 'advisors' (1961), and fifteen when President Johnson ordered the deployment of combat troops and approved the conscription of thousands of (mostly working-class) men per month (1965). In 1968, he was called before the draft board. Like many others on the bus to Newark, Springsteen was determined to play the hippy, drug-addicted misfit card, but in the end, because he had recently suffered a serious concussion, was given a medical exemption. The Vietnam issue – first the fear of being drafted, then the guilt of having been given a way out while many of his friends were shipped out, and finally the pain of observing how the war had changed those who came back – clouded Springsteen's adolescence. The songs that explore this issue – including 'Shut Out the Light', 'Brothers Under the Bridges' and 'The Wall' – are among Springsteen's finest. Springsteen looks at the war very much from a human perspective, sometimes peripherally ('Galveston Bay'), sometimes metaphorically ('Lost in the Flood'), and the songs are the more haunting and powerful because they avoid grand political statements, overt protest or sloganizing. 'Devil's Arcade', a song connected to a later conflict, the Iraq War, occupies the same territory.

2   GUITARS

Years before Springsteen became a songwriter, he wanted to be a guitar player and singer in a band. Like countless boys of his generation, he heard 'I Want to Hold Your Hand' on the radio and saw the Beatles on the Ed Sullivan Show in 1964 and became Beatles-crazy. He had been a fan of rock and roll since first seeing Elvis on television as a child, but it was the music and style of the Beatles that decided his future. Springsteen would sum up the importance of rock and roll to working-class children in a 1978 *Rolling Stone* interview: 'It reached down into all those homes where there was no music or books or any kind of creative sense, and it infiltrated the whole thing. That's what happened in my house.'

Springsteen managed to save up to buy a dirt-cheap guitar and worked laboriously to learn the basics. Like countless novice players, working their way through guitar manuals, the first piece he learned was the English folk song 'Greensleeves'. A little later, his mother used loan money to help him buy the Kent electric guitar he had seen in a music store in Freehold. 'The first day I can remember looking in the mirror and standing what I was seeing was the day I had a guitar in my hand,' he would later reveal.[1] The first solo he mastered was from 'It's All Over Now' by the Rolling Stones. By the time he was in his mid-teens, in 1965, he had joined a local band called the Castiles, managed by a larger-than-life father-figure called Tex Vineyard. Springsteen's focus was directed single-mindedly on music and not at all on his lessons at Freehold High School, where his hair, clothes and introspection made him an outsider. It seems that being a guitarist in a band brought you no kudos at Freehold High, or perhaps Springsteen kept these two worlds deliberately separate. The Castiles' frontman, George Theiss, was seeing Springsteen's sister Virginia. He asked Springsteen to play lead guitar. Tex and his wife Marion gave local kids a place to hang out and the Castiles practised every afternoon after school in their front room. Tex lived on a factory worker's pay but bought equipment and covered costs. He was patron, fixer, flag-waving enthusiast, manager, roadie and blunt-talking critic rolled into one. The members of the Castiles wore their hair like the early Beatles. They played tirelessly in the Freehold area, performing at events such as weddings and school dances. They grew proficient enough to earn a reputation as one of the best groups of their kind. Springsteen was more ambitious than the others. Even at fifteen, this was the real deal for him. Working a regular job and playing in a local band at the

---

[1] *Newsweek* (27 October 1975).

weekends (the extent of his family's expectations) – this would never be enough. He wanted the band to play Rolling Stones songs and to take a turn at the mike. Theiss, though, was a gifted singer, and the main reason for the gaggle of teenage girls hanging around at Tex's. It became clear to people who were watching closely that Springsteen would surpass him, but Tex told him straight that he couldn't sing. Springsteen admired Theiss a great deal, they were friends, and Springsteen wrote his first songs with Thiess when Tex booked the band brief recording time at a local studio in 1966. They completed the songs – 'Baby I' and 'That's What You Get' – in the back of Tex's Cadillac on the way to the studio. By the time he was seventeen Springsteen was ready to move into the adult music scene. (The importance of Theiss and the Castiles to Springsteen would become clear decades later in 2020 when he released the *Letter to You* album.)

Springsteen was something of a historian of pop music, soaking up everything he heard on the radio and on vinyl. Not only the great music of the Beatles, the Rolling Stones, the Who and Dylan, and the 1950s rock and roll of Elvis, Chuck Berry and Little Richard, but also the working-class anger and defiance of the Animals, the blues, sweet soul music and the pure pop of Roy Orbison, Phil Spector and many others: if a record had a great sound, a sweet groove, if it contained craft, art and passion, then Springsteen remembered it (beauty could be found in even the most disposable chart song of the time). Springsteen found encouragement in songs that spoke directly to his own experiences and aspirations – for instance, the Animals' 1965 hit 'It's My Life', a pre-punk declaration of working-class rage and defiance that was like a clarion call to disaffected but ambitious young men from poor families. He would later borrow from all these influences in the creation of his work with the E Street Band.

While Springsteen was earning a reputation with the Castiles, another young guy from the region, Steve Van Zandt, was matching him as a guitarist. Van Zandt, born in Boston in 1950, was seven when his family moved to Middletown Township, a thirty-minute drive from Freehold. Like Springsteen, Van Zandt had been inspired by the Beatles. He was in a band called the Shadows. Inevitably, Springsteen and Van Zandt crossed paths. The Castiles and the Shadows regularly shared the bill at teen dances. They formed a true and life-long friendship. They had an equal passion for music, exchanging their knowledge and enthusiasms and learning from each other. They did not perform together at this time, but the origin of the E Street Band can be traced to the moment they met.

Springsteen and Van Zandt would regularly travel together by bus to New York, where they saw bands in Greenwich Village. These trips also enabled

Springsteen to escape the stress of family life. Douglas Springsteen had no understanding, and very little tolerance, of the long-haired, guitar-playing adolescent his son had become, suspecting that he was 'queer'. When Springsteen was laid up in bed following a serious motorcycle accident, his father brought in a barber to cut his hair.

By 1968, the Castiles had gone as far as their collective talent could take them. Guitar-led trios were suddenly all the rage, playing heavy rock music. Inspired by Eric Clapton, Jeff Beck and Jimi Hendrix, Springsteen bought a Gibson guitar and formed a trio called Earth with a local bassist and drummer and immediately his stock in New Jersey began to rise. Because new trends in music – and the 'Summer of Love' – were slow to arrive in the Garden State, Springsteen was a pioneer, a one-of-a-kind exponent of progressive music. At the same time, Springsteen had started to write songs in the manner of the singer-songwriters he admired and was playing the occasional acoustic gig in local coffee houses. Earth was good enough to play in New York. A record producer showed an interest in Springsteen, recording a demo of his music on two-track tape and encouraging him to drop out of school – Springsteen had been attending Ocean County College to appease his worried mother and aunts. The record producer suddenly stopped taking Springsteen's calls.

TWO: ORIGINS OF THE E STREET BAND

I   ASBURY PARK

The focal point of adult music-making in central New Jersey was Asbury Park, a rundown seaside resort that was, in the late 1960s, more open and liberal than the conservative, slow-to-change towns of the interior. If Asbury Park wasn't exactly Swinging London or LA, it was a place where a young outsider could feel vindicated and liberated. Teen acts like the Castiles were excluded from playing in the clubs and bars of Asbury Park, so for Springsteen, aged eighteen, this was new turf. Of all the places to play music in Asbury Park, the Upstage Club on Cookman Avenue was the place to be, and it was here that the prototype E Street Band was formed.

The club, run by Tom Potter and his young wife Margaret, lead singer of Margaret and the Distractions, was part coffee shop, part would-be Cavern club. The Upstage occupied two floors above a shoe shop connected by a steep stairwell bathed in neon light. The lower room, the café, was for folkies. The long upper room had a stage and a wall of speakers. Narrow and low-ceilinged, this airless sweatbox was perfect for raw, improvised rock music. The club opened at eight in the evening and the music went on all night. Unknown musicians could book a half-hour slot to play their music. Springsteen, at eighteen, was a confidant lead guitarist who played fast and loud; but his real asset was his compelling presence as a frontman. After years of playing, Springsteen knew how to work an audience. So, when, as an unknown kid at the Upstage Club, he plugged in his guitar and began to play (with a borrowed bassist and drummer), the startled spectators took notice. At the club that night were two musicians who would become Springsteen's life-long colleagues in the E Street Band, the bassist Garry Tallent and the accordion and keyboard player Danny Federici. Tallent may have been the bassist who played with Springsteen that night, for he was one of the house musicians who were paid fifteen dollars a night to support the newcomers. Drummer Vini Lopez had a band in Asbury Park, Speed Limit 25, and fifteen-year-old David Sancious, classical pianist, was also building a reputation at the Upstage Club. Tallent, Federici and Lopez, from the moment they saw Springsteen, knew that he was special, and were eager to play with him. Margaret Potter would later write of the young Springsteen:

> There was something magnetic about him that just drew you to him. He was good-looking, with his long hair and hippie look. But the indescribable part of him – the way he led the musicians on or smiled, or the way the guitar hung on his body – made him special. You just knew that he was different from the rest.[1]

Springsteen the performer was now almost fully formed, but there was something else. He was writing enough songs to mean that any band he was in could move away from being a cover act and, with luck, progress beyond the local scene. Springsteen formed a new band with Lopez, Federici and bass player Vinnie Roslin called Child. Tallent was in high demand and had other commitments. This was the true beginning of the E Street Band, for Child would evolve into Steel Mill and then the Bruce Springsteen Band and finally E Street. Van Zandt had joined Springsteen at the Upstage Club and was making his own way as a musician and bandleader. And so it was that a group of friends found a home at the Upstage Club and created a music scene that, in its small way, would become legendary.

Springsteen and Lopez, who came from Neptune Township, received their draft papers at the same time and took the bus together to the draft board in Newark. Vinnie Roslin was also on the bus. A year or so before, Bart Haynes, Springsteen's former bandmate in the Castiles, had told him that he was going to Vietnam and didn't know where it was. Haynes was killed in action in 1967. Springsteen and Lopez shared the fear of being drafted and then the elation of escape. Van Zandt, when his time came, decided the best tactic was to start a political discussion with the unfortunate draft board officer and talk him into submission. Why are we in Vietnam? What's a Commie? I'll fight them if they invade Jersey but I'm not going halfway across the world to shoot people. The officer crossed him off the list.[2]

---

[1] Quoted in Robert Santelli, *Greetings from E Street: the story of Bruce Springsteen and the E Street Band* (San Francisco: Chronicle Books, 2006), p.11.

[2] See Stevie Van Zandt, *Unrequited Infatuations: Odyssey of a Rock and Roll Consigliere* (London: White Rabbit, 2021), p.37.

When Springsteen arrived home from Newark, his parents asked him where he'd been. Springsteen told them he'd been called to the draft board but they didn't take him, not knowing how his father, who was fond of saying 'I can't wait to the army gets you', would react; but his father said: 'That's good.' Springsteen told the story years later in 1985, during a concert in Los Angeles.

When Lopez and Springsteen started Child together, a shaven-headed Lopez had just spent a spell in jail. His wild nature would be an issue going forward. Danny Federici, quiet and enigmatic, but almost as lawless, came from Flemington in northern New Jersey. Born in 1950, he studied classical accordion as a child. He was a natural musician, a fine ensemble player, whose soulful playing of the B3 organ sneaked into the arrangements like a thief into a dark house. Springsteen called him 'Phantom Dan'.

All these musicians struggled to scrape a living. Lopez and Federici and Federici's wife Flo joined Springsteen in his family's house on South Street in Freehold. Springsteen's parents had moved to California with their youngest daughter in search of a better life. Springsteen tried to be philosophical about this latest family trauma, the breakup of the family, with his younger sister Pamela dragged to California and Virginia, just seventeen and pregnant, deprived of her mother when she needed her most. Springsteen's mother had no choice but to go with his father – Springsteen would later write that his father kept his mother 'hostage'. Springsteen, Lopez and Federici's bohemian lifestyle turned the house into a kind of hippy commune. The neighbours complained to the police and the landlord evicted Springsteen and his friends. They loaded their belongings in the back of a truck and headed down Highway 33 to the promised land of Asbury Park.

2 STEEL MILL

Child had acquired a manager, Carl 'Tinker' West, the owner of a company in Asbury Park that made surfboards. Tinker was tough, true-to-his-word and reasonably well connected. An engineer by training, he had no time for work-shy youths trying to escape real life through music but recognised in Springsteen not only talent but also a genuine work ethic. Springsteen and Lopez took up residence in Tinker's factory on Sunset Avenue in the Wanamassa district of Asbury Park, sleeping on mattresses on the concrete floor in a back room. There was another room in which the band could rehearse. The factory was located in an abandoned industrial estate, so they could rehearse as hard and as long as they liked. Child played in bars and clubs along the Shore. When Springsteen discovered that another group had registered the name Child, he took inspiration from Led Zeppelin and renamed the band Steel Mill. Thanks to Springsteen's compositions and charisma, their following grew. Tinker built the band a decent sound system, and soon they had moved on from the seaside bars and were playing their own concerts in parks and sports halls to thousands of fans. Through Tinker's connections, the band began to play gigs at the University of Richmond in Virginia.

Tinker came from California and in January 1970 he took the band west, by truck and van, to San Francisco in search of a record contract and national fame. It was the first time that the band members had travelled beyond their home area and Virginia. They didn't have the money to fly and couldn't even afford overnight stops at cheap motels. On this, the first of many pan-continental road trips that Springsteen would make in the years ahead, he couldn't even drive and didn't have a licence. When the two vehicles became separated, Tinker, in the big truck with Springsteen, had no choice but to ask him to take turns at the wheel: they were lucky to arrive in California in one piece.

The band played at Bill Graham's Fillmore West, rocking the audience and receiving some good notices, and the promoter expressed an interest in signing them. At the Fillmore, Springsteen met a brilliant guitarist with a unique sound and a sweet singing voice who would later join the E Street Band – Nils Lofgren, whose band Grin was also on the bill. Steel Mill recorded 'He's Guilty (The Judge Song)'[1] and two other songs at Pacific Recording Studio, in San Mateo. Graham's support, though, was half-hearted, and the band returned to New Jersey. Vinnie Roslin departed and Springsteen asked Van Zandt to play bass.

If Steel Mill's style of music was based on the heavy blues of British bands of the time, Springsteen's originality was beginning to come through in the musical lines and in the structure of the songs. In songs like 'Goin' Back to Georgia', 'He's Guilty', 'Sweet Melinda', 'The Wind and the Rain' ('now the wind and the rain slashing at my window pane, seems like you have lied again, by now I guess that it's just the same, and I am left with the wind and the rain') and the thirty-minute long 'Garden State Parkway Blues', Steel Mill's playing style could best be described as intense. They had plenty of raw power but could also change the mood on a dime.

Springsteen's lead guitar playing was ferocious and experimental (he would never play like this again), and Lopez's lack of discipline on the drums was not a problem in this context. In one section of 'Garden State Parkway Blues',

---

[1] Included on the *Chapter and Verse* compilation CD in 2016.

Springsteen played running scales over a plaintive three-note descending progression on the organ. The song sounded partly improvised, but its changes of mood and long instrumental passages were clearly carefully composed by Springsteen.

Crossing the country, and experiencing the light, colours and vast blue skies, the silence and emptiness, of the desert, was life-changing for Springsteen. The trip left him doubting Steel Mill and determined to do better. His band, supreme in New Jersey, had been outclassed by the best of the San Francisco groups. He started to view heavy rock as limiting and unsophisticated. His solution was to close Steel Mill down and to start again. In January 1971, Steel Mill played for the last time at the Upstage Club.

3   TRANSITION

Springsteen re-thought a lot of things. He decided to go it alone without Tinker as manager, despite their close friendship. He concentrated on writing lyrics rather than guitar solos. He decided to merge his acoustic song writing with his writing for the band and to follow his muse. He extended his musical palate, writing for piano and horns as well as organ and guitars. His talent as a songwriter was suddenly revealed.

For a short while, Springsteen and Van Zandt treated the band as a cooperative, giving it the name Dr Zoom and the Sonic Boom. Many of their friends were invited to join, including people who weren't musicians and who sat on stage playing monopoly. This only lasted for a few weeks in May 1971. In his memoirs, Van Zandt wrote that Springsteen was momentarily unsure as to whether he wanted to be the leader. The last days of Steel Mill had been anarchic. Local police chiefs had little tolerance for rock bands or pot-smoking hippies and would send in officers to pull the plug if a band played a minute over curfew. At a concert to raise money to bail Lopez out of jail, at the Clearwater Swim Club in Middletown in September 1970, the police charged the peaceful audience in riot gear and Federici pushed a loudspeaker over on one of the officers. He had to be bailed too. Federici at this time was like an 'older Dennis the Menace,' in Van Zandt's evocative phrase.[1] Between May and July 1971, Springsteen played guitar in the band Van Zandt had formed with

---

[1] Van Zandt, *Unrequited Infatuations*, p.52.

Southside Johnny, the Sundance Blues Band, alongside Van Zandt, Garry Tallent and Sancious. But Van Zandt told him that his talent deserved to be recognised. Springsteen became resolved. He wanted to be part of a genuine band, and not a singer with a backing band, but he had grown tired of the creative arguments and the chaos of band democracy. He decided that from now on he was going to call the shots.

At twenty-one, Springsteen was remarkably single-minded in this regard, and capable of being stubborn when necessary. Hence, the future E Street Band would have one songwriter and one lead singer, even when the band included songwriters as talented as Van Zandt and Lofgren. Van Zandt and Lofgren would support Springsteen selflessly. Springsteen was blessed in this respect.

In July 1971, he formed the Bruce Springsteen Band, with Van Zandt, Sancious, Lopez and Tallent. The E Street Band was now almost complete, if unnamed, augmented by horn players and female backing singers. The band's playing was tighter and more refined than before, since Tallent was a first-rate bass player. Born in Detroit in 1949, Tallent, like Lopez, grew up in Neptune City, one of Asbury Park's neighbouring boroughs. He learned the tuba as a boy, but, in common with Springsteen, Van Zandt and most of his bandmates, it was the music of the Beatles that led him to choose the guitar. Inspired by Paul McCartney's lyrical bass-playing he leaned towards that instrument.

The transition was difficult. The 1960s were over. Race riots had split Asbury Park in two and the music scene was in decline. Tom and Margaret Potter split up and the Upstage Club closed. Springsteen moved into the Potters' empty flat above an abandoned beauty parlour. The band rehearsed in a studio built for them by Tinker in his new factory in Highlands. Springsteen's archive contains Tinker's recordings of the band in rehearsal, but only 'The Ballad of Jesse James' has been released (on *Chapter and Verse* in 2016). Springsteen wrote some good songs for the Bruce Springsteen Band, including 'The Fever', but the band struggled to find an audience. The Steel Mill fans wanted Steel Mill not this, and those Asbury music bars still in business wanted cover bands. Eventually Springsteen found a bar that had no music and few customers and persuaded the owner to let his band play there three nights a week. Here, at the Student Prince on Kingsley Street, they built a small following that kept the band going for a few months. One night, during a wild storm, the wind ripped the door from its hinges and in walked a big man carrying a saxophone case. The saxophonist asked to play ('Nobody was going to say no to him,' Springsteen later said), and afterwards disappeared back into the night.

This, according to the myth, was the first meeting of Springsteen and Clarence Clemons, later humorously mythologised by Springsteen during performances of 'Tenth Avenue Freeze-Out'. In fact, they had met a few nights before when Garry Tallent, who sometimes crossed the racial divide into the West Side of Asbury Park to play bass alongside Clemons in the soul band Little Melvin and the Invaders, had taken Springsteen and Van Zandt to a club where Clemons was playing. Springsteen would later reference Little Melvin and the Invaders in his song 'So Young and in Love'. Clemons was a man of many parts. Born in Virginia in 1942, the grandson of a Baptist minister, he attended Maryland State College on a football scholarship until an injury ended his career as a footballer. Later, he moved to New Jersey and worked in a children's home as a counsellor. In the evenings, he played the saxophone in local bands. For Clemons, the meeting with Springsteen was more than good fortune, it was a matter of fate:

> The band were on stage but staring at me framed in the doorway. And maybe that did make Bruce a little nervous because I just said, 'I want to play with your band' and he said, 'Sure, you do anything you want'. The first song we did was an early version of 'Spirit in the Night'. Bruce and I looked at each other and didn't say anything, we just knew. We knew we were the missing links in each other's lives. He was what I'd been searching for. In one way he was just a scrawny little kid. But he was a visionary. He wanted to follow his dream.[1]

It would be a little while yet before Clemons joined the band.

The band moved to Richmond in Virginia in the hope of breaking out from there but made little progress. Springsteen called things to a halt and returned to Jersey and then decided to try his luck once more in California. For a long time, the band didn't know where he was or whether he was ever coming back.

Springsteen spent time with his parents and sister and looked for an opening with a local band. Nothing came of the trip, so he returned home. A few months before, in November 1971, Tinker had introduced him to a music producer in New York called Mike Appel. Appel had co-written songs for the Wes Farrell Organisation, including the Partridge Family's 1971 hit 'Doesn't Somebody Want to Be Wanted', and had 'discovered' the heavy metal band Sir Lord Baltimore, producing their only album in 1970. Appel told Springsteen to come back after he had written enough songs to fill an album. During his stay in California, Springsteen wrote prolifically. The songs combined exuberant word-play – sometimes too exuberant – with sharply observed storytelling based on his experiences in and around Asbury Park and New York. Springsteen's talent as a lyricist seemed to come suddenly. He had a

---

[1] Clarence Clemons interviewed by Phil Sutcliffe, in *Mojo* (May 1998).

writer's natural talent to observe people and places and to extract from these observations a poetic image that resonated. He was able to absorb the lyrics of Bob Dylan and others and then write in a similar way but in his own voice. The best of the songs had a strangeness that was compelling and distinctive. Some were impossible to interpret. Looking back, in 2020, Springsteen would admit: 'The thing about those songs, every line is insane. And somehow they end up making sense about something. I'm not sure how I did it at the time.'[1]

Appel was astonished by their quality when Springsteen returned to see him in February 1972. He offered him an exclusive deal with his company, Laurel Canyon Productions.

Appel's enthusiasm was genuine, but it came at a price. The contract that Springsteen signed gave Appel's company ownership of his publishing rights, and fifty per cent of the royalties. Appel also wanted Springsteen to sign a separate management contract that would give Laurel Canyon fifty per cent of everything he earned. The lawyer engaged to look at the contracts on Springsteen's behalf, challenged this and the figure was reduced to twenty per cent. The deal wasn't unusual for the time, but it was inequitable and exploitative: it denied the artist control and the balance didn't fall in his favour should any real money ever be made. At the time Springsteen focused on what he believed – rightly – that Appel would achieve for him: a record contract and a shot at the big time.

4   'PLAY ME SOMETHING'

Appel proved his value almost immediately, not because of his standing in the music business, which was minimal, but because of his ability as a salesman. He rang up John Hammond's personal assistant and talked about Springsteen with such passion that the assistant thought it was worth taking a punt. John Hammond, the legendary producer and talent scout for Columbia Records who had signed Bessie Smith, Billie Holiday, Pete Seeger, Aretha Franklin and Bob Dylan, agreed to meet this unknown kid from Jersey.

On 2 May 1972, aged twenty-two, Springsteen walked into Hammond's office in New York with a borrowed acoustic guitar in his hands (he didn't have a case) and all the confidence his talent, his ego, and his long apprenticeship could muster. Hammond was an old-school gentleman in a grey suit. His

[1] Quoted in Lindsay Zoladz, 'Bruce Springsteen is Living in the Moment', in *The New York Times* (19 October 2020).

graciousness must have put Springsteen at ease, particularly after Appel had almost wrecked his chances by bragging about his special talent. The pressure must have been intense. One chance in the inner sanctum; one chance to be on Columbia Records. Asked about the audition a few years later, in 1975, Springsteen said: 'I went into a state of shock as soon as I walked in. I'm shrivelling up and thinking, 'Please, Mike, give me a break. Let me play a damn song'.[1]

Hammond smiled kindly and said, 'Play me something'. Springsteen was confident about 'It's Hard to Be a Saint in the City'; he sensed that there weren't many young songwriters out there who could combine imagery and music with such attitude and style. So, he sang 'It's Hard to Be a Saint in the City', hoping that the very first line would pull Hammond in. Next, he performed 'Growin' Up' and he ended with 'If I Was the Priest'. While the first two songs would be cornerstones of Springsteen's first record, the last, easily their equal, was held back by Springsteen until 2020 when the E Street Band recorded the song for *Letter to You*. It seems that Hammond particularly admired 'If I Was the Priest'. Its synthesis of the mythical and the real and its thread of Catholic imagery was inimitable.

When Springsteen had finished he heard Hammond say the seven words that changed the course of his life: 'You've got to be on Columbia records.' That evening Hammond watched Springsteen play at a basement club in the Village (Gerde's Folk City on MacDougal Street), and a few weeks later he introduced him to Clive Davis, the head of Columbia Records. Hammond couldn't have rated Springsteen more highly – 'I only hear somebody really good every ten years,' he would later reveal, 'and not only was Bruce the best, he was a lot better than Dylan when I first heard him'.[2]

Hammond didn't know anything about Springsteen's long apprenticeship as a rock guitarist and bandleader. Watching him sing 'Saint in the City', 'Growin' Up' and 'If I Was a Priest' that night, he knew that he was a natural in front of an audience, a storyteller as well as a singer, but he thought he was a singer-songwriter who would record a solo folk album. Springsteen had other ideas.

---

[1] *Newsweek* (27 October 1975).
[2] *Newsweek* (27 October 1975).

PART II
1972-1989

THREE: THE STUDIO ON ROUTE 303

1   RECORDING SESSIONS 1972

Springsteen's heart and soul resided in band music. When he played his songs on an acoustic guitar, he tried to suggest all the other instruments. Columbia gave Appel an advance of $25,000 and allowed him to produce the album with his business partner Jimmy Cretecos. Columbia wanted at least half of the songs to be solo recordings. Springsteen reluctantly agreed not to use electric guitars on any of the tracks. Appel had no issue with Columbia's demands because, at this time, having not seen Springsteen play in a band, he shared Hammond's vision. Springsteen reconvened the band and in the late June of 1972 they gathered at 914 Sound Studios in Blauvelt, just over the New Jersey state line in New York state.

914 Sound, founded and run by Brooks Arthur, was chosen because its rates were cheaper than those charged by the major studios in New York; and because Springsteen preferred to work in a small-town environment. The studio was a converted petrol station on route 303. It was new but somewhat basic, with poor acoustics and soundproofing. It had some land where the band could play softball during breaks, and even camp out when they didn't want to drive back to the Jersey Shore. There was a diner next door. Instead of working with a Columbia employee, Appel was happy to engage 914 Sound's resident engineer, the inexperienced Louis Lahav. This broke union rules, so in the end the Columbia employee was paid just to turn up.

Federici had moved to Long Island, and was out of sight, and Van Zandt was ejected from the band at 914 Sound because Columbia enforced, with Appel's agreement, the no electric guitar rule. Perhaps Appel didn't want someone in the band who was Springsteen's friend and equal and who said whatever he wanted to anyone without a filter. It hit Van Zandt hard that Springsteen had failed to intercede on his behalf.[1] He decided to quit music and for two years worked for his uncle's construction company. (He would eventually make his way back via touring the oldies circuit with the Dovells and by, back in Asbury, creating the band Southside Johnny and the Asbury Jukes.) This left Springsteen, Sancious (playing organ and piano), Tallent and Lopez. The band tracks – 'Does This Bus Stop at 82nd Street?', 'Growin' Up', 'It's Hard to Be a Saint in the City', 'For You' and 'Lost in the Flood' – were recorded within two weeks. Springsteen then recorded a number of solo tracks, including the five selected for release – 'Mary Queen of Arkansas', 'The Angel' (with piano accompaniment by Sancious), 'Jazz Musician', 'Arabian Nights' and 'Visitation at Fort Horn'. The album was handed in to Columbia. Clive Davis handed it back. He preferred the band tracks and wanted the balance to be adjusted in their favour. He also wanted a song that could be released as a single. Springsteen responded positively. He returned to his spinet piano in the beauty salon and in quick time composed 'Blinded by the Light' and 'Spirit in the Night' (based on an existing song) and returned to the studio. Tallent and Sancious were not available, so Springsteen played bass and a session musician, Harold Wheeler, was brought in to play the piano on 'Blinded by the Light'. A third song recorded during the late August sessions, 'The Chosen', has never been released.

Springsteen wanted a tenor saxophone on both tracks so invited Clarence Clemons to join him in Blauvelt. Springsteen, embolden by Clive Davis's support, also added electric guitar.

'Jazz Musician', 'Arabian Nights' and 'Visitation at Fort Horn' were dropped in favour of the new tracks. Executives at Columbia were learning just how stubborn Springsteen could be. The marketing department wanted to promote Springsteen as a New York City artist: but Springsteen not only refused, he called his album *Greetings from Asbury Park, New Jersey* and insisted on using a seaside postcard of the town on the cover. To some of the executives, it seemed that Springsteen, perversely, was doing everything he could to wreck his own chances: recording at Blauvelt; refusing to use one of Columbia's experienced engineers; using his own musicians; and, now, promoting himself as a product of unfashionable New Jersey. But Springsteen's instincts would be right in the longer term: the Jersey connection helped to make him distinctive.

Greetings from Asbury Park, New Jersey, was released in January 1973 to mixed reviews and negligible public interest. 'There I was, one night, just a normal guy,' Springsteen like to say when introducing the song 'Growin' Up' in concert. 'And then, there I was, the next night… Goddam, I was still just a

---

[1] See Van Zandt, *Unrequited Infatuations*, p.60.

normal guy.'

2 GREETINGS FROM ASBURY PARK, NEW JERSEY

Recorded at 914 Sound Studios, Blauvelt, New York, between June and October 1972. Produced by Mike Appel, Jimmy Cretecos; recorded by Louis Lahav. Released on 5 January 1973.

The album:

Side One:

Blinded by the Light
Clemons (saxophone, backing vocals); Lopez (drums); Springsteen (vocals, guitars, bass)
Additional musician: Harold Wheeler (piano)

Growin' Up
Lopez (drums); Sancious (piano, organ); Springsteen (vocals, guitars); Tallent (bass)

Mary Queen of Arkansas
Springsteen (vocals, acoustic guitar, harmonica)

Does This Bus Stop at 82nd Street?
Lopez (drums); Sancious (piano, organ); Springsteen (vocals, guitars); Tallent (bass)

Lost in the Flood
Lopez (drums); Sancious (piano, organ); Springsteen (vocals, guitars); Tallent (bass)

Side Two:

The Angel
Sancious (piano); Springsteen (vocals)
Additional musician: Richard Davis (double bass)

For You
Lopez (drums); Sancious (piano, organ); Springsteen (vocals, guitars); Tallent (bass)

Spirit in the Night
Clemons (saxophone, backing vocals); Lopez (drums); Springsteen (vocals, guitars, bass, keyboards)
Additional musician: Harold Wheeler (piano) (uncredited)

It's Hard to Be a Saint in the City
Lopez (drums); Sancious (piano, organ); Springsteen (vocals, guitars); Tallent (bass)

Unreleased outtakes include:
Arabian Nights
Visitation at Fort Horn
Jazz Musician
Lady and the Doctor
Cowboys of the Sea
Two Hearts in True Waltz Time
Street Queen
The Chosen

Springsteen's first album is beguiling if a little overwrought. As we have noted, the lyrics were influenced by Dylan, but are too compelling and original to be considered imitations. Nevertheless, the 'New Dylan' tag that was thrown at Springsteen after the record's release would persuade him to change direction.

Springsteen uses alliteration, similes, and internal rhymes. The rapid-fire wordplay creates a kind of delirium. The imagery is constantly unexpected. The music is similarly difficult to categorise. The presentation – in keeping with the wishes of Columbia – is primarily acoustic, but the music has the flamboyance and energy of bar-band rock and soul. As for the subject matter, Springsteen called the album *Greetings from Asbury Park* for good reasons. Most of the songs are about young counter-culture misfits living on the Jersey Shore, streetwise and droll and living under the shadow of racial tension, police aggression and the Vietnam War. Although little of this is made explicit, it informs the album's finest song, 'Lost in the Flood'.

Springsteen wrote the words first and only set a lyric to music once it was completed. He has written that he wrote the songs for himself not knowing whether they would ever be heard.[1] In the opener, 'Blinded by the Light', the

---

[1] See Bruce Springsteen, *Songs* (London: Virgin Publishing, 1998), p.7.

words tumble and the music swings melodically between E, A, Bmaj7, and C$^\sharp$ minor. 'Growin' Up', with its beautiful wordplay and defiant spirit, is more powerful. The song is in C major. It begins with a distinctive sixteen quaver pattern, in four blocks, F-G-C-G, E-G-C-G, D-G-C-G, E-G-C-G, connecting suspended F, C and G chords. This pattern, played by Sancious on the piano, gives way to a strummed acoustic guitar. When the pattern repeats, it is doubled by the guitar. The melody drops to A minor before the refrain.

'Spirit in the Night', in E minor, progressing through C major and A minor, is a soulful evocation of a wild lakeside party on a humid New Jersey summer night, the singer locked in a dialogue with the saxophone. 'Mary Queen of Arkansas' and 'For You' are tortured love songs, sickly and bitter. The former, a stately and mournful dirge in D (linking G major, B minor and F$^\sharp$ minor), combines an ever-present harmonica with Springsteen's distinctive acoustic guitar playing. The latter, in F, moves through A minor, B$^\flat$ major and C major to D minor. 'Does This Bus Stop at 82nd Street?' (in G, passing through B minor and A minor) and 'It's Hard to Be a Saint in the City' (swinging between F$^\sharp$ minor and its relative key of A major) widen out the album's scope to New York. In the latter, the lightning-quick acoustic guitar strumming incorporates suspended seventh chords. 'The Angel' (in G, with E minor and B minor dominating) is perhaps the album's most enigmatic parable, a slow ballad for voice, piano and double bass, about a doomed road rat easy rider.

'Lost in the Flood', in E minor, oscillates between D major and B minor. An almost mythical account of sin, rage and violence, shot through with religious imagery, the song eludes interpretation, for the young Springsteen's use of ambiguity was one of the aspects of his writing that set him apart from ordinary lyricists. The singer is accompanied by solo piano until halfway through the song when the band kicks in, and rocks hard, a portent of the future. Sancious added organ to his piano and for a few bars the band sounds like The Doors. Tallent's precise basslines help to keep Lopez in time. The sound effect that announces the song, achieved using an amplifier, was the work of Van Zandt, his only contribution to the record.

Greetings from Asbury Park, New Jersey has a special status because it was Springsteen's first record, but the music was poorly produced and recorded by Appel, Cretecos and Lahav, men who were little more than amateurs. Some of the writing is strained, unsurprisingly for a first work. If in 'Blinded by the Light' the wordplay seems gratuitous, the song has a great hook and a memorable refrain. 'Lost in the Flood', 'Growin' Up', 'It's Hard to Be a Saint in the City' and 'Spirit in the Night' are classics of their era.

3   THE GREETINGS TOUR

Springsteen took the new songs on the road in October 1972, a couple of months before the album's release. Sancious was unavailable, so Springsteen called Federici. After their years together in Steel Mill there was a real bond between them, but Federici needed convincing that this new phase would last; while Springsteen hoped that Federici would be easier to manage than before, only to find that he was soon being creative with his expenses (and money was tight). It is unknown whether Van Zandt was asked back.

The band rehearsed at a guitar shop in Point Pleasant on the Shore and began the tour opening for a comedy duo at West Chester College in Pennsylvania. The band often appeared as a support act during the pre-*Born to Run* tours.

Clarence Clemons was now a member. It was a powerful combination: the big black ex-footballer and the skinny white kid. They played off each other naturally. Sancious's piano playing was missed, as was Van Zandt's guitar, but Clemons's sax added soul and grit. Springsteen played the piano himself on several songs, including 'Spirit in the Night'. Played live, the songs rocked and came alive. Also of significance, Springsteen was now playing the Fender Telecaster guitar that would be his trademark instrument for the next forty years. He had found the re-built instrument (wooden Telecaster body, dating from the 1950s, and Esquire neck) in a music shop in Belmar.

Springsteen must have been heartened by some of the reviews of the album, if disappointed by the poor sales. A number of serious critics shared John Hammond's view of Springsteen's significance. In the UK, which had had no first-hand exposure to the singer, the album didn't go unnoticed. The music critic of *The Times*, Richard Williams, had been waiting for this moment since the end of the 1960s:

> Since the beginning of the 1970s, pop music's primary search has been for the current equivalents of those major revolutionaries of the previous decade, the Beatles and Bob Dylan. [...] A 22-year-old American named Bruce Springsteen will, within the next few weeks, be dubbed 'the new Dylan'. If he is unlucky, too much attention will be paid to the influence Dylan has had on his work, and he will be damned for it. I hope, though, that listeners remember the way Dylan 'borrowed' much of his inspiration from the genius of the 1950s, Chuck Berry. [...] The torch is simply being passed on to the next runner. Springsteen is special because he's mastered Dylan's Joycean use of imagery. He spits out his verses with a raging intensity and, further, he makes more considered sense than his predecessor

did. Over an imaginative, hard-edged small band, he sings in a tired, abrasive drawl which sometimes switches to a shout of pure youthful arrogance. His stories are riveting, told through vivid description and freewheeling internal rhymes.[1]

Had Springsteen read this review, it might have gone to his head.

With every show, the band's reputation grew: slow but significant progress was made. Alongside the *Greetings from Asbury Park* numbers, Springsteen was singing some of the songs that he would shortly record for his next album, as well as unreleased favourites such as 'Thundercrack'. One early marker was a six-night, two sets per night, stand at Max's Kansas City in New York at the start of February 1973. The band opened for the comedian and singer-songwriter Biff Rose. Halfway through the stand, Rose agreed that Springsteen should play last. David Bowie came to watch Rose. He had never heard of Springsteen, but stayed for his set. He admired the performance and the songs so much that he recorded his own versions of 'Growin' Up' and 'It's Hard to Be a Saint in the City' (during the *Young Americans* sessions, but unreleased at the time).

In April, Springsteen and the band opened for Jerry Lee Lewis and headliner Chuck Berry at the University of Maryland. It was the promotor's task to provide Berry with a backing band, and Springsteen volunteered to back Berry for free. There was no rehearsal, so Bruce and the band had to play by their wits. In May, they flew to Los Angeles to play a support set at the Ahmanson Theatre during a CBS-organised concert series promoting new artists.[2] Their performance, which included 'Wild Billy's Circus Story' (Federici on accordion; Tallent on tuba) and 'Thundercrack' (Springsteen's electric guitar licks recalling Steel Mill), earned a glowing notice in *Billboard*, one of the best of the early reviews:

> If any one artist captured the essence of what the week was really all about it was Bruce Springsteen. [He] has an appeal that borders on the universal. His songs are interesting, thoughtfully worked out and often exciting. Material aside, he has about him that glow, the elusive X factor that spells star. Comparisons to Van Morrison and Bob Dylan have been made but

---

[1] Richard Williams, 'Pop Record: Springsteen is Special', in *The Times* (14 April 1973).

[2] The performance was filmed. Extracts were released on DVD as part of the *Born to Run* box set (2005). Here we see the mark one E Street Band, Springsteen, Clemons, Federici, Tallent and Lopez.

he is no carbon, rather a glowing and vibrant performer in his own right.[1]

Another reviewer wittily proclaimed: 'Was Bob Dylan the previous Bruce Springsteen?'

In May and June, Springsteen supported Chicago on their arena tour, including two nights at Madison Square Garden in New York, playing to hostile Chicago fans. The experience put Springsteen off arena concerts for years.

Between shows and travelling, Springsteen had started to record his second album. In June, Sancious returned to the band. In July, Springsteen and the band returned to Max's Kansas City, this time as headliners of a six-night stand. The supporting act was Bob Marley and the Wailers. In September, the band took a break to complete the new album. By the end of the month they were back on the road. The *Greetings* tour therefore continued as *The Wild, the Innocent and the E Street Shuffle* tour.

---

[1] *Billboard* (19 May 1973).

FOUR: A PLACE CALLED E STREET

I RECORDING SESSIONS 1973

Recording began in May 1973 at 914 Sound and continued until September. It was less than a year since Springsteen had recorded his first album but he was contracted to deliver an album every six months – something that didn't happen, post-Beatles, to established artists. Springsteen's writing was developing at a pace; he had a new batch of songs that were stylistically different to the *Greetings* songs and was keen to release them so that he could shake off the 'new Dylan' label. This time, he was determined to record a true band album, to allow the songs to expand and to rock, if that was what they needed.

Springsteen had written dozens of songs during the previous year but knew which ones he wanted to include on the album. Some fine songs from his live set, including the curiously named 'Tokyo', weren't even recorded during the sessions. The songs were too long for them all to find a place on the album.

Springsteen laid down basic tracks with the current line-up of the band – Clemons, Federici, Tallent and Lopez – during May and June. Then, from July to September, new tracks were added with Sancious in attendance, his delicately soulful piano, half classical, half jazz, intertwining with Springsteen's acoustic guitar. Lahav's wife, Suki, provided backing vocals (uncredited) on 'Fourth of July, Asbury Park', 'Incident on 57th Street' and the unused tracks 'Santa Ana' and 'Zero and Blind Terry'.

Despite the technical issues with the studio, and some less than perfect playing, this was some of the most beguiling music that the band would ever record. The work was exhausting since it had to be fitted in with the band's touring schedule. Springsteen, though, was less exacting and more relaxed, relatively speaking, in the studio than would be the case in the future. He was happy with the results, as was Appel.

The tapes were handed over to Columbia. Clive Davis was no longer there, and John Hammond's influence was on the wane. Springsteen was called in to see the new A & R man, Charles Koppelman. Koppelman was no mug: he had been a musician before moving into the business side of the industry and his signings included Billy Joel and Janis Ian. Koppelman liked his music to have the professional polish of soft rock. The music on *The Wild, the Innocent and the E Street Shuffle* was perhaps too strange, and a little too rough around the edges, to fit into his vision for Columbia. Koppelman and Springsteen listened to the first side together. Koppelman told Springsteen that the album was unreleasable because the musicianship was sub-standard. He didn't hear the appealing community spirit, the warmth and friendship, contained in the playing, let alone the music's soulfulness and poetry. He wanted Springsteen to recut the tracks with professional studio musicians. Springsteen politely refused. He believed in his band. They were his friends; they understood his music, and they played with their hearts. In that case, Koppelman told Springsteen, the record would not be promoted: it would likely disappear, and Springsteen with it.

2 THE WILD, THE INNOCENT AND THE E STREET SHUFFLE

Recorded at 914 Sound Studios, Blauvelt, New York, between May and September 1973. Produced by Mike Appel, Jimmy Cretecos; recorded by Louis Lahav. Released on 5 November 1973.

The album:

Side One:

The E Street Shuffle
Clemons (saxophone, backing vocals); Federici (organ); Lopez (drums, cornet); Sancious (piano, clavinet, soprano saxophone); Springsteen (vocals, guitars); Tallent (bass, backing vocals)
Additional musician: Albany Tellone (baritone saxophone)

Fourth of July, Asbury Park (Sandy)
Clemons (backing vocals); Federici (accordion); Lopez (drums, backing vocals); Sancious (piano); Springsteen (vocals, guitars, recorder); Tallent (bass, backing vocals)
Additional musician: Suki Lahav (backing vocals)

Kitty's Back in Town
Clemons (saxophone, backing vocals); Federici (organ); Lopez (drums); Sancious (electric piano, organ); Springsteen (vocals, guitars); Tallent (bass, backing vocals)

Wild Billy's Circus Story
Federici (accordion); Lopez (drums); Springsteen (vocals, acoustic guitar, mandolin, harmonica); Tallent (bass, tuba)

Side Two:

Incident on 57th Street
Clemons (backing vocals); Federici (second piano, organ); Lopez (drums, backing vocals); Sancious (piano); Springsteen (vocals, guitar); Tallent (bass, backing vocals)
Additional musician: Suki Lahav (backing vocals)

Rosalita (Come Out Tonight)
Clemons (saxophone, backing vocals); Federici (organ); Lopez (drums, backing vocals); Sancious (piano); Springsteen (vocals, guitars); Tallent (bass, backing vocals)

New York City Serenade
Clemons (saxophone, backing vocals); Federici (organ); Lopez (drums, backing vocals); Sancious (piano, string arrangement); Springsteen (vocals, acoustic guitar); Tallent (bass, backing vocals)
Additional musician: Richard Blackwell (congas)

Released outtakes:

Zero and Blind Terry
Clemons (saxophone, backing vocals); Federici (organ); Lopez (drums, backing vocals); Sancious (piano); Springsteen (vocals, guitars); Tallent (bass, backing vocals)
Additional musician: Suki Lahav (backing vocals)
Release: *Tracks* (1998)

Thundercrack
Clemons (saxophone, backing vocals); Federici (organ); Lopez (drums, backing vocals); Sancious (piano); Springsteen (vocals, guitars); Tallent (bass, backing vocals)
Release: *Tracks* (1998)

Santa Ana
Federici (organ); Lopez (drums, backing vocals); Sancious (piano); Springsteen (vocals, guitars); Tallent (bass, backing vocals)
Additional musician: Suki Lahav (backing vocals)
Release: *Tracks* (1998)

Seaside Bar Song
Clemons (saxophone, backing vocals); Federici (organ); Lopez (drums); Sancious (organ); Springsteen (vocals, guitars); Tallent (bass, backing vocals)
Release: *Tracks* (1998)

Unreleased outtakes include:

The Fever
Clemons (saxophone); Federici (organ); Lopez (drums); Springsteen (vocals, guitar); Tallent (bass)

Evacuation of the West
Clemons (saxophone); Federici (organ); Lopez (drums); Springsteen (vocals, guitar); Tallent (bass)

Phantoms
Clemons (saxophone); Federici (organ); Lopez (drums); Springsteen (vocals, guitar); Tallent (bass)
[Melody re-used for 'Zero and Blind Terry']

Fire on the Wing

New York Song
[Lyrics re-used for 'New York City Serenade']

Secret to the Blues

Angel's Blues

The Wild, the Innocent and the E Street Shuffle represented a departure from Springsteen's debut record. He edited his lyrics to make the writing leaner but no less poetic. Musically, the album's jazzy, soulful vibe would not be repeated by the band on record, since Springsteen would very quickly adopt a harder more rock-orientated approach as he settled on a signature style. Alongside acoustic and electric guitars, bass, saxophone, piano and organ, the scoring included parts for Tallent's tuba, Federici's accordion, a recorder, a mandolin, a clavinet and an electric piano.

The album begins with a burst of brass produced by two saxophones and a cornet (played by Lopez). 'The E Street Shuffle', in C major, progressing to A minor via Fmaj7 and Gmaj7 chords, is built on Springsteen's electric guitar and Sancious's clavinet. Springsteen has written that the shuffle of the title represents the kind of dance that people in the song perform to get through life. The music is Springsteen's take on the soul and blues music that blared out from bars all along the Jersey Shore during the early 1970s. The band swings and the vocal line descends like a French *mélodie*. As in several songs on the album, the subtext is of an Asbury Park suffering from economic depression and racial tension, its pleasure domes mostly closed, and the boardwalk life tinged with sadness.

'Fourth of July, Asbury Park', also in C, descending to A minor, is a kind of farewell to the town and to youth. The musical introduction is exquisite. Two obbligato electric guitars duet either side of a strummed acoustic. It has a gentle, relaxed vibe, a melancholy tone, for summer is ending. The accordion conjures the feeling of music played outside on a summer's evening.

'Kitty's Back in Town', in A minor, is not the best song lyrically. The cat metaphor is overdone. The music, combining electric guitar, electric piano and two saxophones, and underpinned by Tallent's superb bassline, swings between suspended and 7th chords (A minor 7, Emaj7sus, D minor, Fmaj6, F$^\sharp$ minor, D major). The song, with its changes of mood and instrumental passages, was designed to be played live. In concert, the band would use 'Kitty' to fuse jazz, rock and Broadway musical elements and then deconstruct them by introducing chromatic scales and dissonances.

Side one concludes with the evocative vignette 'Wild Billy's Circus Story', a song inspired by Springsteen's childhood memory of the annual circus that pitched its tents on the fields outside Freehold. The song captures the allure and mystery of the travelling performer, of an illicit world of illusion and freakery. The circus becomes a metaphor for both freedom and creativity. The song's particular atmosphere is created by an acoustic guitar, mandolin, accordion, tuba and recorder, playing in G major.

Side two begins with 'Incident on 57th Street', a New York-set romance that occupies some of the same territory as *West Side Story*. Unlike the musical, though, Springsteen's song makes effective use of strangeness and ambiguity and takes place during a single summer night. It was Springsteen's most advanced story song up until this point and a good early example of his ability to grip the attention of the listener from the very first line (the first line of 'Incident' is superb) and to create a compelling world in only a few verses. The structure of the song allows for the changes of mood demanded by the narrative, although this is achieved musically within a straight-forward three-chord progression, B♭, E♭ (or E♭maj7) and F. An F major suspended chord is utilised at key moments. The song is a transitional work for in its complex yet lyrical piano part, played by Sancious, the music connects to the songs that Springsteen would write in the coming months for *Born to Run* (indeed, there is a close connection between 'Incident' and 'Jungleland'). Behind the piano's opening theme (which actually combines two intertwining piano parts, the second played by Federici), a rising scale on the organ, played softly by Federici, sets up a second theme, played by Springsteen on the eclectic guitar, which begins to wail at the moment the drums and bass crash in. The musical thinking here, as throughout the song, is highly sophisticated. Crafting a musical introduction that has its own musical line but which leads naturally and logically to the main melody is one of the hardest things for a pop songwriter (untrained in music theory) to do, and many of the greats don't even try. Halfway through the song, the music falls away to leave Tallent's bass and Lopez's deft touches on the cymbals, and then builds up again. In the coda, a long guitar solo drifts away to leave only the piano, playing a gentle theme that quietly reaches F major to segue into the next song, 'Rosalita (Come Out Tonight)'.

The semi-autobiographical 'Rosalita', in F, uses E Street's standard combination of drums, bass, electric guitar, organ, piano and sax, and flows on a foundation of rapidly changing chords, F, B♭, C, A minor, D minor, G minor, Cmaj11, Csus4, and E♭. The singer tries to persuade a girl to defy her parents. The parents see a long-haired small-town punk with limited prospects; but the singer brags to his girl that he is on the brink of rock and roll stardom. The Latin-flavoured music punches hard, and the song's humorous tone is undercut by the singer's desperate need for both the girl and success. 'Rosalita' would work brilliantly in concert. Springsteen used the song as the main set's closing number for many years.

We are back in New York for the album's long closing song, 'New York City Serenade', a dreamlike portrait of the nocturnal city (midnight in Manhattan). David Sancious made his most important contribution to the album, fusing classical and jazz elements in the piano part and arranging the strings (note the use of pizzicato). Springsteen's acoustic guitar combines with the piano. The song is in A major. The melody travels through F♯ minor, B minor, Asus4, A and D. In this moody, impressionistic song, Springsteen makes use of the street vernacular of New York and New Jersey. The poetic lyrics are fragmented and ambiguous. The real and surreal are interwoven. By the time Clemons's sax enters, the harmonies have become richly layered. As the music starts to fade, a new theme, soft and wistful, is played on the piano, rising by fourths, E-A-D and then falling C♯-B-A (in simple chordal terms, Asus4 resolving to A). It is taken up by Springsteen's voice. At the same time, the strings climb the scale. The combining of themes is one reason for the song's significance. Springsteen, at twenty-three, showed extraordinary ambition in composing what can be described as a tone-poem.

3   THE WILD, THE INNOCENT TOUR

Touring resumed at the end of September 1973, a month before the album's release. The band travelled in a van with their equipment following in a truck. They stayed in cheap motels or, when the distances weren't too great, travelled from home. They were making no real money. Springsteen and the band, though, were now playing far fewer shows as a supporting act, especially in the East. On 6 November, following the release of the album, the band returned to Max's Kansas City in New York as headliners of a five-night (two sets per night) stand. Later in the month, they played the Roxy in Philadelphia. A show at the Nassau Community College in Garden City, NY, on 15 December, was filmed. Extracts were included in the *Wings for Wheels* documentary (*Born to Run 30th Anniversary Edition* box set, 2005). The year ended with eight shows at the Main Point Coffeehouse in Bryn Mawr, Pennsylvania.

Before a show at Muther's Music Emporium in Nashville in January 1974, during, but not part of, a Columbia convention in the city, Appel sent leaflets to all of the delegates, inviting them to attend. No-one showed up, but this may have been due to commitments at the convention rather than disdain for Springsteen. Springsteen's relationship with his label was close to rock bottom. As Koppelman had indicated would be the case, *The Wild, the Innocent and the E Street Shuffle* had been released without a sales campaign. Springsteen had started to introduce songs by saying, 'Here's a song off our second album which you can't find anywhere in town'.

Columbia was underestimating the buzz being generated by Springsteen's live performances. During the almost continuous touring since 1972, Springsteen had honed his performing skills. He was now, if the size of the stage allowed, making the shows as physical as possible: he ran about the stage, jumped onto the piano, and interacted with the audience. Girls had started to invade the stage. Performances were intense, manic but also playful. Springsteen, though, had the stagecraft to provide plenty of contrasts. During the slower more reflective songs, he would stand stock-still at the centre of the stage. He wanted the spectators to go crazy, but also, when he asked, to listen in complete silence. And, as a support act, it wasn't in Springsteen's nature to under-perform so that he wouldn't overshadow the headliner. The band gave one hundred per cent every time. Word was getting around that letting Springsteen open could be the kiss of death.

Springsteen had started to talk more during the shows. He contextualised some of the songs by telling long stories, often autobiographical but making some of the details deliberately surreal. The stories were vividly told in the vernacular of a working-class guy from New Jersey, as if Springsteen was talking to the band or a bunch of his friends on the beach or in a bar; and they were integrated into the music with a real sense of the dramatic. During performances, Springsteen could seem a little crazed, and unpredictable, his mood changeable, depending on how things had gone that day or how the spectators were responding. This added to his appeal. As did the fact that he was the frontman of a band, and not a solo artist with backing musicians. Springsteen would play off the others, talk about them to the audience, making sure that they were viewed as a gang, a community. Followers of Springsteen soon came to know the members of his band, although they may have thought Springsteen was exaggerating when, during 'Thundercrack', he introduced Lopez as 'Mad Dog'.

On 12 February, before the band took to the stage at the University of Kentucky, an argument between Lopez and Steve Appel, the band's road manager (and Mike Appel's brother), had turned violent. The band's patience with Lopez's violent temper had been exhausted for some time. One night, Lopez made the mistake of provoking Clarence Clemons: 'It's him or me,' a bruised and humiliated Lopez told Springsteen. The fight with Steve Appel was the last straw. Only Springsteen's sense of loyalty – they had been together since the days of Child in 1969 – had kept him in the band this long. The parting was traumatic but necessary. The rest of the band had outgrown Lopez's level of musicianship. Lopez, for all his flair and passion, didn't have the technical discipline to play in a more rigid style let alone to be adaptable. Federici was, in his own way, just as troubling and demanding to Springsteen, who, as bandleader, was forced into a position where he had to play the role of the responsible one; but unlike Lopez, he was not going to be left behind musically. Lopez, though, believed he was fired because he had accused Appel of cheating the band over money. 'There was nothing I could do except ask for a second chance,' he said later. 'Which I did. But I didn't get it.'[1] A friend of David

---

[1] Vini Lopez interviewed by Robert Santelli, in Charles R. Cross, *Backstreets: Springsteen, the Man and His Music* (London: Sidgwick and Jackson, 1989), p.100.

Sancious, Ernest 'Boom' Carter, was brought in at short notice. Springsteen wanted to cancel a gig at the Satellite Lounge, in Cookson, a bar used by soldiers from Fort Dix, to give Carter time to learn the songs, but the owner told Appel he'd send someone to break everyone's fingers if they didn't play. Such was one of the hazards of playing clubs in the Mafia's backyard.

Carter quickly fitted into the band. In March, they played in Texas for the first time, headlining a four-night, eight concert, stand at the Liberty Hall in Houston. A review of the first night in the *Houston Chronicle*, concentrating on the overall power of the performance rather than the songs (the album isn't mentioned), is typical of the notices Springsteen and the band were receiving:

> Bruce Springsteen is at Liberty Hall this weekend and he has brought with him a celebration of life so intense and vivid that only the most hardened cynic could avoid becoming involved. [He] plays the kind of music that makes you want to dance. It has its roots deep in songs such as 'Walking the Dog' [by Rufus Thomas], which Springsteen sandwiches between his own bittersweet ballads of life in the city. Springsteen's band consists of six pieces, focusing around Springsteen on guitar, Clarence Clemons on sax and Garry Tallent on bass. This is the mainspring that makes the rock machine move. Tallent's bass patterns, of unbelievable force and simplicity, create easily recognisable moods with the fewest notes possible.[1]

During their week in Houston, the band performed a full set for local radio in the studio of KLOL-FM.

A hit in Houston, the band moved on to Dallas, where they played to less than seventy people per show. Overall, the Texan leg of the tour was a success and the band headed home in good spirits. In the van on the long journey east, they started to talk about naming the band. Names were bandied back and forth, but nothing stuck until they pulled up outside the house in Belmar where Sancious was living – on E Street. By the time the band opened for Bonnie Raitt at the Harvard Square Theatre in Cambridge, Massachusetts, a few weeks later, on 9 May, the name was being used officially. The second of the two shows on 9 May was attended by the critic and record producer Jon Landau, whose rave review, in *The Real Paper*, included the phrase 'I saw rock and roll future and its name is Bruce Springsteen'.[2] This well-meaning phrase would generate both good and bad publicity, depending on how it was used. Springsteen knew that Landau was in the audience and premiered a few of his

---

[1] John W. Wilson, 'Springsteen', in the *Houston Chronicle* (March 1974).
[2] Jon Landau, in *The Real Paper* (22 May 1974).

new songs, including 'Born to Run'. Landau had introduced himself to Springsteen between the band's early and late shows at Charlie's Place in Cambridge on 10 April, when he saw Springsteen reading his review of *The Wild, the Innocent and the E Street Shuffle*, displayed beside the club's entrance.

In early June, the band's gig at the Agora in Cleveland was broadcast by the local radio station. This show included the last performance of a lost song from the period, 'Tokyo'. Springsteen was about to side-line the accordion, the tuba, and the mercurial nature of songs like 'Tokyo'. The tour continued, but several shows were cancelled during the summer so that Springsteen could return to the studio to begin to record his third album.

In July, Springsteen hired a new lighting designer, Marc Brickman. Brickman (born 1953) was just out of his teens in 1974 and a real find. He had served an apprenticeship in theatre, ballet and opera in Philadelphia. He turned up before one of Springsteen's shows and asked Appel if he could help with the lighting. Appel and Springsteen were amazed by what he could do and hired him full-time. His designs were theatrical and beautiful, but they always served the songs. Brickman had the gift of interpreting Springsteen's music and lyrics in light and colour, subtly changing the mood as required. When Springsteen started the show with 'New York City Serenade', Brickman would use a single vertical white spotlight, so that the singer was enclosed in a narrow column of light and surrounded by darkness. Only when the other musicians started to sing or play would they be illuminated. With Brickman's lighting, the final element was in place. Springsteen now had a show that was as stylish as it was visceral.

Brickman's outstanding work for Springsteen would make his name, leading to collaborations with Pink Floyd and Paul McCartney, but he would remain, first and foremost, Springsteen's lighting designer until 1984, when, for an undocumented reason, he was let go.

FIVE: LAST CHANCE

I RECORDING SESSIONS 1974-75

Springsteen began rehearsing and recording his new songs in May 1974, during gaps in the band's touring schedule. This first phase of recording continued until October. Given that *The Wild, the Innocent and the E Street Shuffle* had not made his name nationally, Springsteen was essentially starting from zero as a recording artist. His contract with Columbia was for three albums, so the label couldn't drop him before the new album was delivered but it could drop him then. The record needed to be released as quickly as possible and it needed to be the kind of work that Columbia would back and promote. As before, to save money, Mike Appel booked 914 Sound Studios in Blauvelt and the engineer Louis Lahav. Despite the limitations of the studio (the piano would not stay in tune), Springsteen still preferred to work in Blauvelt rather than in New York. Springsteen produced the recordings with Appel.

Most of the *Born to Run* album would be recorded at the Record Plant in 1975, but the album's iconic title track was recorded at 914 Sound. Early versions of 'Jungleland' and 'Backstreets' were also recorded, but they didn't satisfy Springsteen. The lyrics of the latter would change significantly. Having asked Lahav's young wife Suki to sing backing vocals on some of the songs on the previous album, Springsteen now decided to use her talent as a classical violinist. 'Jungleland', in its final form, would be recorded in 1975, but from the 914 Sound versions Springsteen decided to retain some of Suki Lahav's violin part if not her falsetto vocal part, sung over Bittan's piano during the coda. In a studio outtake, Springsteen and Lahav can be heard discussing this ending before rehearsing it with Bittan. Lahav also sang and played the violin on some takes of 'Born to Run' and can be seen in the footage of the band recording the song at 914 Sound included in the *Wings for Wheels* documentary.

The recording of the title track occupied most of the sessions in Blauvelt, from May to October. It is arguably the best arranged and produced track on the album, the layers of sound satisfyingly punchy and remarkably clear given that Springsteen, seeking his own version of Phil Spector's 'wall of sound', recorded seventy-two tracks ('overkill' he would later admit). Without knowing how, Springsteen had achieved the aural atmosphere he wanted for his new material. 'Born to Run' was the last song to be recorded by the original line-up of the band, minus the recently sacked Vini Lopez.

The transition from the soul-infused, semi-acoustic and eclectic arrangements of *The Wild, the Innocent and the E Street Shuffle* to the electric rock sound of *Born to Run*, from experimentation to the mid-era E Street Band sound of glittering piano, glockenspiel and sax, was relatively short and seamless, and must have owed something to the arrival of pianist Roy Bittan, replacing David Sancious, and drummer Max Weinberg. Springsteen was upset by Sancious's sudden decision to leave, mid-tour and mid-album, that August (taking Carter with him) – Sancious had been offered his own record deal by Columbia; but not for long, such was Bittan's superb musicianship and affinity to the style of music he was now composing and Weinberg's musicality, rhythmical precision and ability to follow Springsteen's cues. Bittan deepened Springsteen's piano parts by adding arpeggios and countermelodies. So rich was his playing, Springsteen had to ask him to leave space for the guitars.[1] Both Bittan and Weinberg answered the advertisement that Springsteen's management hurriedly placed in the *Village Voice* and joined the band for the closing months of the tour. The advert was cleverly phrased to attract the right musicians – the pianist would need to be capable of playing styles from 'classical to Jerry Lee Lewis' and the drummer should not be a 'junior Ginger Baker' (i.e., a lover of long solos). Springsteen auditioned over sixty musicians – each had a thirty-minute slot to play with the band – but none of the others came close to Bittan and Weinberg.

Weinberg, from Newark, had played in local bands before earning his professional stripes as the drummer in the *Godspell* pit band on Broadway. Bittan, born in New York in 1949, was classically trained and had also played in pit bands on Broadway. The transforming contribution of these two musicians was noted from their very first shows with the band in September 1974. After the flamboyance of Lopez, Weinberg's controlled power transformed the band's rhythm section. Influenced by Ringo Starr's economical playing, he shared Starr's ability to provide exactly what was needed without foregoing flair or personality. Stage right, everyone was expecting the new pianist to be a

---

[1] See Bruce Springsteen, *Born to Run* (London: Simon and Schuster, 2016), p.240.

poor substitute for the admired Sancious. Such was Bittan's ability to integrate his baroque virtuosity within the band's overall sound, Sancious was almost forgotten. Springsteen nicknamed Bittan 'the professor'.

With the song 'Born to Run' completed in October 1974, the band stayed on the road through the winter. This final phase of *The Wild, the Innocent and the E Street Shuffle* tour, evolving into the *Born to Run* project, was one of the most intriguing and distinctive of the band's career. This was partly because of the addition of Suki Lahav. Springsteen invited her to make a one-off appearance with the band at their Lincoln Centre show in New York (4 October) and she was subsequently asked to stay in the band for the rest of the tour. The band played many college gigs during this leg, mostly on the East Coast. Increasingly, headline acts were asking Springsteen to play last. The concert at West Chester College, Pennsylvania, on 22 November, provoked an insightful review in the college paper, *Quad Angles*. It put into words the intense response Springsteen was receiving from audiences who were effectively discovering a band on the edge of stardom; the revelatory power of the shows of the winter of 1974/75 when the band was buzzing with the excitement of Springsteen's new songs. The reviewer was George Tucker:

> His expressions, his motions, the subtlety of his repetition, the raunchy power of his screaming guitar, the sensual rasp of the sax, the fragile piano, the heartbeat of the drums, the bleeding cry of the violin, the omniscience of the organ, all add up to the amazing presence somewhere between greaser and punk that is Springsteen. Springsteen's music is pure rock 'n' roll unlike anything you've heard before, but then it's everything you've heard before. Every rock tune before Springsteen was looking for a final statement, the ultimate expression of an ultimate goal, trying to synthesize emotion and intellect as only Rock could do.[1]

On 25 November Springsteen got together with David Bowie at Sigma Sound Studios in Philadelphia, where Bowie was recording. The meeting was arranged by the local disc jockey Ed Sciaky. Bowie had been a fan since seeing Springsteen at Max's Kansas City in New York in February 1973 and was recording covers of several of his songs. That evening Springsteen attended Bowie's show at the Spectrum.

With her sweet voice and air of mystery, Suki Lahav was more than just an additional musician: she was the only woman and the only non-American – 'a young girl in a flowing white dress from Kibbutz Ayelet Hashahar in the Upper

---

[1] George Tucker, 'Saint from the City Brings Little Angels to Big State', in *Quad Angles*, vol.43, n.12 (26 November 1974), p.3.

Galilee [Israel], barely out of the army, barely married'.[1] Her allusive presence altered the personality of the band at key moments, reflecting the romanticism that existed in songs like 'Incident on 57th Street'. Springsteen changed that song, slowing the tempo and reducing the accompaniment to leave only Suki Lahav's mournful violin and Bittan's piano accompaniment. A new coda included an unexpected shift to C minor. He would begin the show with the song, so that the opening image was of himself and Suki Lahav in separate beams of blue light. Lahav was also prominent in new covers of Leiber and Spector's 'Spanish Harlem' and Bob Dylan's 'I Want You'. Springsteen's decision to add Sam Cooke's 'Cupid' and Dylan's 'I Want You' to the set at this time didn't go unnoticed. People wondered if a new song called 'She's the One' (longer, richer, and more powerful than the song eventually recorded) was written for the young woman on stage. At this time, Springsteen often made oblique use of his relationships in his work. Mike Appel later claimed that the Lahavs returned to Israel in 1975 because of the attraction that had developed between Springsteen and Suki.

The band's show in early February 1975 at the Main Point Coffeehouse in Bryn Mawr, Pennsylvania, was broadcast on local radio. *The Wild, the Innocent and the E Street Shuffle* songs in concert in late 1974 and early 75 were the basis of the most mesmeric music-making of the band's career. In an epic version of 'New York City Serenade', Lahav added swirling countermelodies, Tallent's bass climbed scales, and Bittan seemed lost in his own world. Springsteen's voice and Clemons's saxophone seemed to be symbiotically linked. 'Thunder Road' was premiered at the Main Point. Then called 'Wings for Wheels', it was played somewhat in the style of *The Wild, the Innocent and the E Street Shuffle*, with Federici's organ delivering fairground swirls of sound and Lahav's violin prominent towards the end. Part of Clemons's sax solo would be removed from the song and turned into the instrumental 'Paradise by the C'. 'Jungleland' had almost arrived at its final form, but it was a little slower and more soulful. The violin introduction was longer, and a tubular bell was struck a few times to emulate the sound of church bells. The central instrumental passage was not a Clemons solo but a magnificent duet for Lahav's violin and Springsteen's guitar. The official release of this, or any, concert from the winter of 1974/75 is long overdue. In a 2007 interview, Suki Lahav gave an affectionate account of her time with Springsteen and the band:

---

[1] David Horovitz, 'Bruce Springsteen's Kibbutz violinist: for a few magical months Suki Lahav played with world's finest band', *Jerusalem Post* (22 October 2007).

[At the studio] they worked nights; they were the main event in our musical lives. We were all young. He wasn't the big star. Not yet. Just a unique artist. [...] Louis sent me along to audition. There were others. Surprisingly, he took me. I didn't think I was very good [...] but maybe I did have my own thing. The music was incredible. The lyrics were so rich; some of the most beautiful lyrics didn't even make it onto the record. Everybody knew that he was going to be this big artist. But we were all poor. Bruce was poor. We were all just completely into this thing. [Some of the bigger concerts were terrifying.] Of course, I hid behind Clarence; held onto him; he was always big enough to hide behind.[1]

The Wild, the Innocent and the E Street Shuffle tour came to an end with a show at the DAR Constitution Hall in Washington DC on 9 March 1975. It was widely believed that the next album would be Springsteen's last if it didn't break through into the mainstream commercially. Everyone, from Springsteen down, felt that pressure as the band began, in March, to record in earnest.

Since the summer recording sessions at 914 Sound, a close friendship had developed between Springsteen and Jon Landau, sparked by his review in *The Real Paper*. Landau was college-educated and seemed older than Springsteen (in fact, he was only older by two years). As one of the editors of *Rolling Stone*, he was influential. His credits as a producer included MC5's second album, *Back in the USA* (1970), and Livingston Taylor's *Liv* (1971). Springsteen told Landau about the problems he was having in the studio, and with his record company, and Landau's advice was helpful. Springsteen benefitted from the passionate advocacy of critics like Landau and Dave Marsh, whose book *Born to Run: the Bruce Springsteen Story*, published in 1979, powerfully described the shows of the 1970s for people who had limited or no first-hand experience of them.

Appel must have viewed Landau as an interloper. Before he knew it, Landau had joined him in the studio booth. Landau's first significant contribution was to persuade Springsteen to record at the prestigious Record Plant on West 44th Street in Manhattan. The sixteen-track desk at 914 Sound wasn't antiquated but it wasn't state-of-the-art either. The studio manager wasn't able to fix the squeaky piano pedal let alone the tuning problem. There was no hiding the fact that the building was a former garage, and while the place, with its diner and backyard, had a vibe that appealed to Springsteen and the band, it was something of a dump to Landau. On the other hand, the technicians at the

---

[1] Quoted in Horovitz, 'Bruce Springsteen's Kibbutz violinist', *Jerusalem Post* (22 October 2007).

Record Plant, seeking a dry, pure, sound, covered everything in carpets, including the walls and the piano, thereby preventing any soulful live sound from being recorded. The bosses at Columbia approved of the move. They were rethinking their position on Springsteen's future. 'Born to Run', played occasionally during the live shows, had started to create a buzz of anticipation.

Landau felt that Springsteen's first two records were let down by their recording quality. He recognised the talent of Jimmy Iovine, a young assistant at the Record Plant who had worked on John Lennon's *Rock and Roll* album, and, without asking Springsteen first, appointed him in place of Louis Lahav.[1] Lahav was a popular figure within the camp – he had even taken on the taxing job of road manager during the recent leg of shows. Appel's claim (made in 1992) that Springsteen and Suki Lahav had fallen for each other, and Louis Lahav 'got crazy',[2] if true, suggests a different reason for his replacement as engineer. We'll never know whether Suki Lahav would have had a future with the band. She returned to Israel with Lahav almost immediately (their marriage ended shortly afterwards). Asked about Suki during a radio interview at the start of the *Born to Run* tour, Springsteen said she was no longer in the band because she had wanted to return home to Israel, a fact that she corroborated in an interview with *Backstreets Magazine* (1985).[3] Years later, though, she suggested that it was, indeed, the growing dominance of Landau over Appel that led to her departure: 'We were really Mike's people.'[4] Asked by an interviewer in 2003 about an affair with Springsteen she gave a cryptic response: 'It was complicated.'[5]

Springsteen was growing out of his need for a man of Appel's particular gifts. In the early days, Appel's passion, aggressive advocacy and ability to break down doors, were exactly what the unknown Springsteen needed; but now he was more in need of someone he could trust totally. Always eager to write analytically and to inform his work with a wide range of influences, Springsteen, who had missed out on a higher education, had been on a process of self-education since he had started to write songs. Landau was someone who could point him in certain directions when it came to cultural references beyond

---

[1] See Springsteen, *Born to Run*, p.220.

[2] See Marc Eliot with the participation of Mike Appel, *Down Thunder Road* (London: Plexus, 1992), p.95.

[3] See 'Suki Lahav interviewed by Steven Allen', in Charles R. Cross, *Backstreets: Springsteen, the Man and His Music*, p.105.

[4] Quoted in Horovitz, 'Bruce Springsteen's Kibbutz violinist', *Jerusalem Post* (22 October 2007).

[5] Yoav Birnberg, Interview with Suki Lahav, 23 July 2003, in Ynet, at https://www.ynet.co.il/articles/0,7340,L-2702675,00.html (accessed 18/9/21).

popular music. Something was lost when Springsteen took on board Landau's ideas on how to edit some of the longer songs so that their impact was more immediate and radio-friendly, but something was gained too. Landau made Springsteen feel confident about decisions he was going to make anyway.

When not on the road, Springsteen was living in a rented house in West Long Branch, on the Jersey Shore not far from Asbury Park. It was here that he spent months writing the songs that the band recorded for *Born to Run*. Springsteen revised his drafts until most of the words were erased from the page. It was a moment of stylistic change, for Springsteen was deliberately making his writing more accessible without surrendering the qualities that made his lyrics distinctive. Musically, too, he was seeking a new direction, and wrote mostly on the piano. He composed introductions and codas so that the music would set up and comment upon the lyrics. He wanted to evoke in his songs the dramatic tension and visual poetry that made the cinema so powerful. His desire to achieve a particular mood or feeling became an obsession in the studio. The project was remarkably ambitious for a twenty-four-year-old.

With so much at stake, and with only four months left to make the album, and with all the people involved lacking essential experience, the process was torturous. Sessions were long, lasting fourteen hours and more, day after day, with Springsteen obsessing over arrangements and requiring parts to be played over and over again. The guitar parts in 'Thunder Road' took fourteen hours to complete. He also changed the lyrics. Things weren't helped by the inevitable tension that existed between Appel and Landau. Appel didn't want Landau to be given the leading producer credit.

Federici was absent so Bittan played the organ parts. Van Zandt came into the studio and added some backing vocals and sorted out the horn parts on 'Tenth Avenue Freeze-Out'. The time had come for him to return to the E Street Band. Van Zandt was something of a rock purist and needed time to accept the dominance of Bittan's piano, but the use of classical piano was just one example of how far his friend had travelled. Van Zandt was astonished by the range of his influences, from James L. Cain to Rimbaud, from Elia Kazan to Jacques Tourneur. He saw that Springsteen was treating rock as an artform, analysing his work and seeking an artistic identity, something that few if any of his great predecessors had done.[1]

Slowly songs were recorded, but not one of them satisfied Springsteen. He collaborated with the band, but always had the final word. An easy-going guy when the work was going well, he could be exacting and overcritical, of himself as well as others, when it wasn't. He became silent and withdrawn and his

---

[1] See Van Zandt, *Unrequited Infatuations*, p.93 and 113.

obsessiveness became intimidating. The young photographer Barbara Pyle, who had befriended the band and who was often present in the studio, witnessed this struggle, later commenting:

> In the studio, Bruce would record something, mix it, remix it, and then dump it. He had a specific sound in his head. He would hum the music and the band would lay down tracks. It was brutal. [...] Clarence played his 'Jungleland' sax solo countless times for Bruce. After each one he would ask, 'That's it, right Bruce?' Bruce would answer, 'Again, Big Man'.[1]

The songs that Springsteen had worked on at 914 Sound and/or tried out in concert between October 1974 and March 1975 – 'She's the One', 'Jungleland', 'Backstreets' and 'Thunder Road' – were revised to become more concentrated and less idiosyncratic. The female choir (created, I suspect, by layering Suki Lahav's voice), violin and bells were excised, the rhythms made squarer and more even, and the improvisational feel (actually there was no improvisation) was replaced by classical form. 'Born to Run' had already gone through this process at 914 Sound. It was part of Springsteen's dilemma that both approaches were artistically valid. However, classical form and directness gave the songs an elegance and power that the seemingly freewheeling approach simply did not.

They recorded right up to the start of the tour. Springsteen and Iovine spent three days and nights mixing the record, and then, at five in the morning, on 20 July, the band rehearsed their set before jumping into a van to drive to the first gig in Providence, Rhode Island. Barbara Pyle took a black and white photograph of the band as they rehearsed, their faces pallid and blank. Springsteen would later say that the photo should have been the album cover.

The record was mastered but Springsteen still wouldn't sign off on it. Iovine took the master pressing to the hotel where Springsteen and the band were staying. After Springsteen had listened to the album he walked outside and threw it in the hotel swimming pool, telling Iovine that he'd record the whole thing live. Iovine felt crushed. He took a sedative and returned to New York.[2] Landau saved the day. He helped Springsteen to stand back from the record, to see things in perspective, and to accept the fact that perfection was impossible.

Landau believed that the work was a masterpiece, but for Springsteen the

---

[1] Barbara Pyle, *Bruce Springsteen and the E Street Band 1975* (Reel Art Press, 2015), p.62. Pyle's fine photographs are published in this book.
[2] See Pyle, *Bruce Springsteen and the E Street Band 1975*.

sound he had in his head had not been achieved on tape. The music didn't breathe as sweetly as he wanted. The recording was mannered and a little muddy. The songs and arrangements generated excitement, but the sound did not. It was a minor issue because the songs, both individually and together, were remarkable; but for Springsteen, so much was resting on the record, not just for himself but also for his bandmates, that he feared that he had failed. This was the moment when all those hours spent in small bedrooms learning to play, to write songs; all those years spent practising in garages, playing in small bars and clubs; when all the promise of young lives lived unconventionally on the edge of subsistence would be judged.

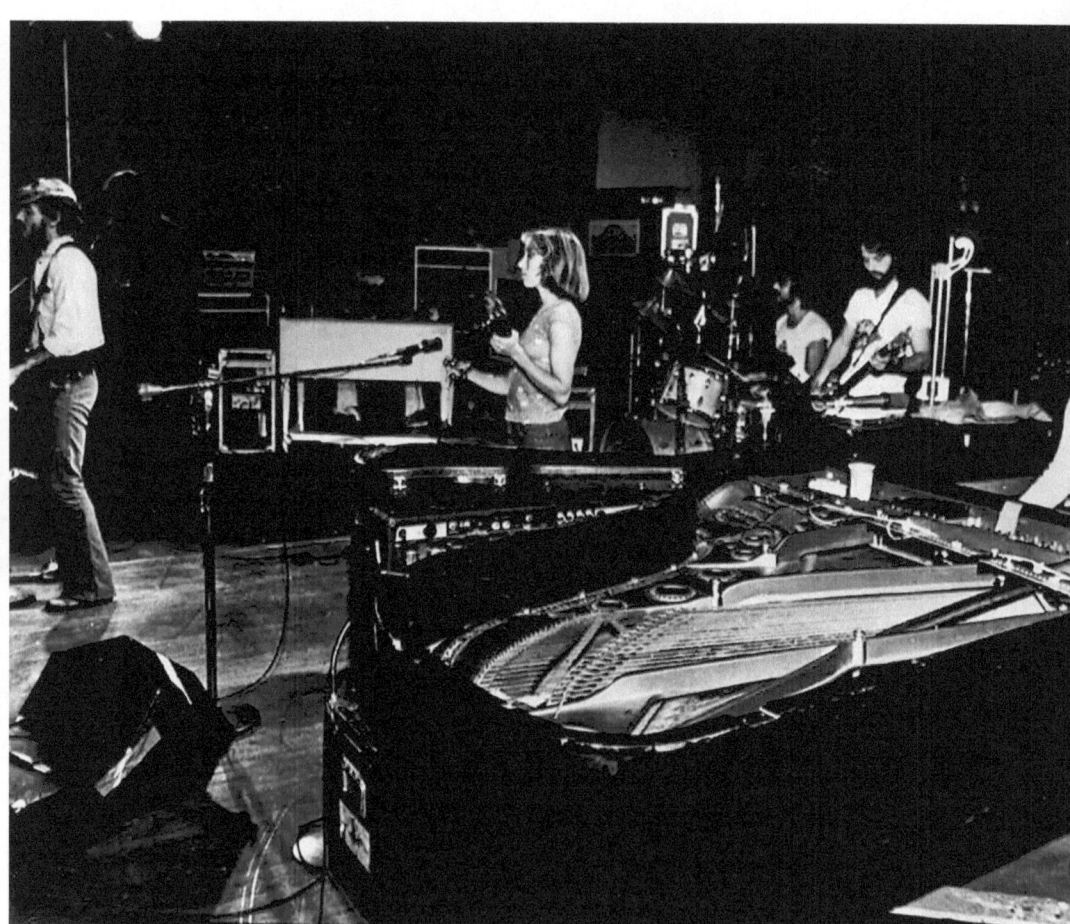

Soundcheck, 1974/75. Springsteen, Suki Lahav, Weinberg, Tallent and Bittan. Photo credit: Unknown.

2 BORN TO RUN

Performed by the E Street Band and recorded at 914 Sound Studios, Blauvelt, New York, and the Record Plant, New York, between May 1974 and July 1975. Produced by Springsteen, Mike Appel, Jon Landau; recorded by Louis Lahav (914 Sound), Jimmy Iovine (Record Plant). Released on 1 September 1975.

Recorded at 914 Sound, May to October 1974: 'Born to Run'.
Recorded at the Record Plant, March to July 1975: All other songs.

The album:

Side One:

Thunder Road
Bittan (piano, glockenspiel, backing vocals); Clemons (saxophone); Springsteen (vocals, electric guitar, harmonica); Tallent (bass); Van Zandt (backing vocals); Weinberg (drums)

Tenth Avenue Freeze-Out
Bittan (piano); Clemons (saxophone); Springsteen (vocals, electric guitar); Tallent (bass); Van Zandt (horn arrangement); Weinberg (drums)
Additional musicians: Wayne Andre (trombone); Michael Brecker (tenor saxophone); Randy Brecker (trumpet); David Sanborn (baritone saxophone)

Night
Bittan (piano, harpsichord, glockenspiel); Clemons (saxophone); Springsteen (vocals, electric guitar); Tallent (bass); Weinberg (drums)

Backstreets
Bittan (piano, organ); Springsteen (vocals, electric guitar); Tallent (bass); Weinberg (drums)

Side Two:

Born to Run
Ernest 'Boom' Carter (drums); Clemons (saxophone); Federici (organ); Springsteen (vocals, electric guitar); Sancious (piano); Tallent (bass)

She's the One
Bittan (piano, organ, harpsichord); Clemons (saxophone); Springsteen (vocals, electric guitar); Tallent (bass); Weinberg (drums)

Meeting Across the River
Bittan (piano); Springsteen (vocals)
Additional musicians: Randy Brecker (trumpet); Richard Davis (double bass)

Jungleland
Bittan (piano, organ); Clemons (saxophone); Suki Lahav (violin); Springsteen (vocals, electric guitar); Tallent (bass); Weinberg (drums)
Additional musician: Charles Calello (string arrangement)

Released Outtakes:

Linda Let Me Be the One
Bittan (piano, organ); Clemons (saxophone); Springsteen (vocals, electric guitar); Tallent (bass); Weinberg (drums)
Recorded during the 1975 sessions at the Record Plant
Release: *Tracks* (1998)

So Young and in Love
Ernest 'Boom' Carter (drums); Clemons (saxophone); Springsteen (vocals, electric guitar); Sancious (piano); Tallent (bass)
Recorded during the 1974 sessions at 914 Sound
Release: *Tracks* (1998)

Unreleased Outtakes recorded at 914 Sound, 1974, include:

Walking in the Street
A Love So Fine
A Night Like This
Janey Needs a Shooter

Unreleased outtakes recorded at the Record Plant, 1975, include:

Lonely Night in the Park

When people talk about an E Street Band signature sound they're really talking about this album. Throughout his career, Springsteen has ensured that each record has its own sound world. *Born to Run* would not be repeated. As the album that broke Springsteen into the mainstream, its flowing classical piano, glockenspiel, layered electric guitars and saxophone solos combined to create one of the most recognisable sounds in rock, much imitated by lesser bands. *Born to Run* was the last Springsteen record to be romantic in the broad sense of the word, romantic in the way people are when they are young and still discovering each other and the world. And yet the album is imbued with a feeling that the skies have already started to darken, that possibilities are few and easily missed. Springsteen placed the songs to suggest connections, taking the listener from a small beach town during a hot afternoon to the violent streets of New York at night, from light into darkness. He wanted the feeling of a long summer evening. He would later say that all the stories could be taking place on the same evening and night, at different places.[1] These are tales of love and rebellion, of outsiders and misfits: youth is brief and transitory, that is both its beauty and its tragedy.

Bittan was the key musician on the album, followed by Springsteen, who played all the guitar parts, and played them hard, and Clemons; but Tallent's melodic basslines and Weinberg's controlled power were hardly less important. Listening to the album again, I'm surprised by how fast the band plays. Bittan took Springsteen's already intricate piano parts and embellished them with arpeggios and added notes. The opening track, 'Thunder Road', in F major, is one of Springsteen's most lyrical expressions of longing. Thematically, it is a companion piece to 'Rosalita', but whereas 'Rosalita' is humorous and bold, 'Thunder Road' is serious and tender. It is summer, a boy has just graduated. He asks a girl to run away with him, a simple enough theme, but it is the details in the lyrics, the metaphors, and the feelings evoked, that make the song. Roy Orbison singing on the radio, the hem of a girl's dress swaying as she dances, a dusty beach road, a graduation gown discarded in the dust. Musically, the expansive melody moves between F, B♭ and C, but replaces B♭ with D minor at key moments (replicating the piano introduction) and increasingly relies, too, on A minor. Bittan streams a waterfall of notes, syncopated and contrapuntal, beneath Springsteen's vocal.

'Tenth Avenue Freeze-Out' is also in F major but D minor dominates. With added horns, the song's hook (F to D minor, B♭ to G minor) has a real punch. The second part of the melody moves through C and B♭ on its way back to F. This is soulful pop music, designed to showcase the band during live performances. Springsteen would reveal later that he had no idea what Tenth Avenue freeze-out meant. The song, referencing Clemons and Springsteen himself, is in part about the creation of the band. 'Night' completes the album's F major opening. In this ferocious rocker, built on blocks of repeated fast notes on the

---

[1] *Wings for Wheels* documentary (2005).

piano, stacked guitars, and Tallent's dancing bass, F suspended 4 chords resolving to F dominate. Saxophone, glockenspiel and harpsichord combine. The theme is a simple and well-trodden one in American popular culture – working-class men, trapped in life-sapping jobs, find release in building and racing cars on the streets at night – but the music has a sophistication that belies its power.

Placed strategically at the end of side one, 'Backstreets' is the album's finest song as well as its darkest and most eloquent treatment of the overarching theme of dislocation, of young lives lived in the shadows, of nocturnal pain and pleasure, in streets, parks and beaches, of redemptive love failing. The beauty of the piano introduction, underpinned by rumbling bass, builds a tension that is released by the guitar, playing a six-note riff. Bittan adds funky licks on the organ. The verses move between G major and E minor, resolving through D to C; the choruses, between G and C, resolving through A minor and E minor before returning to G. The middle eight begins with an ascending scale on the piano, an outstanding modulation to A major. The melody travels from A to F# minor, E major, and D major, and then back to G.

'Born to Run' opens side two. Named the greatest rock song of all time by *The Times* of London, it does appear to have everything. Wall of sound power, glittering classical flourishes, and a perfect rock band arrangement. It is mysterious that a track that was the result of gruelling, repetitive work lasting many months sounds spontaneous and not laboured. It is mysterious that the one song on the album recorded by Louis Lahav at 914 Sound Studios sounds better than any of the tracks recorded, by his replacement, Jimmy Iovine, at the Power Plant.

The song is in E major. The music incorporates Bmaj7 suspended and F# minor chords before dropping to C# minor. The bridge consists of suspended 4 chords (D, G, A, C). The song is a *tour de force* that fuses American B movies with lyrical poetry (John Keats: 'Now more than ever seems it rich to die, to cease upon the midnight with no pain'). The characters seem older than those in 'Thunder Road': the urge to flee has become a reductive way of life, for flight offers false hope. The characters are born to run but they have nowhere to go. This irony is easy to miss given the music's power.

Springsteen's preoccupation with women and desire was surprisingly rarely commended upon at the time, despite a song like the achingly raw 'She's the One'. A syncopated Bo Diddley-style beat, combining piano, guitars and drums, is given a baroque flavour by the addition of a harpsichord. The main melody incorporates suspended 4 chords, resolved, and oscillates between E and A. In the bridge, the music drops down to G# minor and F# minor.

'Meeting Across the River', in E♭ major, is a special song. Nowhere else in his output does Springsteen base a melody so hauntingly around suspended 2 (inverted) and major seventh chords (E♭sus2 and C♯maj7), as well as F minor 7 and B7, and its beauty is enhanced by the pared-down arrangement – elegant piano accompaniment, melodic bassline and Randy Brecker's melancholy trumpet used as an obbligato instrument. It is one of the songs of Springsteen that I call 'classical' because it transcends the limitations of pop music. The lyrics turned a movie that Scorsese might have made into a nineteen-line poem. Springsteen almost left the song off the album and has rarely performed it in concert. He showed that he could handle the piano part when he performed the song during his solo *Devils and Dust* tour in 2005.

'Meeting Across the River' is followed by the album's finale, 'Jungleland'. Nearly ten minutes long and structurally advanced, 'Jungleland' remains E Street's grandest musical statement. The song evolved over many months as Springsteen tried out different versions in concert and then in the studio. One admires the evocative opening images, the descending musical phrase of the refrain, the long sax-led instrumental section, the solo piano theme that introduces the final verse and the cry of protest that concludes the narrative. The short instrumental prelude pairs Bittan's piano with Suki Lahav's violin. The main melody descends from C to E minor 7, before progressing through F and G. It then drops to D minor and A minor. The refrain descends from D minor via A minor and F to C. There is an unexpected shift to B♭ before the first repeat of the refrain. Following Springsteen's guitar solo, a new section takes the music back to C via B♭, F and G minor. A sudden, striking modulation to E♭ announces Clemons's long sax solo, meticulously composed by Springsteen. The solo progresses through A♭ to B♭. At its end, Bittan's piano takes over, and as the music rises chromatically he plays a countermelody on the organ. In the final vocal section, we progress from B♭, via C minor and A♭maj7 until we reach D minor for the final, almost whispered, repeat of the refrain. There are a few (for Springsteen) sub-standard lines ('ballet' rhymed with 'alley'). Springsteen avoids realism, turning a cinematic scenario into a parable. What is so remarkable about 'Jungleland' is its tenderness.

3   THE BORN TO RUN TOUR

Suki Lahav was gone so the E Street Band was once more a boy's gang from New Jersey. The band now felt complete, for Van Zandt was on board to provide support and to share the guitar parts, allowing Springsteen to sing without playing when he wanted. Given that there had only been that one early morning rehearsal at the Record Plant, it took a little time on the road to properly integrate Van Zandt into the show.

The tour started on 20 July 1975 at the Palace Concert Theatre in Providence. At the end of the month, the band played three open-air concerts at Rock Creek Park in Washington DC, and in August they returned to the Bottom Line in New York for a five-night residency. Springsteen's monologues were an essential part of every concert. He would start to speak at the beginning of a song, break off to start singing, and then continue halfway through with musical backing from Bittan and Federici, the music rising and falling and the whole band entering on cue. One of the shows was broadcast on WNEW-FM, the source of the bootlegs that were soon circulating. The Bottom Line stand was an important marker in the band's rise to prominence. *Born to Run*, released a couple of weeks later, was met with widespread acclaim and public attention. Mike Appel, John Hammond and Clive Davis, the men who had recognised Springsteen's talent, were finally vindicated. The company that had failed to support its artist only a few months earlier, now went in the opposite direction and unleashed an advertising campaign that hyped Springsteen to such an extent that some commentators accused this most authentic of artists of being a media-manufactured fake. The record company got one important aspect dead right: the album's white double spread cover, designed by John Berg and featuring Eric Meola's photograph of Springsteen leaning against Clemons, had real visual impact. It was as stylish and compelling as the record it contained. For Springsteen, it made a statement about the band. Once the cover was opened, a story began.[1] Springsteen took this idea onto the stage. For the first time, Clemons left his microphone stand to interact with Springsteen. The physical presence of Springsteen and Clemons together, the Scooter and the Big Man, made a powerful anti-racist statement.

The influential critic Greil Marcus, writing in *Rolling Stone*, declared that *Born to Run* was magnificent. He cited the band's 'majesty' and stressed the darkness that existed at the heart of Springsteen's romanticism. In a nod to Jon Landau, his *Rolling Stone* colleague, he even praised the album's sound.

Marcus's review was representative of the other raves in proclaiming, after Landau, that Springsteen had revived rock music while creating something new. Leading British critics like Philip Norman, biographer of the Beatles, were also enthusiastic, but in a style that was slightly more measured.

In October, the schedule took Springsteen and the band back to New Jersey for a two-night stand at Monmouth Arts Centre in Red Bank, playing to the

---

[1] See Springsteen, *Born to Run*, p.242.

converted, and then to the opposite side of the country, where they were still not well-known even in the major cities. A triumphant four-night stand at the Roxy Theatre in Los Angeles, with members of the Hollywood elite in attendance, was instrumental in changing the fortunes of the band on the West Coast. It was perhaps the fact that they were playing to people for the first time that made the final two shows of the stand so noteworthy (the first show was somewhat deadened by all the industry insiders and guests present). On night one, Springsteen spotted Carole King in the audience and covered her song 'Goin' Back' as the first encore, a superb E Street arrangement with jangling guitars, romantic piano, and the voices of Springsteen and Van Zandt combining powerfully. The song was played throughout the run, but never again.

On the second and third nights the band played two sets. Columbia arranged for the third night early show (18 October) to be recorded using a mobile unit (the engineer was Ray Thompson), in the hope that Springsteen would release a live album as his follow-up to *Born to Run*. This didn't happen, but years later Springsteen began the *Live 1975-85* box set with the opening song of this Roxy performance, 'Thunder Road'. The whole performance was finally released in 2018 as a CD and digital download. As well as capturing the nightclub atmosphere of the Roxy, this gives us official recordings of both the heartfelt 'Goin' Back' and the band's cover of the Searchers' 1963 hit 'When You Walk in the Room', a song they had premiered at the Bottom Line. Announcing 'Goin' Back' Springsteen referenced a future member of the band: 'This is a Carole King song. It was done on one of the early Byrds albums. Also Nils Lofgren did a nice job with the song on his last album.'

A few weeks later, the band made their first overseas trip. 'We stepped out of the plane into the land of our mystic heroes,' Springsteen wrote in 2005. 'A London that seemed very foreign and exotic to a bunch of provincial Jersey Shore beach bums and musicians.' Springsteen felt the pressure of meeting the expectations of the sceptical British. The last thing he needed was his record company's 'Finally London is Ready for Bruce Springsteen' publicity campaign. That one sentence ensured bad reviews from the specialist music papers – *Sounds* and *NME* – irrespective of how the band played, and Springsteen knew it: 'The whole city, or at least the part that was interested in pop music, seemed primed for... a party? a funeral? a coronation? a hanging? All of the above? With the shadow of the crown and the noose upon my neck, I stood in the middle of it, this week's Next Big Thing.'[1]

The band took to the stage of the Hammersmith Odeon on 18 November.

---

[1] Springsteen, Sleeve notes, *Bruce Springsteen and the E Street Band, Hammersmith Odeon, London '75*, DVD, 2005.

Springsteen had rarely, if ever, felt as nervous. Such was the level of personal trauma playing out inside his mind that he performed a lot of the show on autopilot.[1] However, it only really showed when he spoke (and he hardly spoke at all). 'So how are things going over here in England and stuff?' he quietly asked between nervous chuckles. 'It's the first time. I've never been here before.' But he aborted the monologue that should have followed and launched into 'The E Street Shuffle'.

At the time Springsteen and the band didn't realise how well they had played. In his review in *The Times*, Philip Norman wrote:

> Even the music business is astonished by Bruce Springsteen. An industry, peerless in the generation of legend around nonentities, of vast conceit around minimum competence, has seen its most carefully nourished protégés eclipsed at a stroke by a New Jersey loafer aged 26 who seems in every way to be the antithesis of star material. [...] Having seen Springsteen at Hammersmith, and attempting how to weigh my words, I can say only that he is wonderful. He is as devastating a talent as popular music has ever produced. His records, good as they are, leave one unprepared for the strength of his stage performance. He is discovered alone in a spotlight, a small, unkempt figure in baggy trousers, a woollen hat. No studio has yet captured the resonance of his voice. Of all analogies, the one with Bob Dylan is most appropriate, and most misleading. There is the same originality, uncontrollable, raging, uttered in its own unmistakable voice. But Dylan was a convert where Springsteen was born. He is a child of rock and roll, and of all its clichés; the motorcycles, the funfairs, the drag racers. He sees them with both illusion and disillusion, with punk love and weary hindsight. In rock's terrible conformity there is the further excitement to be felt at the birth of an entirely new character. [...] Whatever we see, it does represent extraordinary hope. Let us hope also that he remains ignorant of his power for a little time yet.[2]

The great Derek Jewell, writing in *The Sunday Times*, admired Springsteen too, but not uncritically. Because his admiration was considered, and based on wider cultural influences, it cut more deeply than anything previously written about Springsteen's work:

> He can whisper and command silences more effectively [than Bob Dylan].

---

[1] See Springsteen, *Born to Run*, p.226-33.

[2] Philip Norman, 'Bruce Springsteen, Hammersmith Odeon', in *The Times* (9 November 1975), p.8.

He doesn't moralise much. He simply describes – scenes of rough touch urban New Jersey life, the bleak sidewalks and the scruffy beaches and the hellholes of chemical living and the hot-rod no-hopers in language so evocative it sets him apart from the street, no longer its child. [...] His lyrics are the thing: the surprising, extravagant language is as poetically remarkable in its context as was Dylan Thomas's for his particular world. So, powerful as Springsteen's stage show is, his three albums remain his glory.[1]

Jewell undervalued Springsteen's melodies and the E Street Band (he would later revise his opinion of both) and bristled at some of the stuff being written about him: 'Springsteen is compared to Bob Dylan, Mick Jagger and a largish cast. "He's a rock 'n' roll punk, a Latin Street poet, a ballet dancer, an actor, a poet joker, hot rhythm guitar player, extraordinary singer and a truly great rock 'n' roll composer." Thus Jon Landau of *Rolling Stone*. Rock's hyperboles make one fall about.'

Success came with its own issues. Between the Roxy stand and the London shows, the two most influential American weekly magazines, *Newsweek* and *Time*, ran cover stories that were as much about the forces that were making Springsteen a star as they were about his music. Springsteen, encouraged by both Appel and Landau (who knew the two journalists), had reluctantly agreed to be interviewed, but he was dejected by this aspect of his success. The band simply kept playing throughout it all.

The Hammersmith show was filmed by the BBC on 16mm film for a possible *Old Grey Whistle Test* special. It is not clear whether Appel pitched the idea to the producer of the *Whistle Test*, Mike Appleton, or the other way round. Appleton wasn't happy with the picture quality of the footage. Anyway, it is certain that Springsteen would not have wanted the film to be shown. Thirty years later, he asked Thom Zimny to look at the footage and, if possible, restore it for release as part of the *Born to Run* box set. Springsteen was amazed by the result. The film quashed his fear that the band had played below its best. It is the best document we have of the mid-1970s E Street Band.

The concert began with the solo piano version of 'Thunder Road', with Springsteen standing stock-still in a blue spot and Bittan hunched beneath his wide-brimmed panama hat. The performance was immaculate. The pressure of the occasion prompted Springsteen, Bittan, Van Zandt and Clemons to embrace at the end of the song. The musicians kicked into 'Tenth Avenue Freeze-

---

[1] Derek Jewell, 'Springsteen Off the Streets', in *The Sunday Times* (23 November 1975).

Out' and played with an intensity that was only just reigned in. An extraordinary version of 'Lost in the Flood' was also played breakneck fast. Sartorially, the band would never look this cool or eccentric again. Springsteen – woollen hat (worn perhaps as a kind of security blanket) and baggy trousers; Van Zandt – red suit and white carnation; Clemons – white suit and red carnation. Marc Brickman isolated each musician in a separate colour, and flooded the stage with reds, greens and blues. It was only after the masterly 'Backstreets' that Springsteen took off his hat (briefly) and the band started to relax into the hypnotic groove of the extended version of 'Kitty's Back'. During the long instrumental break Bittan quoted Van Morrison's 'Moondance'.

The band played in Stockholm and Amsterdam and then returned to Hammersmith for a second show. This time there was less pressure, and Springsteen was happy with the performance. The band played twenty-two songs, six more than on night one. All the songs from the first night were performed again apart from 'The E Street Shuffle'. 'Lost in the Flood' and a nine-minute-long solo piano 'For You' were definitive. The added songs included 'Growin' Up' and seven covers programmed to reveal the band's American and British influences: Elvis's 'Wear My Ring Around Your Neck', Chuck Berry's 'Carol' and 'Little Queenie', Manfred Mann's 'Pretty Flamingo' and 'Sha-La-La', the Searchers' 'When You Walk in the Room' and the Beatles' 'Twist and Shout'.

It was important to the band that they belonged in the country of the young men of the 1960s who had so inspired them. They returned home feeling that perhaps they did. Those London gigs were an important rite of passage.

The US tour resumed in Boston and continued to the end of the year and a four-night stand at the Tower Theatre in Philadelphia. The band's New Year's Eve concert was recorded by Jimmy Iovine for possible release.[1]

The band had three months off before starting the second leg of the *Born to Run* tour, targeting the southern states, at the end of March 1976. Springsteen hadn't intended to prolong the tour, but his dispute with Appel had started, delaying a return to the recording studio. He wanted to keep the band busy, telling *Rolling Stone* magazine: 'It's a lot easier for me than the rest of the guys when we're not playing. I've got my piano at home, so I can write.' Despite the success of the record, the logistics hadn't changed. They were still travelling in a Greyhound bus, converted to contain eight beds. After a show in Memphis, Springsteen and Van Zandt decided to call on Elvis at his Graceland mansion. Springsteen climbed the gates but was stopped by security guards. They told him that Elvis was in Lake Tahoe. The leg came to end in May with a show in Annapolis, Maryland.

---

[1] The recording was officially released as a CD/digital download in 2015.

Born to Run tour, Hammersmith Odeon, London, 18 November 1975. Springsteen and Van Zandt. Photo by Andrew Putler (Getty Images).

SIX: TROUBLE IN THE HEARTLAND

I RECORDING SESSIONS 1977-78

Mike Appel advocated the quick release of a live album to capitalise on the success of *Born to Run*. Springsteen had other plans. He wanted to start recording his next album in August, with Landau and not Appel. He wasn't necessarily seeking to break with Appel as his manager, but was determined to renegotiate the original contracts and to take back ownership of his songs. There was now real money; real money that went into the bank account of Appel's company, for, under the terms of the deal, Springsteen was paid by Appel and not directly. Such an arrangement was untenable for the major artist Springsteen had become.

The new contracts that Appel wanted Springsteen to sign didn't even redress the balance. Appel tried to talk Springsteen round. Worried about Landau, he tried to shore up his position before it was too late. Despite his affection for Appel, Springsteen wouldn't be persuaded. He wanted to come to an equitable agreement based on trust, but Appel held back. He enforced his legal rights, preventing Springsteen from recording his next album with Landau. The dispute ended up in court. Springsteen's lawyers sued Appel for fraud and breach of trust. For Springsteen, the dispute was principally about control (in future, his manager would work for him and not the other way around). Sympathetic and grateful to Appel in many ways, it understandably enraged him that Appel could withhold money or go against his wishes in deciding who could or could not quote his lyrics in a book.

The fear was that any significant delay in releasing a follow-up to *Born to Run* would damage Springsteen's career. In those days, momentum was key. If a band went away for a few years, their time could pass. Springsteen, as bandleader, worried about the impact on everyone else: he would later reveal that he felt that he had failed his bandmates. During the two years since *Born to Run*, the British music scene had undergone one of its frequent revolutions in style and something similar had happened in the States. It seemed for a while that 'punk' might prove to be genuinely radical and divisive. Bands like the Sex Pistols, The Damned, the Ramones and especially The Clash were producing angry and anarchic music that challenged the existing rock order on both sides of the Atlantic. Springsteen did not seek to be a part of this movement, but punk's seeming authenticity appealed to the working-class outsider he still partly was.

Springsteen was renting a former farm in Holmdel, not far from Asbury Park. He continued to live a normal life, spending time with his girlfriend and drifting around the bars on the Shore. He was also writing prolifically. The band gathered at the Telegraph Hill Road property. The house was large and comfortable, and remote enough for the band to play as loud as they liked. They rehearsed in a converted barn. Van Zandt revealed in his memoirs that there was very little money and a danger that the band would split up. Van Zandt asked his agent and friend, the legendary Frank Barsalona, boss of Premier Talent, to help Springsteen and the band and Barsalona provided the funds that enabled them, in August 1976, to return to the road. The tour began with a six-night stand at the Monmouth Arts Centre in Red Bank. The innocence had been taken away. Springsteen was now clean-shaven; he often dressed in black and the woollen hat was nowhere to be found. At the Monmouth Arts Centre, he premiered a new song called 'The Promise'. This song, along with the Animals' classic 'It's My Life', played frequently, would come to represent the year-long period when Springsteen was forced to place his recording career on hold and to endure the stress of a legal process that required hour upon hour of depositions. Also premiered was an early version of 'Something in the Night'. This song would be re-worked during the next few months. There were no shows over Christmas and the New Year.

In January 1977, the E Streeters, including Springsteen, gathered at Columbia Studios to record a version of Billy Joel's 'Say Goodbye to Hollywood' with one of their heroines, Ronnie Spector. Van Zandt produced. This was both a great pleasure and a means of making money during the tour break. The song was released as a single that April. Springsteen was uncredited because of the lawsuit.

Touring resumed in February 1977 with shows in Albany and Rochester, NY.[1] Springsteen inserted a new section into the coda of 'Backstreets', spoken and sung, over piano and bells, describing a bitter breakup that was so intense it sounded personal. The section would be further developed during future concerts, but it would never again sound as raw. The *Born to Run* tour and its

---

[1] The discovery of soundboard tapes of both shows led to their release in 2017.

unplanned extension (popularly named 'The Lawsuit Tour') finally came to end with a string of shows in Boston in March.

Springsteen's legal battle with Appel was finally settled out of court on 28 May 1977. His contracts with Appel's company were annulled. Appel was granted a financial settlement and fifty per cent of the publishing rights to the songs recorded during the period Springsteen was contracted to his company, but no role in managing them. Springsteen was allowed to re-negotiate his recording deal with Columbia. Nearly all of the *Born to Run* profits had been spent on the lawyers, but Springsteen was free. Appel's share of the songs on the first three albums only lasted until 1983, when, seeking quick money, he sold his rights to Springsteen.

Four days after the case was settled, on 1 June, Springsteen and the E Street Band started to record the new album at Atlantic Studios in New York.

Despite the stress of the *Born to Run* sessions, Jimmy Iovine agreed to return as engineer. Appel had gone, but mistakes continued. It is unclear why they decided to make the album at Atlantic Studios. Problems quickly emerged with the sound quality and the facilities in the building. They decided to return to the Record Plant, but the studio was mostly booked so they couldn't switch until September. Most of the tracks that make up *Darkness on the Edge of Town* were recorded at the Record Plant between the middle of September and the end of December. Springsteen then spent nearly three months mixing the recordings.

The band worked on over fifty songs during the sessions. Some remained uncompleted, and of these, 'Independence Day', 'Drive All Night', 'Ramrod' and 'Sherry Darling' would be revised and re-recorded during the sessions for *The River*, and 'Frankie' would be re-recorded, but rejected, for *Born in the USA*. Eighteen of the others would be released as a 'new work' called *The Promise* in 2010. Out of this wealth of material, much of it eclectic, vibrant and joyful, Springsteen chose ten broodingly sombre songs to create *Darkness on the Edge of Town*.

Multiple versions of most of the songs were recorded as Springsteen tried out different melodies and instrumentation. Some of the songs evolved during the sessions, without anyone knowing which version would be finally chosen. In the end, fine songs, and fine arrangements, were rejected if they didn't have the tone and meaning that Springsteen was after.

Springsteen's thoughts had already moved on from *Born to Run*. He didn't want to repeat the sound-world of that album. With the exception of 'Racing in the Street', the new songs were not composed on the piano as Springsteen used his electric guitar as the primary instrument for the new work. The drums and Federici's organ were also prominent. Bittan's piano parts were as elegant as ever, but less prominent in the mix. The songs, lyrically, were more direct; some were even rock anthems. There was only one song over six minutes in length – 'Racing in the Street' again. Springsteen wanted a sparser sound. He wanted the album to grip from the first note and not let the listener go: to contain a sense of foreboding. He wanted to get to the essence of the band, with few overdubs, so for the first time in the studio the band played the songs live as a unit. Some of the songs weren't fully composed before the band played. Springsteen let each musician find his place in the music, something that, because of their years of playing together, they did naturally. They didn't want to repeat the dense textures of *Born to Run*; this time, they wanted to leave spaces between the notes. This was probably the first record where the band members had a significant voice. It was the first with Van Zandt, and Van Zandt always had strong opinions and was a brilliant arranger. Springsteen listened to both Van Zandt and Landau before making up his own mind. Springsteen and Landau would talk for hours, which drove Van Zandt and Iovine crazy.

They were holed-up in the studio for months. Like a sculptor, Springsteen chiselled away at his block of material in search of his album. It was by now clear that he needed to work in this way because of the pressure he placed on himself to make the most meaningful and the most exciting record that he was capable of making. It would be years before he could work in any other way in the studio. The process was all-consuming, and stressful for everyone. There were moments, though, of levity between takes. The others would have fun at Springsteen's expense by making bets at the start of each session as to which songs would be discarded, which brought back, which re-written. In *The Making of Darkness on the Edge of Town* documentary there is studio footage of Springsteen and Van Zandt clowning around at the piano, singing 'Talk to Me' and 'Sherry Darling', two of the dozens of great pop songs that Springsteen had in his notebook that Van Zandt loved. Their joy at making music shines through.

Springsteen still struggled to achieve the recorded sound he was after. In particular, he wanted a great drum sound. No-one in the studio knew how to achieve it but they spent weeks trying. The sound they were after was unattainable through the mikes. The mixing process went on for weeks: it defeated Iovine, probably because he was too exhausted to think. Finally, Springsteen sought help from the experienced producer Chuck Plotkin. Plotkin came in and immediately changed the balance of the instruments so that the music came alive. He couldn't eradicate the pronounced hiss that can be heard at the beginning of 'Racing in the Street'.

Bruce Springsteen at the time of *Darkness on the Edge of Town*, 1978/79. Photograph: Everett Collection.

2 DARKNESS ON THE EDGE OF TOWN

Performed by the E Street Band and recorded at Atlantic Studios, New York (June–August), and the Record Plant, New York (July–March), between June 1977 and March 1978. Clemons (saxophone); Bittan (piano); Federici (organ, glockenspiel); Springsteen (vocals, lead guitar, harmonica); Tallent (bass); Van Zandt (guitar, backing vocals); Weinberg (drums). Produced by Springsteen, Jon Landau; with Production Assistance by Van Zandt; recorded by Jimmy Iovine; mixed by Jimmy Iovine, Chuck Plotkin. Released on 2 June 1978.

The album:

>Side One:
>Badlands
>Adam Raised a Cain
>Something in the Night
>Candy's Room
>Racing in the Street
>
>Side Two:
>The Promised Land
>Factory
>Streets of Fire
>Prove It All Night
>Darkness on the Edge of Town

Released outtakes:

Tracks (1998)
>Don't Look Back
>Hearts of Stone
>Iceman
>Give the Girl a Kiss

The Promise (2010)
>Racing in the Street ('78)
>Gotta Get That Feeling
>Outside Looking In
>Someday (We'll Be Together)
>One Way Street
>Because the Night
>Wrong Side of the Street
>The Brokenhearted
>Rendezvous
>Candy's Boy
>[Save My Love]
>Ain't Good Enough for You
>Fire
>Spanish Eyes
>It's a Shame
>Come On (Let's Go Tonight)
>Talk to Me
>The Little Things (My Baby Does)

Breakaway
The Promise
City at Night
The Way

Unreleased outtakes include:
Preacher's Daughter
I'm Goin' Back
Break Out
Crazy Rocker
Down by the River
Frankie (1977)
Independence Day (1977)
Sherry Darling (1977)
Drive All Night (1977 vocal)
Ramrod (1977)
Don't Say No
I Wanna Be With You (1977)
Castaway
Our Love Will Last Forever
Cheap Thrills
Triangle Song
I Got My Eye on You
After Dinner
King's Big Chance
Blue Moon
(I Love) Everything About You

If *Born to Run* was partly about the urge to escape, *Darkness on the Edge of Town* was about making a stand. Springsteen would later say that he wanted the record to be angry and rebellious but also about adult life. For Van Zandt, the record expressed something of the spirit of the John Wayne character in *The Searchers*: 'I know who I am, I know right from wrong, the clarity that we all search for.' If *Born to Run* was essentially about urban life, in New Jersey and New York, *Darkness* evoked the wide-open spaces of the American heartlands. The songs are connected by questions of doubt and faith and sin and redemption, with religious references to promised lands and fathers and sons (Cain and Abel, Abraham and Isaac) inserted into American scenarios in the manner of John Steinbeck.

The opening track, 'Badlands', in E, is, structurally, as straight-forward as it gets, a three-chord (E-A-B) anthem for the dispossessed that contains a guitar into saxophone break that never fails to galvanise arena crowds. Musically, the guitars and drums dominate. Weinberg's pounding beat sets the tone for the album. The view of life expressed on the album is often bleak. But can a work of art be existential if it also expresses hope? Such is the paradox of *Darkness*. Some of the songs have a defiant spirit. This is true of 'Badlands', 'Promised Land', opening side two, and the title track.

'Adam Raised a Cain' is a brooding rocker built upon a three-note pattern – E minor, G and A minor – played in unison by the guitar and bass. There is a lovely shift from A minor to C, while a B7 chord sets up the chorus. Springsteen, Bittan, Tallent and Weinberg play with a controlled ferocity that matches Springsteen's throat-tearing vocal. At the end, the voices combine to produce an E minor 7 chord over the E minor-G-A minor riff. Nowhere else in his work does he turn memories of childhood into a howl of rage. The oppressive power of the church over working-class communities, the violent power of fathers over sons, inspires a parable of violence and sin without redemption. This was a cathartic song for Springsteen. He would continue to address the issues that underpin 'Adam Raised a Cain' in his work, but philosophically in a search for meaning and understanding.

The music momentarily quietens for 'Something in the Night'. In the prelude, Bittan plays an elegant three-note phrase (B, down to A then climbing a fourth to D) moving between Cmaj7 and Cmaj9, then repeated in G. The music of the verses passes from the home key of G through C, A minor and D7. Both the music and the lyrics are subtly different from the first version of the song performed in concert in 1976. Both versions are fine. The first was just as complete and slightly larger in scale. Springsteen's dissatisfaction meant that here, as elsewhere, he considered every detail in seeking a very particular tone. The final version has a more austere tone and benefits from the singer's lonely howl and the very fine syncopated piano motif that begins and closes it. The change to the melody makes the song more distinctive.

The opening lines of 'Candy's Room' are spoken over the piano as Bittan plays the melody that the singer will soon take up. There is a musical ambiguity in the progression of this melody, which moves from G through D minor 7 to C and back to G. It is the mode of D minor that dominates. The singer describes his passion for a promiscuous young woman who reciprocates but who won't, or can't, make a commitment. She may be a prostitute. She may be controlled by a pimp. She is certainly vulnerable and damaged. It is the most intimate song on the album, equalling 'Adam Raised a Cain' for raw power but surpassing it for ambiguity. The music switches to B minor, A and F♯ minor as, halfway through, Springsteen's guitar wails and burns. The song belongs to Weinberg. He plays a very fast single stroke roll throughout most of the song, beginning on the cymbal and then on the snare. The four bars of hissing cymbal at the beginning creates the tension, the anticipation, that is a vital element of the song's power. For the last verse the guitar doubles the voice and then plays a new theme (B♭, A minor, G, D minor and C) while the piano takes over the main theme underneath. The final note on the guitar is suspended in ambiguity.

This note sets up the elegant ballad 'Racing in the Street'. In *Born to Run*, *Darkness* and later in *The River*, Springsteen used the car as a metaphor for freedom but also for criminality, recklessness and death. In 'Something in the Night', a car chase ends violently at a police roadblock. Commenting on his own work at this time, Springsteen said that the characters were 'in transit' but were going from 'nowhere to nowhere': 'There's no settling down, no fixed action. You pick up the action, and then at some point [...] the camera pans away, and whatever happened, that's what happened. The songs I write, they don't have particular beginnings and they don't have endings. The camera focuses in and then out.'[1] The quote confirms the influence of the cinema on his writing.

In 'Racing in the Street', though, the car represents self-expression and purpose. The characters in the song are not running, fighting, rebelling: they are searching for meaning and redemption. 'Racing' and the similar 'The Promise', left off the album, were the last of the great piano songs that Springsteen wrote in his twenties. Federici played a fine countermelody on the organ and Tallent, Weinberg, Clemons and Springsteen added touches of colour, particularly during the coda, but the song would work just as well when performed only with the piano. Bittan once again provided syncopation and endlessly creative counterpoint, but his accompaniment never overshadowed Springsteen's superb vocal. In the introduction, the musical line moves from the home key of F, through D minor 7 and C4 to G minor. The motif is bittersweet. The main melody connects F, B♭ and G minor. Springsteen makes the components of an engine sound poetic and uses drag racing as the starting point for a song about sadness and nobility of spirit. The exquisite coda fades away too quickly. In concert it would be extended.

'Promised Land', opening side two, returns the listener to the badlands of the opening track. The compelling melody swings between G, its relative key of E minor and C, before moving momentarily to A minor. The song is a perfect example of how the band members give each other space. The instrumentation contains many deft touches. Picking patterns on the electric guitars; the piano and organ playing in unison and then separating; Tallent's bass and

---

[1] Quoted in Paul Nelson, 'Springsteen Fever', in *Rolling Stone* (13 July 1978).

Weinberg's drums locked together but also independent. Best of all is the short instrumental passage at the song's heart, in which the music is passed between the instruments with sublime artistry. Bittan plays a syncopated pattern on the piano over which Federici produces a descending melody. This sets up Springsteen's guitar solo. A rising scale on the guitar sets up Clemons's saxophone solo, which in turn hands the music back to the harmonica.

Springsteen's father worked for long periods in a factory. Springsteen grew up registering the way the 'working life' affected his character. It was a life he was determined to avoid, but the extent to which he understood what it could do to someone was revealed by the sombre and profound 'Factory', one of the finest songs written on this theme. An unfulfilled life breeds despair and violence. 'Factory' has a simple country music melody, utilising only two chords, C and F, but this was a deliberate choice: the melody has a nakedness and a nobility that suits the theme. Surrounded as it is by more flamboyant songs, it is easy to miss what is perhaps the most important song on the album.

The quality drops in the next two songs. 'Streets of Fire', in F# minor, and 'Prove It All Night', in A, fit on the album but as individual songs they are relatively weak. In an extended form, 'Prove It All Night' remains popular in concert, but there is no disguising the substandard lyrics. 'Streets of Fire' was played during the *Darkness* tour, but rarely thereafter. Many finer songs were recorded during the sessions. 'Because the Night' was given to Patti Smith and, as we have noted, 'The Promise' was too similar to 'Racing in the Street' to make the cut. (The widely held belief that the song was about the Appel lawsuit, and discarded for that reason, was false. The song was written before the case. 'I don't write songs about lawsuits,' Springsteen told a journalist.) Most of the others wouldn't have worked in context in *Darkness*. 'Iceman', an ominous, enigmatic tale in the unusual key of D# (a four-note motif on the piano is repeated as the melody travels an unexpected course), and the majestic 'Breakaway', if placed correctly, perhaps would have.

Darkness on the Edge of Town ends on a high with the title track. The song resolves the album's duality, combining darkness and loss with stoicism and defiance. It shares with 'Promised Land' a G-C-E minor progression, although added 9 chords are utilised with a G added to the chords. Bittan plays a G to F# decoration before each verse. In the chorus, the melody drops to D with an unexpected move through D minor 7 to C. Springsteen's guitar and Bittan's piano dominate the instrumentation, but Federici plays a haunting phrase on the organ during the final verse and the melancholy coda: here Springsteen's voice combines beautifully with the piano, producing a long E note above the melody of the chorus in D major.

3   THE DARKNESS TOUR

The E Street Band was already on the road when *Darkness on the Edge of Town* was released with relatively little publicity on 2 June. The touring strategy was cautious, with no European dates, although it seems likely that an autumn trip to Europe was considered. Springsteen was determined to proceed without any kind of hard sell. He would promote the album by playing the songs live and by giving interviews with trusted radio stations. The legend of Bruce Springsteen and the E Street Band was still in the making. However, although Springsteen was expecting a dip in his popularity because of the three-year gap since *Born to Run*, the initial sales of the album were disappointing. For people expecting a repeat of *Born to Run*, the new songs were underwhelming. Because of the perceived hype of three years before, some reviewers were cautious. Robert Christgau, in *The Village Voice*, wrote that 'Promised Land', 'Badlands' and 'Adam Raised a Cain' were 'models of how a limited genre can illuminate a mature, full-bodied philosophical insight', continuing: 'Lyrically and vocally, they move from casual to incantatory modes with breath-taking subtlety, jolting ordinary characters and details into a realm charged with meaning.'[1] Despite this high praise, Christgau wondered whether Springsteen was an 'important minor artist or a very flawed and inconsistent major one'.

In England, the influential weekly *New Musical Express* rated *Darkness* as the number one album of the year. Preparing an article, the young NME journalist Tony Parsons, who had a punk-sensibility and whose writing was considered cool and credible, interviewed Springsteen after a show in New York. Springsteen's anxiety about the album being misunderstood became clear when he asked Parsons for his opinion. 'After repeated playing it stands up as by far the best thing you've ever done,' Parsons replied. Parsons published Springsteen's response in his 1978 profile of the artist: 'That's good... that's what we want people to react like when they hear it. [...] People tell ya so many different things... I just want the people who care about me to know what I'm trying to do. See, it couldn't be an innocent album like *Born to Run* because things ain't like that for me anymore.'[2]

The album's reputation would build. Parsons was right, repeated listens revealed the album's power, as did the live performances. The shows were now

---

[1] Robert Christgau, 'Christgau's Consumer Guide', in *The Village Voice* (26 June 1978).

[2] Tony Parsons, 'Bruce: the Myth Just Keeps on Coming', in *New Musical Express* (14 October 1978).

three-hour-plus epics, cut in two by a brief intermission. The band rehearsed at the Paramount Theatre in Asbury Park, and began their tour in Buffalo, New York, on 23 May, followed by two nights at the Spectrum in Philadelphia and three at the Music Hall in Boston. The first weeks included shows in Indianapolis, Bloomington, Iowa City, Kansas City, and St Louis. On 20 June, the band played the Red Rocks Amphitheatre in Morrison, their debut in Colorado. Following shows in Portland, Seattle, and Vancouver, the band visited California, Arizona and Texas, with concerts in San Jose, Berkeley, Los Angeles – at the Forum in Inglewood and the Roxy in West Hollywood –, Phoenix, San Diego, Dallas, San Antonio and Houston. The show at the Roxy, on 7 July, was recorded by Jimmy Iovine in the Record Plant Remote Truck and broadcast live on KMET-FM. When Springsteen finally released live recordings, with 1986's *Live 1975-85* box set, he chose eight of the Roxy tracks to represent the *Darkness* tour. Part of the show in Phoenix at the Arizona Veterans Memorial Coliseum, on 8 July, was filmed by Arnold Levine. This resulted in the official promo clip of 'Rosalita' shown on the *Old Grey Whistle Test* in the UK. The other filmed songs were later released as part of the *Darkness* box set in 2010. In the South, the itinerary included concerts in New Orleans, Memphis, Nashville, Birmingham, Miami and Louisville. The exhausting schedule next took the band to Toronto, Cleveland – the show at the Agora, on 9 August, would be released on CD in 2015 – and Chicago. In the middle of August, they returned east to Philadelphia, New York (three nights at Madison Square Garden followed, a short while later, by three at the Palladium), Pittsburgh and Passaic, where the first of their three homecoming shows at the Capitol Theatre was broadcast live on WNEW-FM New York and other radio stations.

After shows in Boston and at the Fox Theatre in Atlanta, broadcast live on radio, the band took a break that lasted for all of October. October may have been left blank originally in case Springsteen decided to tour Europe. The tour resumed at the start of November at Princeton University. This last leg saw the band return to key cities in the South, Midwest and West, as well as to cities yet to see a *Darkness* show such as Montreal and San Francisco. The band's concert at the Summit Theatre in Houston on 8 December, filmed on the theatre's in-house video, was included in the *Darkness* box set. The two performances at the Winterland Arena in San Francisco, on the 15 and 16 December, were recorded by Pete Carlson and Iovine. The first was broadcast live on KSAN-FM. Like the other *Darkness* shows relayed on the radio, the Winterland broadcast was illegally recorded by bootleggers. This trade was only ended in 2019, when the last of the relevant shows was transferred from the original tapes and officially released by Springsteen.

The tour ended with two shows in Richfield, Ohio, over the new year. Rare performances of 'Meeting Across the River', 'The Fever', 'Heartbreak Hotel' and the Rolling Stones' 1965 classic 'The Last Time' were highlights of the longest show of the tour.

Making *The River* at the Power Station, NYC, March 1980. L-R: Jon Landau, Springsteen, Clemons, Tallent, Van Zandt, Neil Dorfsman, Federici. Photo by David Gahr (Getty Images).

SEVEN: COME TOGETHER

1   RECORDING SESSIONS 1979-80

The members of the band were soon back in the studio (March 1979). Springsteen hoped that an album would be ready for release by the end of the year, and he did sign off on a record called *The Ties That Bind* in September. However, he quickly changed his mind – the work was not ambitious enough – and the band returned to the studio for a further six months of work. Fifty-three songs were recorded.

First, though, Springsteen recorded ninety-five home demos on cassette tape. He rehearsed the songs with the band at his Holmdel property and recorded them with basic equipment: one hundred and four band demos were produced. Everyone was in a happy frame of mind. After the stress of the court case and the making of the *Darkness* album, the *Darkness* tour had been liberating: by its end the band's reputation was higher than ever and the *Darkness* album had been acknowledged as a modern classic. Springsteen was writing songs at an astonishing rate, and the new music was less controlled and more varied than before. Folk and country music-influenced songs flowed naturally in the rural setting of Telegraph Hill Road; but there was also a strand of songs inspired by the Beatles and other British bands. Springsteen was happy with the music but struggled to complete the lyrics to his satisfaction.

Springsteen decided to record at the Power Station in New York, a studio that was newer and more technologically advanced than the Record Plant. Van Zandt joined Springsteen and Landau as co-producer, but the engineers at the Power Station, Bob Clearmountain and Neil Dorfsman, were new to the team. Clearmountain had been involved in designing the Power Station, while Dorfsman was recording his first major work. Dorfsman would later comment:

> I was a huge fan of Bruce's from early on. When I heard they were coming in, I went to the studio manager and, basically, begged to be on the date.

> Bob Clearmountain started the project, did a track or two, then had to leave for a prior commitment, and they gave me a shot. I was so nervous the night he walked in, I was shaking. I was sure the first night would be my last. Little did I know it would go on for something like sixteen months.[1]

Springsteen and Van Zandt wanted to capture the band's live sound, and the Power Station had a spacious wood-panelled room (Studio A) in which the band could continue the *Darkness* practice of playing the songs as a unit with a much better chance of achieving the open sound they were seeking. Clearmountain and Dorfsman placed the microphones to record the instruments and the ambient sound in the room. Both naturally gifted, they were the first engineers to capture on tape the excitement of the band's overall sound without losing clarity for each instrument. (Dorfsman would go on to work for Paul McCartney, Dire Straits, Bob Dylan and Sting.)

Between March and September 1979, the band recorded twenty-eight tracks, of which eighteen were rejected and ten sequenced. Clearmountain mixed the tracks in quick time and Springsteen signed off on *The Ties That Bind*. As well as the vibrant title track, the album contained 'Cindy', 'Hungry Heart', 'Stolen Car', 'Be True', 'The River', 'You Can Look (But You Better Not Touch)', 'The Price You Pay', 'I Wanna Marry You' and 'Loose End'. There were some very fine songs on the album, but the work lacked the gravitas and scope that Springsteen wanted his new album to encompass. In pulling the record, he rejected the evocative and tender 'Stolen Car' (he would re-write the song as a chilling study in alienation), and the Beatles-inspired 'Be True' and 'Loose End', a glorious pop music mix of melody, ringing guitar interplay, vocal harmonies and late-night saxophone. The standout track, 'The River', survived, along with 'The Ties That Bind', 'Hungry Heart', 'I Wanna Mary You' and 'The Price You Pay'. The band resumed work at the Power Station in October, but without Clearmountain, who was finding it difficult to abide Springsteen's method of working.[2] Clearmountain made everything too quick and easy to fit into Springsteen's world. Dorfsman persevered and now occupied the hot seat.

During a break in recording, in June 1979, the band gathered in Los Angeles to celebrate lighting man Marc Brickman's wedding at the Whisky a Go Club on Sunset Boulevard (they played for three hours); and in September, they played their first public gigs since the end of the *Darkness* tour, headlining two

---

[1] Quoted in Maureen Droney, 'Classic Tracks: Bruce Springsteen's The River', in *Mix* (1 October 2003).

[2] See Springsteen, *Born to Run*, p.279.

of the *No Nukes* concerts at Madison Square Garden in New York, during which they premiered 'The River'. The concerts were organised by Musicians United for Safe Energy (MUSE), a collective founded by Jackson Browne, Graham Nash, Bonnie Raitt and John Hall in the wake of the Three Mile Island nuclear disaster of March 1979. Springsteen had no experience of political activism, or bill-sharing benefit jamborees. His participation was a surprise. He had to agree to play for little more than an hour and to be recorded and filmed, although he retained approval. He allowed the release of the band's performances of 'Stay' and the 'Detroit Medley' on the *No Nukes* album and 'Thunder Road', 'The River' and 'Quarter to Three' in the *No Nukes* movie.

The issue of nuclear energy safety concerned him (he wrote the powerful song 'Roulette' shortly after the shows) but it's unlikely that his position was ideological. He knew Jackson Browne (Landau had produced Browne's album *The Pretender* in 1976) but had little in common with the other organisers, who were LA-based and from the rapidly fading musical aristocracy of the late 1960s and early 70s. Backstage, the concerts were stressful, with so many egos clashing. Nash and others were not happy that they were being overshadowed by Springsteen and the E Street Band, an act that ripped through the event like a runaway train, making Crosby, Stills and Nash's languor seem like mediocrity. The chants of 'Brooce' understandably upset some of the artists who performed before Springsteen. 'Too bad his name isn't Melvin,' Bonnie Raitt remarked sardonically. Springsteen surely felt the stress of being placed in such an awkward position (while perhaps enjoying it at some level).

During the second concert, Springsteen's private life momentarily became public when he jumped down from the stage to evict the photographer Lynn Goldsmith. He pulled her from the pit, onto the stage and into the wings, telling the crowd mid-manoeuvre: 'This is my *ex*-girlfriend.' Goldsmith had gone back on a promise not to take photographs. It was Springsteen's thirtieth birthday and his mood had been erratic all night. When an audience member handed him a cake, he lobbed it high into the crowd and said: 'Send me the laundry bill.'

The film created from Springsteen's sets, released in 2021, confirmed that the band came to the *No Nukes* festival to conquer. They had that kind of ambition. Despite the difficulties, or perhaps because of them, the band's playing was magnificent. The film beats the Hammersmith Odeon film for picture quality if not for historical importance.

At some point during the final phase of recording, which lasted from October 1979 to May 1980, Springsteen decided that he was making a double album. Now that he had enough space to incorporate the whole range of his material, from interior monologues to bar-band music, the project started to fall into shape. Around thirty songs were recorded during this phase.

With the recording finally over, Springsteen started to mix the record at Chuck Plotkin's studios in Los Angeles, but it would be months before he signed off on the work of Dorfsman, Plotkin and Plotkin's ace engineer Toby Scott. The correct placement of Springsteen's vocal was one of the final issues to be resolved. Scott was deeply affected by some of the songs, particularly 'The River': 'It really got to me, the story of this kid who got a girl pregnant and trapped them both into a miserable life. I was sitting there, actually sobbing away at the console.'[1]

In terms of production and engineering, Springsteen and Van Zandt, despite their doubts, achieved nearly everything they were seeking. Rarely since the time of George Martin and Geoff Emerick at Abbey Road had a rock band sounded so right on record, raw, tender, wild, spontaneous, sophisticated, timeless. So let's give credit to Clearmountain, Plotkin, Scott and especially Dorfsman.

The songs recorded during *The River* sessions amounted to an embarrassment of riches. Springsteen was focused on his goal and had the discipline to reject songs like 'Loose End(s)', 'Roulette', 'Restless Nights', 'The Man Who Got Away' and 'Stray Bullet', to name just some of them. Perhaps he knew that he would be able to release the outtakes further down the road. This finally happened in 2015 with the release of *The River* box set. However, a fair number of songs are still in the vault.

2   THE RIVER

Performed by the E Street Band and recorded at the Power Station, New York, between March 1979 and May 1980. Clemons (saxophone, backing vocals); Bittan (piano, organ on 'I'm a Rocker', 'Drive All Night', backing vocals); Federici (organ, glockenspiel); Springsteen (vocals, electric guitar, 12-string electric guitar, harmonica, piano on 'Drive All Night'); Tallent (bass); Van Zandt (electric guitar, lead guitar on 'Crush On You', acoustic guitar, 12-string acoustic guitar, backing vocals); Weinberg (drums). Produced by Springsteen, Jon Landau, Van Zandt; recorded by Neil Dorfsman, except 'The Ties That Bind' Bob Clearmountain, and 'Drive All Night' Jimmy Iovine; mixed by Toby Scott, Chuck Plotkin, except 'Hungry Heart' Bob Clearmountain. Released on 17 October 1980.

---

[1] Quoted in Droney, 'Classic Tracks: Bruce Springsteen's The River', in *Mix* (1 October 2003).

The album:

    Side One:
    The Ties That Bind
    Sherry Darling
    Jackson Cage
    Two Hearts
    Independence Day

    Side Two:
    Hungry Heart
    Out in the Street
    Crush on You
    You Can Look (But You Better Not Touch)
    I Wanna Marry You
    The River

    Side Three:
    Point Blank
    Cadillac Ranch
    I'm a Rocker
    Fade Away
    Stolen Car

    Side Four:
    Ramrod
    The Price You Pay
    Drive All Night
    Wreck on the Highway

Released outtakes:

[I] *Tracks* (1998)
    Be True
    Roulette
    Bring on the Night
    Restless Nights
    Dollhouse
    Where the Bands Are
    Loose Ends
    Living on the Edge of the World
    Take 'Em as They Come
    Ricky Wants a Man of Her Own

I Wanna Be With You
   Mary Lou
   Stolen Car (Alternative Version)

[II] *The Ties That Bind: The River Collection* (2015)

[II.a] *The Ties That Bind* (the rejected 1979 album)
   The Ties That Bind
   Cindy
   Hungry Heart
   Stolen Car (Alternative Version)
   Be True
   The River
   You Can Look (But You Better Not Touch) (Alternative Version)
   The Price You Pay
   I Wanna Marry You
   Loose End

[II.b] Outtakes
   Held Up Without a Gun
   Roulette
   Restless Nights
   Dollhouse
   Where the Bands Are
   Living on the Edge of the World
   Take 'Em as They Come
   Ricky Wants a Man of Her Own
   I Wanna Be With You
   Mary Lou
   From Small Things (Big Things One Day Come)
   Meet Me in the City
   The Man Who Got Away
   Little White Lies
   The Time That Never Was
   Night Fire
   Whitetown
   Chain Lightning
   Party Lights
   Stray Bullet
   Paradise by the C

The River is a pivotal work. Whereas *Darkness on the Edge of Town* is mostly about the individual, isolated but defiant, *The River* is mostly concerned with connection and community, albeit with failure and the pull of isolation still ever-present for some of the characters. The shift is subtle but undeniable. The album is about the loss of innocence. About facing up to things *as they are*. It contains a philosophical view of life, something which neither the Beatles nor Bob Dylan attempted, and shows that Springsteen was operating within an American literary tradition – Steinbeck, Faulkner, Kerouac – as well as drawing on the American cinema of John Ford and others to create images in music. The album contains Springsteen's deepest songs of love and loss, as well as some of his most personal writing. The title track draws on his sister's life; 'Independence Day' is his deepest meditation on his relationship with his father. There is a strand of songs on the fragility of life, from the rocker 'Cadillac Ranch', about death, to the country ballad that ends the album, 'Wreck on the Highway', about the fear of losing a loved one. Sonically, Springsteen used the E Street Band in a new way, almost as a chamber ensemble. Each instrument is clearly defined but used economically. Every note matters. The music sounds nocturnal, mysterious. Some of the rockers are not of the stature of the album's finest songs, most of which are ballads, dark in tone, but Springsteen knew that the contrast was necessary. Musically, they fit. He wanted *The River* to include all aspects of the band's live concerts. It's revealing how some of the lesser songs have a sting in the tail. After listening to *The River* from beginning to end, it is the melancholy that lingers longest. 'All you can do is say there are possibilities,' Springsteen remarked to Fred Schruers during *The River* tour. 'Dreams and possibilities make you strong. That's what I hope people get from our music. That's what I got from the Drifters, say, 'Under the Boardwalk'. As full as the singer sounds, it always had that little sadness that made you love it, made you recognise it as being true.'[1]

The album features wonderful guitar playing in the mid-1960s style of the Beatles, fast picking patterns and melodic riffs, as well as Beatlesque vocal harmonies. Nowhere is this more apparent than in the fast opening track, 'The Ties That Bind'. Following a sharp snap on the snare and four Csus2 chords, two duetting electric guitars play the introductory melody, underpinned by Tallent's bassline. The guitars dominate, taking on the role previously assigned to Bittan's piano. The music moves between C, F, and G, before dropping to A minor in the middle eight. Clemons's sax solo surfs above the syncopated electronic twang of Springsteen and Van Zandt's intertwining guitars. The key changes to D for the final verse.

---

[1] Quoted in 'Bruce Springsteen and the Secret of the World', in *Rolling Stone* (5 February 1981).

'Sherry Darling', in F, is a piece of (high class) bubble-gum summer pop, replete with party noises and driven by Clemons's sax. It is also a comic monologue, for to be with his girl the singer has to put up with her mother, her 'big feet' in the car and her constant yapping. The joy of the music is contrasted with the cruelty of the lyric. It is telling how that one image about the size of the mother's feet and the detail about driving her to the unemployment agency, is all Springsteen requires to convey the characters and the situation.

The next song couldn't offer a greater contrast. In the enigmatic 'Jackson Cage', the view of life is extremely bleak. It is unlikely that Springsteen was thinking of the town near Freehold in New Jersey. 'Jackson cage' could be an oblique reference to William Faulkner's *As I Lay Dying*, for one of the characters is placed in a 'cage in Jackson' (Jackson being an insane asylum). Springsteen's cage is a metaphor for the circumstances faced by the young woman and man in the song, 'handed life' (condemned by the hand dealt to them at birth) and crushed to such an extent that they 'turn the key' themselves. 'Jackson Cage' connects with 'The Ties That Bind' and, particularly, 'Point Blank'. There is, in this work, a preoccupation with young women who have been hurt, who are fatalistic and wary of the ties that bind. Musically the song is among E Street's finest achievements. Ringing guitar work from Springsteen and Van Zandt and swirling organ licks from Federici are supported by Tallent's rhythmical bassline and Weinberg's intense drumming. Bittan's piano enters after the first verse. The music is balanced between $C^{\sharp}$ minor and E major. The $C^{\sharp}$ minor-A-E melody ends with $F^{\sharp}$ minor rather than the expected B. In the chorus the $C^{\sharp}$ minor to E progression is reversed before the music moves to $G^{\sharp}$ minor.

The fast rocker 'Two Hearts' is based on a C to Csus4 pattern. In some of the songs on *The River*, for the first time in his work, Springsteen wrote very direct lyrics, unconcerned that some listeners would find the words corny. When compared to the finest songs on the album, 'Two Hearts' is nothing at all, but the music is exuberant, and the song would work in concert as a duet between Springsteen and Van Zandt.

In 'Independence Day', one of Springsteen's greatest songs, the words and music are perfectly matched. This melancholy song is in F and uses major keys throughout. The attractive melody is built on three chords, $B^{\flat}$, F and C. After the drop to C, the phrase ends with the ambiguity of $B^{\flat}$ rather than the resolution of F (deceptive cadences often feature in Springsteen's songs). The introduction, played by Federici on the organ, rises and falls by thirds, each rise and fall ending with a suspended chord, resolved. Van Zandt's acoustic guitar provides the backing. As Springsteen starts to sing, Bittan produces deft touches on the piano. Drums, bass and an electric guitar, all played subtly, are added. The instrumental break contains one of Clemons's finest solos. The sax is played lyrically. During the penultimate verse, somehow complementing the loneliness of the words, Bittan adds a lovely countermelody beneath the vocal: a single-note phrase that begins with G to F, then climbs a fourth to B♭ and finally descends an octave.

Side two opens with another of the direct songs. 'Hungry Heart' is the catchiest song on *The River*, the emotional slogan of its title slightly deeper than the previous side's 'Two Hearts'. The seemingly straightforward melody is in the difficult key of C♯ major. Bittan plays eight quavers in the bar, combining with punchy bass, organ licks, glockenspiel, and superb vocal harmonies.

'Out in the Street' is an invitation to dance and sing in A major. The introduction, though, ends with a drop to G. The infectious melody begins simply enough with a D-E-A-D progression before surprising with C♯ and F♯ minor. The chorus is introduced by a powerful F♯ minor, B minor, F♯ minor, F♯ major progression. The chorus returns us to the home key but reverses the order (A-D-A-E). The instruments combine thrillingly. The guitars and keyboards often play in unison. Weinberg pitches his drumming perfectly and Tallent provides yet another outstanding bass pattern. Clemons plays a signature solo. Vocal harmonies are used very effectively.

'Crush on You' changes the mood. Unromantic sexual desire is the theme of what may be the most raucous, dirty-sounding guitar-and-drums-based music ever recorded by the E Street Band. An E-A-E riff is concluded by C♯ minor and B major. 'My masterpiece,' Springsteen would proclaim ironically before singing the song during complete performances of the album in 2016. The two-chord (C and F) rocker 'You Can Look (But You Better Not Touch)' is droll in a dark kind of way, for there is bitterness at the song's heart.

'I Wanna Marry You' is a subdued love song in which sentimentality and realism find an unlikely balance. The music has an old-fashioned charm. The theme is romantic sexual desire ('Crush on You' and 'I Wanna Marry You' have both sides of the male psyche covered). The swinging melody is in D. In the Beatlesque middle eight, there is a swooning modulation to F♯ minor 7 and B minor 7. The character in the song is in love with a young single mother, working a low paid job and perhaps ostracised by her local community. In concert, the song would follow a prologue, sung by Springsteen, Clemons and Van Zandt, suggesting that the girl in the song represented someone the young Springsteen had seen walking by, someone he had never forgotten even though he had never spoken to her (the kind of memory we all share). In this sense, the song is not a wedding proposal but a dream.

'The River', ending side two, and 'Point Blank', beginning side three, are the key songs on the album. They link to 'Jackson Cage', on side one, and

'Fade Away' and 'Stolen Car' (closing side three) and 'Drive All Night' and 'Wreck on the Highway' (closing side four). It was at the first of the *No Nukes* concerts in 1979 that Springsteen premiered 'The River', introducing it with the words, 'This is my brother-in-law and my sister'. Perhaps Springsteen's most beautiful song, 'The River' is a fine example of his concise, evocative storytelling as well as a heartfelt gift to his sister Virginia. Influenced, in part, by the songs of Hank Williams, Springsteen imagined that a man was telling his story to a stranger in a bar. In E minor, the melody takes in G, D, Cadd9 and A minor. Springsteen's harmonica is prominent, but the song is carried by Van Zandt's twelve-string acoustic guitar and Bittan's delicate piano. There is a masterly change to the structure – a double-verse before the final chorus – and one of the great rhymes – 'brother's car' with 'reservoir'. The river is used poetically, as a metaphor for youth, hope and beauty, for a woman's body, for desire and intimacy. The young lovers marry when the girl gets pregnant, and they persevere through hard times. But the river is dry. What a devastating final line that is. In an episode of BBC Radio 3's poetry programme, *The Verb*, Ian McMillan spoke of how the image of the river 'helps Springsteen to talk about time and change' (2019).

Side three opens with another masterpiece. The grave 'Point Blank', in B minor, is placed at the centre of the work. It is a night song, acutely tender, and a memory song, haunted by the past, by missed opportunities, longing and regret. Springsteen's writing reveals a sensitivity to the experiences of young women during the transition from teenage life to adulthood.[1] The last verses are particularly fine. A man snatches a moment of tenderness with a girl on the dance floor of a bar, and some years later sees her on the street, alone, sheltering from the rain in a doorway, like a stranger. He calls out her name, but she looks away. It is unknown whether Springsteen drew on a particular relationship or used his writer's imagination. The song is a passacaglia, built on Tallent's elegant bass ostinato and Bittan's classical piano, the music following a B minor, G, A, F$^\sharp$ minor and F$^\sharp$7 pattern. The sound produced by Federici on the organ and Van Zandt or Springsteen on the guitar evokes a distant siren or alarm.

'Cadillac Ranch', in G, is a blast, until you realise that the Cadillac represents a hearse and the Cadillac ranch a graveyard. 'I'm a Rocker' is a piece of joyful nonsense that is used to momentarily lighten the mood. In 'Fade Away' a love affair has ended, and the singer feels as if he is disappearing. The strong melody uses G, A and D. There is a fine transition before the final verse. The

---

[1] The National Organisation for Women, however, objected to Springsteen's use of the term 'little girl' in his songs.

music travels from B minor to E minor 7 and then from Asus4 to A. Van Zandt's twelve-string guitar and Federici's organ are the featured instruments.

The music in 'Stolen Car' moves between G and an inverted C (with G forming the bass note). An electric guitar strums the chords and Bittan plays falling bell-like phrases on the piano. The song is a duet for voice and piano. Sustained vocal harmonies enhance the song's eery tone. Haunted as it is by desperation and loneliness, 'Stolen Car' is the one song on the album that takes the listener into a chasm from which there is no way back. The stark music matches the words. The singer could be the character from several of the other songs, including 'Fade Away'.

The final side of *The River* begins with a burst of rock and roll guitar, introducing the hypnotic riff, played by Federici, that repeats throughout 'Ramrod'. The song is in the rarely used key of F♯ (six sharps) and has a great groove. Springsteen and Van Zandt's voices combine for the final verse. The song, though, is insubstantial. The mysterious 'The Price You Pay', in G, is a kind of summation, as well as a hymn, a metaphorical journey from the city to the desert and finally to a new frontier, a river at the edge of a chosen land. Acoustic and electric guitars underpin the pleasing melody and beautiful vocal harmonies. The music softens for the penultimate verse. Tallent's bass and Federici's accordion accompany the singer before the guitars and piano kick back in. There is an unexpected move to E minor during the final line, and a single snap on the snare before the return to G. The meaning of the song is unresolved, but the images resonate, particularly the final plea to tear down the signs that keep people boxed in and written-off.

'Drive All Night' is an intense love song. In the key of F, the melodic line swings through B♭ and C. Springsteen plays the piano part, a motif that repeats throughout the song over a simple but effective drum and bass pattern from Weinberg and Tallent. The space between the notes is as important as the notes themselves. Bittan plays a descending phrase on the organ, doubled by Federici's glockenspiel. The song is a slow-burn that darkens as Springsteen sings about dances for the dead. Clemons's sax rips into the song. Springsteen used the recording made during the *Darkness on the Edge of Town* sessions but overdubbed a new vocal.

The River concludes with the sombre ballad 'Wreck on the Highway'. In a few short verses, the song speaks for all of us in expressing the most profound of our fears – the fear of losing the people we love. The music is built on Tallent's dotted bass ostinato and Federici's country organ, with delicate guitar work at the heart of the mix. Once the A to D melody has concluded the music drops to F♯ minor for the loneliest of codas. The music slowly fades.

The River tour, Bingley Hall, Stafford, England, 20 May 1981.
Photo by Steve Rapport (Getty Images).

3   THE RIVER TOUR

At the end of September 1980, the band rehearsed for four nights at a rehearsal facility in Lititz, Pennsylvania. The tour began a few days later, on 3 October, in Ann Arbor at the University of Michigan's Crisler Arena. *The River*, released on the 17th, was a commercial and critical success, climbing to number one in the charts, a first for Springsteen and the band. Reviewing 'the longest awaited and most anticipated record of all' in *The Guardian*, Robin Denselow wrote: 'It took me hours to get through this album, for I kept re-playing the tracks I'd just heard. It's that good. [...] He ends with 'Wreck on the Highway', a vivid country-tinged ballad in which the themes of fate and cars come together. It adds up to the classic we've been waiting for.'[1] Vic Garbarini, writing for *Musician*, found that the album, with its 'skeletal textures' dominated by Springsteen and Van Zandt's jangling guitars, came over as opaque at first, until the listener tumbled in like Alice through the looking glass. 'It's a work of uncommon courage – an open confrontation with the fears, failures and insecurities that we all try to shove under the carpet of our waking consciousness.'[2]

Now widely considered to be the greatest band of its generation, the tour would take the band back to Europe for the first time since 1975. It was at this time that Springsteen started to address in his work, subtly and without fanfare, political and social issues.

From Ann Arbor, the band travelled to Cincinnati, Detroit, Chicago, St Paul, Milwaukee, St Louis, Denver, Seattle and Portland. In California, two shows in Oakland were followed by a four-night stand at the Memorial Sports Arena in Los Angeles, 30 October to 3 November. Bittan was regularly prefacing 'The River' with a new piano introduction as well as quoting from Bach's C major prelude during the band introductions. On nights when 'The River' and 'Badlands' were played back-to-back, the two became a single suite of music thanks to Bittan's prelude to 'The River' and the linking music based on Morricone's 'Once Upon a Time in the West'. The band's performance at Arizona State University in Tempe on 5 November, the day after Ronald Reagan's election as President, was recorded and partially filmed. Finally released in 2015, as part of *The River* box set, the film remains the only officially

---

[1] Robin Denselow, 'Blue collar blues: Robin Denselow reviews new work from Springsteen and Bowie', in *The Guardian* (8 October 1980), p.10.
[2] Vic Garbarini, 'Bruce Springsteen: The River', in Musician, *The Year in Rock, 1981-82* (LSP Books, 1981), p.217-18.

approved visual record of the tour.¹

Next came shows in Dallas, Austin, Baton Rouge, Houston and Largo. At the end of November, the band gave two concerts at Madison Square Garden in New York, and then travelled to Pittsburgh, Rochester and Buffalo. On 8 December, during the band's show at the Spectrum in Philadelphia, John Lennon was murdered. The road crew didn't tell them while they were on stage – 'They saved it from us till after the show,' Federici recalled. Van Zandt was so devastated he wanted to cancel the 9 December show at the Spectrum, but Springsteen argued that it was more important than ever to go on stage. At the beginning of the concert, Springsteen told the audience: 'It's a hard night to come out when so much has been lost. The first record that I ever learned was 'Twist and Shout' and if it wasn't for John Lennon, we'd all be in some place very different tonight. It's an unreasonable world and you have to live with a lot of things that are just unliveable. And it's a hard thing to come out and play but there's just nothing else you can do.' Fred Schruers, who was present, wrote about the extraordinary intensity of the band that night and the feelings the concert provoked. The next day Van Zandt told him: 'I've heard those songs a million fucking times, and it was like I never heard them before. I've watched him write, months and months of digging, but last night was a weird feeling – like you were in exactly the same place he was when he wrote them.'²

Springsteen was unaware that Lennon considered him to be the great young artist of the time, and especially admired *The River*. Lennon had spoken about Springsteen to *Rolling Stone* on the day he was killed. 'God help Bruce Springsteen when they decide he's no longer God,' he had said. The quote is poignant because he was surely in part thinking about himself. Lennon's murder prompted Springsteen to make the concerts more sombre and reflective. He still included episodes of slapstick and tales of romance; he still ended the night with a joyful divertissement – but there was a sense that the joy had to be earned. Returning to Madison Square Garden, Springsteen introduced a new song, Creedence Clearwater Revival's anti-war, anti-corruption, classic 'Who'll Stop the Rain', often sung as a protest against social injustice. The band ended the year with a remarkable three-night stand at the Nassau Coliseum in Uniondale, New York, 28, 29 and 31 December. By now, the concerts were regularly featuring thirty songs or more and lasting well over three hours. Highlights of the 29 December show included a rare 'Incident on 57th Street',

---

¹ The ten songs not included in the film, mixed by Bob Clearmountain, were released on CD/digital download in 2016.

² See Fred Schruers, 'Bruce Springsteen and the Secret of the World', in *Rolling Stone* (5 February 1981).

full-band, and meaningful pairings of 'Factory' with 'Independence Day' and 'Stolen Car' with 'Wreck on the Highway'. The New Year's Eve show consisted of thirty-eight songs, among them Guthrie's 'This Land Is Your Land', 'In the Midnight Hour' and 'Twist and Shout'. The three shows were officially recorded by Toby Scott, only to collect dust in the archives. They were finally transferred from the tapes and released during the digital era.[1]

The *No Nukes* appearances had been the first indication that Springsteen was willing to address contemporary political issues directly, and the inclusion in the set of Fogerty's 'Who'll Stop the Rain' and Guthrie's 'This Land Is Your Land' in the days following the rise of Ronald Reagan's neo-conservatism in a country still suffering the consequences of the economic recession of the late 1970s, was an oblique form of protest. Springsteen would continue to perform these songs during the rest of *The River* tour.

Following a two-week break, the band resumed the tour in Canada with shows in Toronto, Montreal and Ottawa. The itinerary then took them to St Louis, St Paul, Southern Illinois University, Kansas City, Mississippi State University, followed by a trio of shows in Florida. The leg came to an end with performances in Atlanta, Memphis, Nashville, Greensboro, and Indianapolis (on 5 March).

On 17 March, Springsteen and the band were due to start their first European tour since the very brief 1975 visit to England, Sweden and the Netherlands with a show in Brighton. For the first time, the band would perform in Germany, Switzerland, France, Catalonia, Belgium, Denmark and Norway. The stakes were once more very high. Whether solely because of exhaustion following a bronchial infection (the official reason) or partly to delay the high-profile and significant British concerts, the long UK leg was postponed until May and June. Springsteen and the band started the tour in Hamburg on 7 April, before travelling on to Berlin, Zurich, Munich, and then to Paris for two shows at the Palais des Sports in the 15th arrondissement. Here Springsteen premiered his version of Elvis's 'Follow That Dream'. Next came Barcelona, Lyon, Brussels, and Rotterdam, where Springsteen sang an original song based on Creedence's 'Run Through the Jungle', written in response to the 11 April race riot in Brixton, south London ('Well now the land is on fire, it's written in blood in the sky'). Shows in Copenhagen, Gothenburg, Drammen and Stockholm brought the continental leg to a close. Springsteen hadn't known what to expect from European audiences, since in nearly all these countries he was playing for the first time; but everywhere, people were wildly

---

[1] Released on CD/digital download in 2019 and 2021.

enthusiastic and knowledgeable about the music. Some of the European reviewers, however, allocated few words to the music, preferring to use their columns to write about their idea of Springsteen as a new American icon. 'He arrived in Paris to give two concerts at the Palais des Sports, this little guy from New Jersey, the one they call the boss,' wrote Alain Wais in *Le Monde*. 'We would finally be able to judge the stature of the man, this new American hero with his Italian-American face straight out of a Scorsese film and his angelic smile, with his hooligan demeanour and charismatic presence, with his guitar poised to produce the surliest riffs.'

At the beginning of May, the band arrived in England for the start of a month of concerts in the UK. At the City Hall in Newcastle, Springsteen inserted a line about the Brixton riots into 'This Land Is Your Land' – 'Now they're dying on the streets of New York and down in Liberty City, in Harlem County and the streets of Brixton, people wonder, people worry, if this land was made for you and me'. Two nights at the Apollo Theatre in Manchester, during which Springsteen debuted 'Johnny Bye', about Elvis's death, were followed by shows in Edinburgh, at the Playhouse, and Stafford, at the Bingley Hall. The band then headed south for their first UK show in an arena, the Brighton Centre in Brighton.

At the end of May, they arrived in London for a six-night residency at the iconic Wembley Arena. Six long years after a nervous Springsteen had taken to the stage of the Hammersmith Odeon, much had changed. His body of work was now substantial, and his writing had the depth to appeal to creative artists and commentators who were not normally interested in rock music (beyond the work of the Beatles and Dylan). Pete Townshend, Elvis Costello, and the young members of U2 were among the many artists who attended the shows. In 1975, Townshend had recognised that Springsteen was the coming man: 'Until the British Punk-rock movement kicked off there were just two contenders for our crown: The Rolling Stones and the upstart Bruce Springsteen.'[1]

But there was something about London that made Springsteen feel like he was auditioning for a place at the top table, and which put everyone in the band on edge. One senses, from the relative shortness of the performances, that the band didn't truly start to relax until the third show, and then never looked back. Reviewing the opening night for *The Sunday Times*, Derek Jewell wrote:

> No performer in the world personifies the life-force of popular music more vividly than Bruce Springsteen. His searing and exhausting three-hour concert at Wembley Arena on Friday proved that conclusively. […]

---

[1] Pete Townshend, *Who I Am* (London: Harper Collins, 2012), p.281-82.

His concert, indeed, was as much a celebration as a performance [...]. This frenetic activity was married to outgoing songs like 'Cadillac Ranch'. His demeanour during contemplative pieces was even more striking. He would stand quietly in mid-stage, silencing the thousands with the excoriating lyrics born of his maturity. Such songs, sung in that hoarse and expressive voice, which burns itself on the memory, are his greatest glory. 'Independence Day', 'The River', 'Stolen Car', 'Point Blank', 'Factory', all of them gaunt or tragic or terrifying in their different fashions, and arranged with telling economy. The brilliant playing [...] by the E Street Band was an essential element of a memorable evening shot through with contrasts of pace and mood. So was the lighting, used continually as an understatement, with soloists caught in gentle glimmers that emphasised the blackness around them.[1]

'Trapped', based on a song by Jimmy Cliff, and 'Jolé Blon' were premiered in London. The final London show, on 5 June, was released as a digital download and CD set in 2018. Springsteen and the band closed out their European tour with two shows at the National Exhibition Centre in Birmingham. Pete Townshend joined the band onstage during 'Born to Run' on night one. Night two (8 June), the band's European finale, included 'Trapped', 'Follow That Dream', 'Johnny Bye', 'Who'll Stop the Rain', as well as 'Jackson Cage' and 'Jungleland'. The show ended with 'Rockin' All Over the World'.

The European tour was special for fans of the E Street Band, old and new. UK concertgoers had Springsteen and the band to themselves for a whole month and saw them in theatres and arenas. Because of the mega-success of *Born in the USA*, and the need to make tours profitable (the sold-out European tour made a loss because the ticket sales didn't cover the high cost of the touring operation), the band played in football stadiums when they returned in 1985 and 1988. Arenas were chosen for the UK leg of the Reunion Tour in 1999 but there have only been a few indoor shows in Europe in all the years since.

Before returning to the States, Springsteen attended, with Townshend, U2's show at the Hammersmith Palais in London (9 June). On 22 June, everyone gathered in East Orange, New Jersey, to celebrate Max Weinberg's wedding. On 2 July, the band began a six-night stand at the new Brendan Byrne (Meadowlands) Arena in East Rutherford (an inner-suburb of New York on the New Jersey side of the Hudson), playing to 20,000 home fans per night. Springsteen's version of Tom Wait's 'Jersey Girl' was premiered. 'We couldn't hear

---

[1] Derek Jewell, 'The Man Who Was Born to Run', in *The Sunday Times* (May 1981).

ourselves on stage,' Springsteen said after the first show. 'I felt like the Beatles.' Next came a residency at the Spectrum in Philadelphia. The tour's final leg took the band to Largo, Washington DC, Detroit, Morrison (two shows at the Red Rocks Amphitheatre), and Los Angeles (a six-night stand at the Memorial Sports Arena). The first LA show was a benefit for the Vietnam Veterans of America Foundation, a cause close to Springsteen's heart. The idea of using a concert to support the VVA came out of Springsteen's chance meeting with Ron Kovac, Vietnam veteran and author of the book *Born on the Fourth of July*, in LA during a short break in the touring schedule following the European leg. The concert included 'Who'll Stop the Rain' and the band's only known cover of the Byrds' 'Ballad of Easy Rider'. It was after the experience of meeting veterans at the concert, that Springsteen started to address the legacy of the Vietnam War in his work.

During the final LA show, the band played, for the first and last time, Woody Guthrie's 'Plane Wreck at Los Gatos (Deportee)'. The year-long *River* tour came to an end with shows in San Diego, Rosemont (Illinois) and Cincinnati (on 14 September).

EIGHT: REASONS TO BELIEVE

I   RECORDING SESSIONS 1982-84

If Springsteen's bandmates, gathering in New York at the beginning of 1982, hoped that the process of making their new album would prove to be less protracted and less stressful than had been the case with its two predecessors – after all, nearly a decade's experience in the recording studio should count for something – they were quickly disappointed. Springsteen, as usual, post-*Born to Run*, had written so many songs (over seventy in fact) that he was confronted by a myriad of possibilities.

But there was another pressure. Following the very successful *River* tour, Springsteen was potentially on the brink of tabloid fame, and superstardom was something that he was deeply ambivalent about. He would eventually decide to take his shot at fame, but only after he had delayed the studio record by releasing the low-key *Nebraska* demos instead. Most significant of all, Springsteen suffered a profound personal crisis towards the end of 1982. Springsteen has confessed that, off stage, he rarely felt comfortable in his own skin at this time. The process of making a record was, in fact, the least difficult aspect of his life during his early thirties. This was a period when Springsteen was seeking to make sense of his life outside of rock music.

The process of making the new album began in December 1981, when Springsteen decided to record some home demos before going into the studio with the band that January. This was his way of trying to speed up the recording process. He had been writing a series of intimate songs, inspired in part by his reading of the short stories of Flannery O'Connor, that drew on his childhood experiences in and around Freehold. In *The River*, Springsteen, influenced by the economy of expression and frank truthfulness of the finest folk and country music, had started to pare down his writing style, turning songs into evocative monologues or poetic short stories in which places were evoked, people described and feelings expressed in a few telling details or a strikingly representative image: 'Point Blank', 'Stolen Car' and 'Wreck on the Highway' are good examples. He continued this approach in an even starker style in the songs he wrote in his rented ranch house in the wooded country of Colts Neck, Monmouth County. The house was situated beside a reservoir, perhaps the reservoir that features in the final stanza of 'The River', for Springsteen had chosen to live in his old stomping ground, less than ten miles from Freehold. Despite their intimacy, some of these short-story songs seemed to magically expand until they had the visual resonance of whole movies. Springsteen was exploiting one of his greatest gifts as a lyricist, a gift that had been apparent even before *The River* in songs such as 'Meeting Across the River' from *Born to Run* or 'Factory' from *Darkness on the Edge of Town*.

If some of the songs he taped on a Teac Tascam four-deck cassette recorder in his house in Colts Neck – 'Mansion on the Hill', 'Used Cars', 'My Father's House' – were haunted by his childhood memories, and told from a child's point of view, others were concerned with outsiders and small-town criminals. Springsteen was influenced here by the noir novels of James M. Cain and Terrence Malick's films *Badlands* and *Days of Heaven*. 'Nebraska' may be the most chilling expression of existentialism ever committed to tape by a contemporary songwriter, while 'Highway Patrolman' is a humane tale of two brothers on either side of the law.

In March, the E Street Band began committing the Colts Neck demo songs to tape at the Power Station. Chuck Plotkin joined the production team, and Toby Scott took the engineer's seat. The band continued the *Darkness* and *River* method of recording the songs live as a unit, and 'Born in the USA' was recorded in one take, created on the spot from two chords. 'Downbound Train' also lent itself to a full band arrangement. Springsteen used most of the lyrics of the Colts Neck demo 'Child Bride' but completely changed the music and tone to create 'Working on the Highway'. These three tracks would eventually be selected for the studio record. Springsteen decided that the others, even in the subtle arrangements that he had composed for the band, did not: their delicate aural atmosphere was lost. (The band recordings of the *Nebraska* songs will hopefully one day be released.) Springsteen made solo recordings of the songs in the studio, but still wasn't happy. He asked Toby Scott if the recordings on the demo tape – a cassette he had been carrying around in his pocket for weeks – could be improved but otherwise released as they were.

While this was being considered, the band carried on into the early summer recording other songs. 'Darlington County', 'I'm on Fire', 'I'm Goin' Down' and 'Glory Days', all recorded in May, would – along with 'Cover Me' (recorded right at the beginning of the sessions in January) – make it onto the studio record, but only after other track listings had been considered. Among the other songs recorded were 'Lion's Den', 'Murder Incorporated', 'My Love Will Not Let You Down', 'Wages of Sin', 'This Hard Land' and 'Frankie'. For a short while, Springsteen considered the idea of releasing a double album, one record devoted to the Colts Neck recordings, and the other consisting of the band songs 'Born in the USA', 'Murder Incorporated', 'Downbound Train', 'I'm Goin' Down', 'Glory Days', 'My Love Will Not Let You Down', 'Working on the Highway', 'Darlington County', 'Frankie', 'I'm on Fire' and 'This Hard Land'. Against the odds, Scott and Bob Ludwig were able to transfer, mix and master the demo recordings onto vinyl, and Springsteen, with the support of Van Zandt and Landau, signed off on a September release of *Nebraska*. Intriguingly, two of the demo songs, 'Child Bride' and 'The Losin' Kind', were left off the album, and have never been released.

Following the release of *Nebraska*, Springsteen halted the E Street recording sessions, broke up with his young girlfriend of the last few years, and spent most of the autumn and winter of 1982/83 in Los Angeles. Many years later, in one of the most powerful passages of his autobiography, Springsteen would reveal how, on the road trip to LA, at a country fair in a little Texan town (the kind of scene that he had tenderly evoked in several songs – for instance, the alternative version of 'Stolen Car'), an epiphany forced him to confront issues relating to his personal life and character. Soon after arriving in California, he sought the professional help that would enable him to cope with severe depression.[1]

Depression didn't hamper Springsteen's creativity, in fact it seemed to feed into it. Here, in his house in the Hollywood Hills, between January and April, he embarked on a new round of solo recording. Over twenty new songs were recorded, and Springsteen briefly considered releasing them as a follow-up to *Nebraska*. Only two of the songs, 'Johnny Bye' and the masterly 'Shut Out the Light', have been released. 'Shut Out the Light', about a soldier returning home from Vietnam, psychologically traumatised and unable to adjust to normal life despite the love of the uncomprehending people around him, had a personal dimension.

That spring, Springsteen returned east, finally committed to making and releasing a commercial E Street Band studio album. The band reconvened at the Hit Factory in May 1983. Tensions between Springsteen and Steve Van Zandt came to a head at this time. Van Zandt, a brilliant songwriter and record producer, as well as a singular man of ideas with a powerful personality, wanted a bigger role in decision-making, something that Springsteen instinctively resisted, although he did listen to his friend, adopting his ideas when he felt they

---

[1] See Springsteen, *Born to Run*, p.301-12.

were right. He had made Van Zandt co-producer of both *The River* and *Born in the USA*, and, during the former, had shared his wish for the recordings to have a rawness to them, a live feel. Van Zandt made a significant contribution when it came to arrangements. He wrote in his memoirs that Springsteen had stopped listening but didn't go into the specifics. It is likely that Van Zandt was seeking an equal say over production, arrangements, and especially song choices, since we know that Van Zandt felt that too many great songs had been rejected during the making of *The River*.

Despite their natural affinity, their natures were different. Off the stage, Springsteen was still somewhat shy, whereas Van Zandt was a straight-talking extrovert. This helped Springsteen. He had relied greatly on Van Zandt during his rise to prominence, benefitting from his insights, talent, daring and absolute support. However, they didn't always agree artistically. Van Zandt had grown tired of losing arguments by default, particularly when he believed, unequivocally, that he was right. Perhaps brotherly rivalry was a factor. Springsteen was wary of handing over even a modicum of real power because he wasn't prepared to compromise when it came to his own work. The boundaries he had established early on to ensure that band democracy didn't wreck the whole thing, were still firmly in place. His bandmates gave everything to the cause, and Springsteen gave everything back, except any real power. The bond was mutually dependent. Even with the boundaries, the early E Street Band had been a 'madhouse' (Springsteen's own word).[1]

Springsteen and Van Zandt talked things through late one night in Springsteen's New York hotel room. At the end of the discussion Van Zandt rashly quit the band. The outcome was devastating for both men, but they had boxed themselves into a corner. Springsteen took Van Zandt's departure hard. It is lonely on stage without the people who make you feel safe. On his side, Van Zandt hated leaving and missing out on E Street's next adventure. He felt he was betraying his friend. Springsteen and Van Zandt had started as equals, but when Springsteen's genius had revealed itself, Van Zandt had chosen to support him and to place his personal ambitions on hold. The break with Springsteen was unplanned and unnecessary. Van Zandt felt like he was entering the wilderness.

For years, Van Zandt had chosen to give his own songs to Southside Johnny and the Asbury Jukes and to act as the band's producer, a role he continued to fulfil after he joined the E Street Band if the schedule allowed. Van Zandt produced Southside Johnny's debut album *I Don't Want to Go Home* in 1976, writing three of the tracks, including the title track (Springsteen donated 'The

---

[1] Springsteen, *Born to Run*, p.253.

Fever' and 'You Mean So Much to Me'). He provided nearly all of the songs on Southside's second album *This Time It's for Real* (1977), and seven of the songs on *Hearts of Stone* (1978). Springsteen provided the title track and 'Talk to Me'.

In 1981, though, Van Zandt started to record a solo record. Members of the E Street Band, including Springsteen (uncredited), played or sang on some of the tracks. Van Zandt completed the album, called *Men Without Women*, while Springsteen finalised *Nebraska* for release. From the summer of 1982, he toured under the name Little Steven and the Disciples of Soul. He planned to prioritise the E Street Band while continuing with his solo projects on the side.

Then came the rupture with Springsteen. On leaving the E Street Band, Van Zandt recorded a second album, *Voice of America*, and began to combine music with effective political activism, establishing Artists United Against Apartheid, writing the protest song 'Sun City' and producing the album of the same name.

With only a short break in August, the band continued to record until February 1984. Of the songs recorded during the July to February period, 'My Hometown', 'Bobby Jean', 'No Surrender' and 'Dancing in the Dark' would make it onto the *Born in the USA* album, forming most of the second side. 'Bobby Jean' and 'No Surrender' were, in part, songs of farewell written for Van Zandt; while 'Dancing in the Dark', the last track recorded (on 16 February), was composed in a single night because the album needed a potential hit single. Rejected songs included 'Pink Cadillac', 'Car Wash', 'None But the Brave', 'TV Movie', 'Cynthia', 'Stand On It', 'Janey, Don't You Lose Heart', 'Brothers Under the Bridges', 'Man at the Top' and 'Rockaway the Days'. It took time to decide on the track listing of *Born in the USA*. 'Cynthia', 'Nothing But the Brave', 'Shut Out the Light', 'Johnny Bye', 'My Love Will Not Let You Down', 'Janey, Don't You Lose Heart' and the yet to be released songs 'Sugarland' and 'Follow That Dream' were serious contenders. Speculation about when an album would appear had been building for months. When *Rolling Stone* asked Van Zandt about it, he said: 'With forty-two wars going on in the world, I don't worry about it.'

The final choice made cohesive sense. The songs of *Born in the USA* belonged together, connected by themes of friendship and stoicism in the face of hard times, but, as Springsteen has said, with *Nebraska*'s black pit of isolation and alienation waiting just beneath the surface. It is a rock record, but its finest songs – 'Downbound Train', 'I'm on Fire' and 'My Hometown' – are interior monologues. The music was brilliantly recorded and mixed by Toby Scott and Bob Clearmountain. Even today, in comparison with so much 1980s music, the recording style – particularly the drum sound – remains thrillingly current.

The synthesizer parts, played by Roy Bittan, were subdued but lyrical. It was a record designed to break the E Street Band into the big time, and if there is a criticism, it is that one suspects a measure of calculation in the song selection (if so, it was a calculation that Springsteen resisted for over two years). It is true that, as with *The River*, a number of the finest songs recorded during the sessions were rejected in favour of lesser music. For me, a different record consisting of 'Frankie', 'Shut Out the Light', 'Wages of Sin' and 'Janey, Don't You Lose Heart' in place of 'Darlington County', 'I'm Goin' Down' and 'Glory Days', would have meant more; but this is to miss the point, for *Born in the USA* is more than the sum of its parts.

On 4 June 1984, two-and-a-half years after Springsteen and the E Street Band had started to record songs for their new album, *Born in the USA* was finally released.

2   NEBRASKA

Recorded at Springsteen's house in Colts Neck, New Jersey, between 17 December 1981 and 3 January 1982. Springsteen (acoustic guitar, electric guitar, mandolin, glockenspiel, harmonica, tambourine). Produced by Springsteen; recorded by Mike Batlan. Released on 20 September 1982.

The album:

> Side One:
> Nebraska
> Atlantic City
> Mansion on the Hill
> Johnny 99
> Highway Patrolman
> State Trooper
>
> Side Two:
> Used Cars
> Open All Night
> My Father's House
> Reason to Believe

Released outtakes:
>   The Big Payback

Release: B Side of 'Open All Night' single (1982)

Born in the USA
Release: *Tracks* (1998)

Unreleased outtakes include:
Child Bride
The Losin' Kind
Pink Cadillac

Nebraska is not a rock record, a concept album, or even a folk music experiment. In its ambition and aesthetics, it has more in common with a classical music song-cycle than with rock and roll.

The title track sets the tone for much of the rest of the work, a tone revealed by the singer's voice, hushed, withdrawn, deliberately monotonous. Springsteen has written that the songs were composed to be played in the dark, late at night. He wanted the listeners to feel like they were inside the minds of his characters.[1] The first of these adult lullabies is the bleakest of all. As with all the songs on the album, it is not an easy listen. The listener has to want to engage with the men who haunt the record, has to concentrate to register the succession of images, both mundane and dreamlike, that bring the songs to life, from a grand mansion with lighted windows rising above fields of corn, to a boy noticing how his mother plays nervously with her wedding band; from a teenage girl twirling a baton in a summer garden, to an old man poking a dead dog with a stick. Half of the songs are informed by Springsteen's childhood memories and by an America of limited possibilities and moral uncertainty. The characters are alienated from family and friends, love and faith. They are isolated and there is no way back.

Springsteen uses a major key for all but one of the *Nebraska* songs. D major, shared by 'Nebraska', 'Mansion on the Hill', 'Highway Patrolman', 'Used Cars', and 'My Father's House', dominates. The faster, more rock style songs are in A ('Atlantic City'), B ('Johnny 99') and F$^\#$ ('Open All Night' and 'Reason to Believe'). The brooding 'State Trooper' is in A minor. The subject matter and mood of the songs led Springsteen to compose minimally. However, while the music initially seems to be based on triad chord progressions, added chord notes and suspensions, along with unusual guitar patterns and muted strings, are used very subtly and precisely. These progressions, deliberately plain and repetitive, match the characters and situations they describe. There is a beauty in the music's austerity.

[1] See Bruce Springsteen, *Songs*, p.138.

Terrence Malick's 1973 film *Badlands* inspired Springsteen to research and then write a song about Charles Starkweather, the youth who murdered eleven people during a two-month killing spree in rural Nebraska and Wyoming in 1958. In thirteen lines, the killer makes his confession without any regret: only the sentimental memory of his teenage girlfriend (and accomplice) has any meaning for him. The tinkling of a glockenspiel underlines the killer's banality. The repeated picking pattern on the guitar, utilising an Aadd9 chord, and with the four beats of each bar consisting of a crotchet followed by six quavers, also gives the impression of something off-kilter.

The melody of 'Nebraska' recalls Woody Guthrie's 'This Land Is Your Land', surely intentional. Guthrie's songs, along with those of John Lee Hooker and Robert Johnson, had been meaningful for Springsteen for some years. He admired Joe Klein's biography of Guthrie and had regularly played 'This Land Is Your Land' during *The River* tour. By alluding to 'This Land Is Your Land' in 'Nebraska', Springsteen gave his song both a mythical pedigree and a sense of the most painful irony. In place of Guthrie's utopian 'this land was made for you and me' we have the stark nihilism of there's just a meanness in this world. Springsteen's guitar is tuned a little below standard pitch. Whether this was deliberate or not, it adds to the song's sense of foreboding.

'Nebraska' is followed by the work's most outward-looking song, 'Atlantic City'. Here, the acoustic guitar is strummed rhythmically with colour provided by a mandolin, and the appealing melody moves between A, F# minor and D. As in 'Meeting Across the River', from *Born to Run*, an ordinary man drifts into crime. There is, in the song's beautiful refrain, an expression of hope that lifts the song out of its localism and which challenges the nihilism of the proceeding track. The song cries out for band treatment, and the E Street Band perform it regularly in concert.

'Mansion on the Hill' is the first of the semi-autobiographical songs. Springsteen borrowed the title, if not the tone, from Hank Williams's 1947 classic. Whereas Williams's song has a jaunty country-music character, Springsteen writes a slow folk melody that moves between the major chords of D, G and A. The song is written from a child's viewpoint. The private mansion on the hill, gated and grand, is a symbol for everything that the family of the children in the song will never have; but for the children, it is a place of wonder and mystery. During summer night parties, music and laughter drift over the fields; the boy and his sister hide in the corn, 'listening' to the mansion on the hill.

'Johnny 99' introduces the album's second murderer, but the circumstances are different. Johnny loses his job and can't pay his mortgage; he gets drunk and shoots a night clerk during an attempted robbery. Johnny doesn't ask for sympathy but tells the judge: 'It was more than all this that put that gun in my hand.' Responding to the sentence of ninety-nine years, he asks for the death sentence. The classic rock and roll riff that Springsteen utilises for the song turns Johnny into a kind of rebel or working-class hero: but this is more ironic than boastful. The exuberant music of the harmonica provides a marked contrast to the bleak subject matter.

'Highway Patrolman' forms the humanistic centre of the work. It is a superb story song, remarkable for covering so much ground in six verses. The sombre melody of the verses, backed by an arpeggio figure on the acoustic guitar, are separated by a lyrical chorus. The setting is rural Michigan, close to the Canadian border, during the 1960s. Some details are specific, others imaginary. Joe Roberts, the highway patrolman of the title, tells the story of his wayward brother Frank, the girl they both love, Maria, and what befalls them during the years of the Vietnam War. The details selected by Springsteen imply so much more. Frank goes into the army in 1965 and returns in 68. Springsteen doesn't need to spell out that the war changes him. The narrative has a mythical quality. Joe is given a farm deferment and settles down with Maria. Forced out of farming by the economic recession of the late 1960s, he takes a job as a policeman. Discharged from the army, Frank can't adjust to normal life and is estranged from his brother. One night, Joe gets a call to say that Frank has badly hurt a man in a fight over a girl in a roadhouse. He drives through Michigan County [sic] until he sees the car Frank is driving heading towards the Canadian border. Instead of attempting to apprehend his brother, he pulls over to the side of the highway and watches as the car's taillights disappear.

Springsteen creates a dignified character in Joe Roberts, an ordinary joe who is instantly recognisable and likeable. The final verse provides one of Springsteen's most poignant endings. 'Highway Patrolman' was covered by Johnny Cash, and turned into a film by Sean Penn. The E Street Band played the song during two concerts in New Jersey in 1984, in an evocative arrangement for acoustic guitar, mandolin, piano and drums.

In the next song, 'State Trooper', we are taken into the cabin of Frank's car and we hear his voice (or at least the voice of someone like him). The song is closely aligned to 'Stolen Car' on *The River*. The singer lives on the outside of the law and is driving alone late at night. Over a hypnotic two-chord pattern on the guitar, played *pianissimo*, the singer's angst is expressed in a half-awake murmur until bursting into several high-pitched cries after the desolate phrase 'deliver me from nowhere'.

Side two opens with 'Used Cars', the second of the semi-autobiographical songs. A boy observes his father, mother and sister, as his father buys a used car from a car lot and then drives them home. On the surface, the tone is wryly humorous, but one can feel the boy's underlying rage and embarrassment as he senses his father's humiliation and his mother's unease.

'Open All Night' features an electric guitar and musically could be an old Chuck Berry outtake. A dreamlike evocation of the New Jersey Turnpike at night, it is a lighter take on the subject matter of 'State Trooper' and the least substantial song on the album.

The last of the songs that connect in some way to Springsteen's own life, 'My Father's House', occupies the penultimate track. We are back in the home key of D major. The singer is estranged from his father. One night, he dreams that he is a child again, and the dream takes the form of a dark fairy tale: a boy is lost in a forest and trying to find his way home. He runs through the trees, with the devil snapping at his heels. Finally, he reaches his house and falls into his father's arms. Deeply affected by the dream, the singer drives to his father's house only to discover that his father no longer lives there. The final image is of the house's windows throwing light across the highway. The forlorn melody is in waltz time. A tambourine and a synthesizer are used sparingly.

'Reason to Believe', the ambiguous final song, acts as a coda: despite everything that happens to us, we find a reason to believe. This is perhaps both a declaration of hope and a wry acceptance of the ironies of life. A repeated bass note underpins the vocal line; isolated notes on an electric guitar offer some colour.

3 BORN IN THE USA

Performed by the E Street Band and recorded at the Power Station and the Hit Factory, New York, between January 1982 and February 1984. Clemons (saxophone, backing vocals); Bittan (piano, synthesizer); Federici (organ, glockenspiel); Springsteen (vocals, guitars, harmonica); Tallent (bass); Van Zandt (guitars, mandolin, backing vocals); Weinberg (drums). Additional musicians: La Bamba (backing vocals 'No Surrender'); Ruth Jackson (backing vocals 'My Hometown'). Produced by Springsteen, Van Zandt, Jon Landau, Charles Plotkin; recorded by Toby Scott ('Cover Me' recorded by Bill Scheniman); mixed by Bob Clearmountain. Released on 4 June 1984.

The album:

> Side One:
> Born in the USA
> Cover Me

Darlington County
Working on the Highway
Downbound Train
I'm on Fire

Side Two:
No Surrender
Bobby Jean
I'm Goin' Down
Glory Days
Dancing in the Dark
My Hometown

Released outtakes:

[I] *Tracks* (1998)
    Lion's Den (recorded by Neil Dorfsman)
    My Love Will Not Let You Down
    Wages of Sin
    This Hard Land
    Frankie
    Johnny Bye (Springsteen solo, recorded by Mike Batlan)
    Shut Out the Light (Springsteen solo, with Suzie Tyrell, violin, recorded by Mike Batlan)
    Cynthia
    Car Wash
    Pink Cadillac
    TV Movie
    Janey, Don't You Lose Heart (Lofgren backing vocal added summer 1985)
    Stand On It
    Brothers Under the Bridges
    Man at the Top
    Rockaway the Days

[II] *Greatest Hits* (1995)
    Murder Incorporated

[III] *The Essential Bruce Springsteen* (2003)
    None But the Brave

Unreleased outtakes:

    Full band *Nebraska* songs:

Atlantic City
Highway Patrolman
Johnny 99
The Losin' Kind
Mansion on the Hill
Nebraska
My Father's House
Open All Night
Reason to Believe
Used Cars

Other unreleased outtakes include:

Baby I'm So Cold
Bad Boy
Bells of San Salvador
Betty Jean
Body and Soul
Club Soul City
Common Ground
Delivery Man
Don't Back Down
Fade to Black
Follow That Dream
Fugitive's Dream
Hold On
Glory of Love
Gone (Seeds)
A Gun in Every Home
I Don't Care
Ida Rose
Invitation to Your Party
James Lincoln
Johnny Go Down
Just Around the Corner to the Light of Day
King's Highway
The Klansman
Little Girl Like You
Love's on the Line
The Money We Didn't Make
On the Prowl

One Hundred Miles from Jackson
One Love
Out of Work
Protection
Refrigerator Blues
Richfield Whistle
Robert Ford
Roll Away the Stone
Savin' Up
Seven Tears
Shut Down
Stop the War
Sugarland
Summer on Signal Hill
Swoop Man
True Love is Hard to Come By
Under the Big Sky
Unsatisfied Heart
William Davis
Workin' On It
Your Love is All Around Me

The first side of *Born in the USA* is aligned to *Nebraska*, although the music is mostly upbeat in character. The title track and 'Downbound Train' were written during the Colts Neck sessions.

The pivotal songs on each side, 'Born in the USA' and 'Dancing in the Dark', are in B major. Side one oscillates between B major ('Born in the USA') and B minor ('Cover Me'), and G major ('Darlington County') and G minor ('Downbound Train'). 'Working on the Highway' is in C; 'I'm on Fire' is in E. Except for 'Dancing in the Dark' and 'No Surrender' (which is in F), all the songs on side two are in A. The key selections help to unify the songs while creating musical momentum. Connecting the songs is the theme of blue-collar life at a time of recession.

The Colts Neck version of 'Born in the USA' was a two-chord (A and B) blues howl of rage, lacking melody or refinement. Weinberg's whip-snap snare and Bittan's melodic synthesizer riff transformed the song into a Copeland elegy. It seems that the band plugged in their instruments and played instinctively. Because Bittan played the synthesizer, Federici sat at the piano, placing a single repeated note strategically within the mix. Tallent's bass suggested the stutter of helicopter blades. The song is brilliantly conceived – a patriotic anthem hijacked by a protest singer. The song burns with anger on behalf of the men sent to Vietnam.

'Cover Me', the first of the album's relationship songs, is in the parallel minor key. Springsteen's electric guitar drives the music along with Federici's artistry on the organ and Tallent's perfect bassline. Following the two-chord attack of 'Born in the USA', the melody of 'Cover Me' travels between minor and major chords and is built upon a B minor-D-A riff. Male vulnerability is the unusual theme of the song. 'Darlington County' and 'Working on the Highway' are closely aligned, their characters picking up young women (in the case of the latter an underaged girl) and drifting between temporary low paid jobs and jail time. The bravado of the characters chimes with the major key classic rock and roll bluster of the music but there is tension given the darkness in both tales. The two intimate songs that conclude the first side show a different attitude to hard times. In the forlorn 'Downbound Train' a relationship breaks down because of economic hardship. The character's isolation, pain and longing for the woman he has lost are poignantly described during the final double verse. 'I'm on Fire' takes us inside a man's head. In both songs, Bittan's synthesizer parts are essential. In 'Downbound Train' the verses move from G minor to F via B$^\flat$ followed by a terrific shift to E$^\flat$maj7. In 'I'm on Fire', the progression is from E to C$^\sharp$ minor, followed by a cadence of A-B-E. The muted electric guitar pattern, moving from chord to chord the whole length of the song, conveys the tension in the singer's head. It is played by Lofgren in concert. Bittan creates a wonderful harmony by hanging a mournful F$^\sharp$ over the opening E major pattern (creating an Esus2 chord). Weinberg plays a locomotive rhythm on the drums and Clemons uses a woodblock to add colour. In both its music and lyrics, the song is a lesson in economical writing, on how to create atmosphere in music. This short piece is arguably the album's finest moment.

Side two begins with two life-affirming odes to friendship and ends with a portrait of Freehold. There is a surprising tinge of nostalgia given that Springsteen was not yet thirty-five. The songs on side two are semi-autobiographical: Springsteen references his youth and his friendship with Van Zandt in 'No Surrender' and 'Bobby Jean', and then takes an ironic look at fame in 'Glory Days'. 'I'm Goin' Down' and 'Dancing in the Dark' continue the love song strand from side one. The first is about the end of an affair, the second about the beginning.

Some of the most rousing music ever recorded by the E Street Band can be found on side two of *Born in the USA*. The playing has extraordinary vibrancy and elan. 'No Surrender' is a fast rock anthem that finds hope in both friendship and romantic love and just manages to avoid banality in its use of clichés and combat metaphors. Beginning with four cracking blows on the snare, the

F-C-B♭ melody is driven by Weinberg, Springsteen's rhythm guitar and Tallent's bass. The only change in the musical pattern comes at the end of the penultimate singing of the refrain when the music moves unexpectedly to the subdominant, B♭, and not F.

Like 'No Surrender', the glittering 'Bobby Jean' was in part inspired by Van Zandt's departure from the band. Springsteen says *au revoir* to Van Zandt metaphorically. The stirring melody is built on a four-chord progression: A-C♯ minor-D-B7. In the bridge, the music moves from D to E via F♯ minor. At the end of the final verse, as Springsteen sings the key line, the melody lingers on an unexpected D before returning to the tonic via E. Bittan's piano is more dominant here than elsewhere on the record. He plays a repeated pattern on each change of chord and adds syncopation during the final verse. Clemons delivers a fine solo to end the song. 'Bobby Jean' would often be paired with 'Born to Run' during the *Born in the USA* tour.

The two songs that follow are more than they seem. 'I'm Goin' Down' uses the chords of A, E, F♯ minor and D and sounds like a piece of throwaway pop. It is, in fact, an exercise in irony for the tone of the lyric is very dark. True to the world it depicts, 'Glory Days' is constructed as a bar-band song. Built on an A-F♯, D-G, riff on the electric guitar, organ and bass, the melody moves between three major chords, A, D and E. A mandolin, played by Van Zandt, adds colour. 'Glory Days' is a deceptive song. The music is upbeat, but the words are about ageing and how the glory of being young fades away and leaves a bitter aftertaste.

Like 'Hungry Heart' before it, 'Dancing in the Dark' is a striking pop song with a wide appeal. The chord structure of the melody travels from major keys to their relative minor keys – B to G♯ minor, E to C♯ minor. The elegant opening phrase, played on the synthesizer before being passed to the singer, climbs three notes from B to D♯. In the refrain, the melody moves from F♯ to E and then to C♯ minor 7. With its French horn synthesizer part, flowing melody and metronomically precise beat, the music is both silky smooth and percussive: the band finds a perfect groove and doesn't let go. Best of all is the syncopated melody that Clemons weaves through the B-C♯-D♯ riff as the music fades.

Springsteen brings *Born in the USA* to a close with the exceptional 'My Hometown'. In this song Springsteen tells the story of Freehold (the song could be about any similar town) from the 1950s to the 1980s, from post-war boom to depression, in four concise verses. The theme is the circle of life. At the beginning, the singer sits on his father's lap as he drives; at the end, he does the same with his son. The glowing melody uses suspensions. It is built an Asus2 to A, Esus4 to E, inversion, with Bittan's warm synthesizer harmonies backed by an acoustic guitar, tambourine and delicate percussion from Weinberg. For the middle eight, the music makes a very effective shift to the relative key, F♯ minor.

While many of the themes expressed in the songs are universal, *Born in the USA* is, in part, a protest on behalf of working-class communities: a protest on behalf of the men who were sent to Vietnam; a protest on behalf of the men and women who suffer the most during economic recessions. The people in the songs struggle but persevere. An album that begins with the adrenalin rush of 'Born in the USA' ends with the quiet, contemplative 'My Hometown'. This is something of a masterstroke, for 'My Hometown' prompts the listener to reconsider all of the songs that have gone before.

Among the fine songs that didn't make the cut were 'Wages of Sin' and 'Frankie'. The intimate and bitter 'Wages of Sin' was forgotten by Springsteen until he revisited his archive of unreleased music during the late 1990s. It was released on the *Tracks* box set in 1998. Interviewed at the time, Springsteen said of the song: '[It] was a real find. It may have been one of those songs that cut close to the bone at the time, so I put it to the side.'[1] 'Wages of Sin' achieves a unique *noir* feel despite being scored for a standard E Street configuration of guitars, keyboards and drums. A repeated Esus4 chord, strummed on an electric guitar, underpins the musical progression, establishing from the first note a sense of unease as well as a droning melancholy. It is one of those inward-looking songs that reveal just how subtle the E Street Band can be when Springsteen pares things down to achieve a stark minimalism. In the coda, Federici plays a descending phrase on the organ.

'Frankie' was written some years before and first recorded during the *Darkness on the Edge of Town* sessions. It is remarkable that Springsteen couldn't find a place for this beautiful song on any album.

4 THE BORN IN THE USA TOUR

Steve Van Zandt's departure presented Springsteen and the band with a major problem, but, by chance, an ideal (and permanent) solution was found. Springsteen and Nils Lofgren had kept in touch over the years, and Lofgren was visiting Springsteen in New Jersey in February 1984 when news of Van Zandt's departure broke. Lofgren, in passing, and in a typically modest way, told

---

[1] *Billboard* (November 1998).

Springsteen that, if he needed someone, he would be interested in auditioning to join the band. Given Lofgren's talent as an artist in his own right (songwriter, singer and master guitarist), Springsteen must have been surprised at first by the offer. Despite his early promise, Lofgren hadn't enjoyed the lasting commercial success that his talent deserved, and was in something of a career lull, but his desire to join the E Street Band wasn't about this. A musician's musician, he had supported Neil Young back in the early 1970s, was passionate about playing in a great band and had a love of Springsteen's music.

Lofgren, born in Chicago in 1951, grew up close to Washington DC in Maryland. He mastered the classical accordion and the guitar while still at school and began his professional life as a musician at the age of seventeen. He formed the trio Grin in 1968 and a year later Neil Young invited him to play guitar and piano in his band. Lofgren played on Young's album *After the Goldrush* (1970) and toured with the singer. Grin released their debut album in 1971 and recorded three further records during the next few years. Lofgren pursued a solo career from 1974. His debut album, *Nils Lofgren*, released in 1975, is a classic of its era.

In May, during a week of rehearsals with Lofgren at a venue on Monmouth Street in Red Bank where Clemons had until recently owned a club, Lofgren was officially welcomed into the band. On 8 June, Lofgren made his debut with the band at the Stone Pony in Asbury Park. Set and lighting rehearsals then took place in Lititz, followed by further rehearsals back in Red Bank. It had been ten years since the brief period when Suki Lahav had been in the band. Springsteen knew the band would benefit if it contained a female member. Patti Scialfa, a talented local singer (she was born in Deal in Monmouth County in 1953), was invited to join during the Red Bank rehearsals. Scialfa attended NYU and started her career as a singer while still in her teens, busking in Greenwich Village with her friends Soozie Tyrell and Lisa Lowell before progressing to perform at the Village's coffee houses and folk clubs. In Asbury Park, she sometimes sang with the house band at the Stone Pony. Springsteen had first become aware of Scialfa when, at the age of seventeen, she applied to join the Bruce Springsteen Band. He told her over the phone that the job was full-time, and she should finish high school (she was attending Asbury Park High School at the time). Then, in 1974, when Springsteen was considering adding a female singer to the band on the eve of *Born to Run*, she applied again, this time getting to sing with the band. Springsteen, though, changed his mind about adding a singer, or perhaps he was thinking of Suki Lahav stepping up to this role. Springsteen and Scialfa's paths crossed again in 1984 at the Stone Pony.

Springsteen and his management were right to believe that *Born in the USA* had the commercial appeal to be a game-changer. Annie Leibovitz was engaged to take the photographs for the artwork, and Springsteen signed-off on using the American flag on the cover. The cover image could easily be misunderstood as a simple declaration of patriotism. This boosted sales of the record in the US. And those sales, in the millions, were unlike anything Springsteen had experienced before: they were kept rolling by the timed release of singles, MTV-friendly videos and the band's world tour. The album stayed at number one on the Billboard chart for seven weeks; in the UK, it debuted at number two and eventually climbed to the first spot. The critical response to the album was mostly enthusiastic. Debby Miller, writing in *Rolling Stone*, admired the mixture of exuberance and contemplation, the humour and the bleakness, the new musical textures delivered by the synthesizer, and, especially, the quality of the writing, which she compared to Sam Shepard: 'Springsteen has always been able to tell a story better than he can write a hook, and these lyrics are way beyond anything anybody else is writing. They're sung in such an unaffected way that the starkness stabs you. [...] That you get such a vivid sense of these characters is because Springsteen gives them voices a playwright would be proud of.'[1]

In the UK, Robin Denselow felt that the work's undoubted power wasn't sustained during the second side (*The Guardian*). Richard Williams noted that Springsteen was deliberately juxtaposing upbeat music with bleak lyrics: 'I'm Goin' Down' sounds at first like the sort of zestful nonsense Gary US Bonds might have confected in 1961: in fact, the story is suspicious, doubting, with intimations of tragedy.'[2] Williams admired the album, but viewed it as a continuation of themes that Springsteen had explored in earlier works. He would later see the album as a cynical simplification of Springsteen's gifts to make the music more commercial. The use of the flag on the cover may have been an error of judgement; but cynicism just isn't one of Springsteen's vices. Springsteen himself was divided about *Born in the USA*'s quality, particularly when compared to *Nebraska*, and aware that its meaning could be misinterpreted.

The tour began at the end of June 1984 in St Paul, Minnesota, with three concerts at the Civic Centre Arena. During the first show, a camera crew, directed by Brian De Palma, shot the video for 'Dancing in the Dark' (filming had also taken place the day before in front of extras). A young actress – the then-unknown Courteney Cox – was engaged to dance with Springsteen at the

---

[1] Debby Miller, 'Bruce Springsteen: *Born in the USA*', in *Rolling Stone* (19 July 1984).

[2] Williams, 'Green Grass and Parables of the Badlands', in *The Times* (2 June 1984).

end of the song. The band played five songs from *Nebraska* and nearly all of *Born in the USA*. The tour continued in Ohio, buoyed by the news that the album had reached number one in the charts. The first phase of the tour covered the Midwest and Canada.

In August, the band returned to New Jersey and performed ten shows at the Meadowlands Arena in East Rutherford. Highlights of the residency included an extended version of 'Pink Cadillac' with a comic monologue about the garden of Eden, 'Jersey Girl', 'Highway Patrolman', 'Atlantic City', reinvented as a rock classic, an acoustic 'No Surrender', and the debut of the band's cover of the Stones' 'Street Fighting Man'. The shows were recorded using the Power Station Mobile Truck with Toby Scott at the controls. Springsteen released 'Nebraska' (6 August), 'Reason to Believe' (19 August), 'No Surrender' (6 August) and 'Tenth Avenue Freeze-Out' (20 August) on *Live 1975-85*. Between 2015 and 2020, three of the concerts were released in their entirety – the first (5 August), second and last (20 August). The recordings reveal that Lofgren, after little more than a month down the road, had become a crucial member of the band without any kind of self-advertising, his guitar work complementing Springsteen's beautifully – listen to their joint attack on 'Street Fighting Man'. At the same time, Van Zandt was still missed. On the final night of the stand he returned to the band (along with the Miami Horns) during the encores, joining Springsteen at the microphone for 'Two Hearts' and the debut of the old Dobie Gray hit 'Drift Away', a song chosen specifically for this moment. Springsteen and Van Zandt shared the lines. Springsteen: 'And when my mind is free, just a melody can soothe me'; Van Zandt: 'Listen Brucie, when I'm feeling blue, guitars coming through to soothe me'; Together: 'Thanks for the joy, the twenty years you've given me. I believe in your song, rhythm and the rhyme and the harmony. You help me along, making me strong.'

In September, the band gave five concerts at another of their favourite venues, the Spectrum in Philadelphia. The presidential election campaign was in full swing, and Ronald Reagan's advisors thought they'd tap into Springsteen's popularity. They heard the chorus of 'Born in the USA', but not the verses, and therefore didn't register that, in Springsteen's song, being born in the USA meant being drafted to fight in an unjust war; it meant either dying or coming home to indifference and unemployment and a lifetime of mental trauma. On 19 September, during a speech in Hammonton, NJ, Ronald Reagan said: 'America's future rests in a thousand dreams inside your hearts; it rests in the message of hope in songs so many young Americans admire: New Jersey's own Bruce Springsteen. And helping you make those dreams come true is what this job of mine is all about.' At this stage Springsteen wasn't the articulate political player he was to become. His instinct was to keep playing his song in the hope that people would start to listen to the words. However, he did respond to Reagan two nights later, during the band's show at the Civic Arena in Pittsburgh. 'The President was mentioning my name the other day, and I kind of got to wondering what his favourite album must've been,' he told the audience. 'I don't think it was the *Nebraska* album. I don't think he's been listening to this one.' Springsteen then sang 'Johnny 99'. The presidential challenger, Walter Mondale, then claimed that Springsteen was backing his campaign, which wasn't true.

In October, the band headed west. During a seven-show stand at the Los Angeles Memorial Sports Arena Springsteen dedicated a rare performance of 'Shut Out the Light' to Ron Kovic. The year ended in December with performances in Tennessee and Atlanta. After a break for Christmas and the New Year, the tour continued with more shows in the South. The first American leg ended in Syracuse, New York.

In March, the band travelled to Australia and Japan for their first-ever shows in Sydney, Brisbane, Melbourne, Tokyo, Kyoto and Osaka. Before heading to Europe at the end of May, the band dispersed for a month, during which Springsteen married the actress Julianne Phillips in Lake Oswego, Oregon. Van Zandt and Clemons were the best men. News of the marriage leaked out and generated the kind of intrusive media interest that Springsteen found difficult to take. Springsteen had met Julianne Phillips in Los Angeles a few months before.

In Europe, the band performed only outside in stadiums before audiences of seventy thousand plus people. Springsteen was, understandably, maximising his earning potential. *The River* tour of European theatres and arenas had lost money despite being sold-out; the *Born in the USA* tour of stadiums would amass a fortune.

The shows were communal events, magical on fine evenings. Springsteen's approach was to make as few compromises as possible, selecting at least some of the quiet songs and refusing to sacrifice nuanced playing even though it tended to get lost in the air. However, gestures and movements that came over as ironic, quirky, and self-deprecating indoors were hard to read in stadiums where big gestures are needed and performance easily succumbs to cliché and parody. This wasn't a good tour to see Springsteen for the first time. It was hard to square the bandana-wearing, iron-pumping, garage mechanic stadium Springsteen with the skinny, eccentric, droll, possessed young guy of 1981. Seeing the band in a stadium was nobody's first choice.

During the first show, at Slane Castle in County Meath, Ireland, overcrowding meant that people were in danger of being crushed at the front of the stage. That night, Springsteen debated cancelling the whole tour. The safety issues were addressed and the first show in England, at St James's Park stadium in Newcastle, went well. Shows in Sweden, the Netherlands and West Germany followed. The band next played their first-ever show in Italy, at the San Siro in Milan. In France, because the authorities were worried about crowd control, the venue of the band's two Paris concerts was changed from the Stade de Colombes to the Parc de la Courneuve in the northern suburbs (Saint-Denis).

On reaching London at the beginning of July, Springsteen realised that he had become a celebrity rock star: his picture was splashed all over the pages of the British tabloids. In public he seemed relaxed about it all (he wasn't), for the band's three concerts at Wembley Stadium (with Van Zandt in attendance) were among the finest of their stadium career. Springsteen premiered a new song – 'Seeds' – and began the 4th of July show with an acoustic version of 'Independence Day'. 'Highway Patrolman', Elvis's 'Can't Help Falling in Love' and the Stones' 'Street Fighting Man' were given rare performances. The European tour ended with a show at Roundhay Park in Leeds.

Back in the States, the final leg of the *Born in the USA* tour included six shows at the Giants Stadium in East Rutherford, 18 August to 1 September, and four at the Los Angeles Memorial Coliseum, 27 September to 2 October, recorded by Toby Scott. *Live 1975-85* relied heavily on two shows from these stands – 19 August at the Giants Stadium and 30 September at the Memorial Coliseum. The Los Angeles stand brought the *Born in the USA* tour to a close. The band played to over 80,000 people per night in LA: they had come a long way since their appearances at the Roxy seven years before. On opening night, the band played the achingly lovely 'Janey, Don't You Lose Heart' for the first time in concert. Springsteen premiered his cover of Edwin Starr's 'War', played after a version of 'The River' that was prefaced by the true story of how he escaped the draft and the response of his parents. Spoken over Lofgren's elegiac acoustic guitar, it was an example of Springsteen's refusal to forego intimacy when playing to vast crowds. The two songs amounted to a passionate anti-war statement. This concert was released as a CD and digital download in 2019. Erik Flannigan, in his essay on the show (nugs.net blog), makes a telling observation on Nils Lofgren: 'LA 1985 is an opportunity for reappreciation of how much of the load he carried on the tour and the many spots when he shined. His intro to 'Seeds' oozes dirtier than you might recall, and the hypnotic prelude to 'I'm on Fire' alters the tone of the song significantly.'

In reaching the peak of their popularity, Springsteen and the E Street Band had lost something of their mystery, their eccentricity and their coolness. Where would they go from here?

NINE: DOUBTS

I RECORDING SESSIONS 1987

After the *Born in the USA* tour, Springsteen and Julianne initially lived in California. Springsteen recorded a number of songs at his home studio in Los Angeles in the summer of 1986 and worked on the live box set that was released that November. *Bruce Springsteen and the E Street Band Live 1975-85* contained forty tracks recorded during the band's American tours. Springsteen sequenced the songs so that the album represented a single concert. Fans had been craving a live album for ten years. While many were disappointed that Springsteen had decided to release a retrospective miscellany (utilising overdubs) rather than a single concert in its entirety, the handsomely produced box contained many pleasures.

Returning to New Jersey, Springsteen bought a house in the wealthy neighbourhood of Rumson, where, from January to May 1987, he recorded the songs that would form the *Tunnel of Love* album. Members of the E Street Band added additional parts at the Hit Factory. Then, in the summer, back on the West Coast, further recording sessions took place. Springsteen's marriage was already in trouble, and its disintegration influenced most of the new songs. Springsteen's reaction to the *Born in the USA* juggernaut was to create a work that was smaller in scale and more intimate than its predecessor. Now that he could work at home in a state-of-the-art studio (Thrill Hill East), built by Toby Scott in a detached garage on his Rumson estate, the recording sessions were markedly different from the gruelling marathons of old. The calm and wise Charles Plotkin joined Toby Scott in the recording booth. *Tunnel of Love* is a solo record but the contributions of members of the band were not insignificant. The title track was almost a full band recording, and Federici, Tallent, Weinberg, Bittan and Lofgren played, in various combinations, on seven of the other eleven tracks.

2 TUNNEL OF LOVE

Recorded at Thrill Hill East, New Jersey (with additional recording at the Hit Factory, New York) and A&M Studios, Los Angeles ('One Step Up' only), between January and July 1987. Produced by Springsteen, Jon Landau, Charles Plotkin; recorded by Toby Scott; mixed by Bob Clearmountain. Released on 6 October 1987.

The album:

Side One:

Ain't Got You
Springsteen (vocals, acoustic guitar, harmonica, percussion)

Tougher Than the Rest
Federici (organ); Springsteen (vocals, acoustic guitar, electric guitar, keyboards, bass, harmonica); Weinberg (drums, percussion)

All That Heaven Will Allow
Springsteen (vocals, acoustic guitar, electric guitar, keyboards, bass, harmonica); Weinberg (drums)

Spare Parts
Federici (organ); Springsteen (vocals, acoustic guitar, electric guitar, keyboards, percussion); Tallent (bass); Weinberg (drums)
Additional musician: James Wood (harmonica)

Cautious Man
Springsteen (vocals, acoustic guitar, mandolin, synthesizer)

Walk Like a Man
Springsteen (vocals, acoustic guitar, electric guitar, synthesizer, bass); Weinberg (drums)

Side Two:

Tunnel of Love
Bittan (synthesizer); Federici (organ); Lofgren (lead guitar); Scialfa (vocals); Springsteen (vocals, acoustic guitar, sound effects); Tallent (bass); Weinberg (drums)

Two Faces
Springsteen (vocals, acoustic guitar, electric guitar, synthesizer, bass, woodblock); Weinberg (drums)

Brilliant Disguise
Bittan (piano); Federici (organ); Springsteen (vocals, acoustic guitar, electric guitar, bass, woodblock); Weinberg (drums)

One Step Up
Scialfa (vocals); Springsteen (acoustic guitar, electric guitar, synthesizer, bass, drums, percussion)

When You're Alone
Clemons (vocals); Lofgren (vocals); Scialfa (vocals); Springsteen (vocals, acoustic guitar, synthesizer, bass, drums, percussion)

Valentine's Day
Springsteen (vocals, acoustic guitar, mandolin, synthesizer, bass, percussion)

Released outtakes:

Tracks (1998)

Lucky Man
Springsteen (vocals, acoustic guitar, electric guitar, synthesizer, bass, drums, percussion)

Two For the Road
Springsteen (vocals, acoustic guitar, electric guitar, synthesizer)

The Honeymooners
Springsteen (vocals, acoustic guitar, synthesizer, harmonica)

The Wish
Springsteen (vocals, acoustic guitar)

When You Need Me
Springsteen (vocals, acoustic guitar, mandolin, synthesizer, bass, harmonica, percussion)

Unreleased outtakes include:
Pretty Baby, Will You Be Mine
Things Ain't That Way
Part Man, Part Monkey

Walking Through Midnight

Tunnel of Love is Springsteen's most directly self-revealing work. It was something of a turning point. He had written similar songs before, but never an entire album devoted to introspection and affairs of the heart. Love, doubt, betrayal, self-knowledge and human frailty, inform all the songs. The music is tender and shimmering: there is no anger or bitterness on the album, but rather regret and self-deprecating humour. Most of the songs are scored for acoustic guitar, electric guitar, bass, synthesizer, woodblock and drums. These instruments, used with subtlety, combine like a chamber ensemble and not a rock band.

Four of the twelve songs are in G, the key of benediction, and five are in F. One song is in F's relative key, D minor. The connected keys, along with the shared scoring elements, give the work a tonal unity.

'Ain't Got You' is a two-chord rumble, G and C. The first verse is sung acapella. The instrumentation is basic: acoustic guitar, harmonica, woodblock and tambourine.

'Tougher Than the Rest' is motored by a memorable bass riff, played by Springsteen on the synthesizer, and by Weinberg's heavy rock beat. Federici's organ produces layered chords. Springsteen adds electric guitar and harmonica solos. The main melody, in F, incorporates C and B♭. In the middle eight, the music falls to D minor.

'Tougher Than the Rest' is followed by 'All That Heaven Will Allow', a gentle love song in G major. The short instrumental introduction (reminiscent of the Beatles' 'Eight Days a Week') is formed from Cadd9, G, Dsus4 and D. It is repeated at the end of the song with A minor 7 inserted. The middle eight introduces E minor. Springsteen plays the syncopated bass pattern and the internal guitar riffs. The moodily raw 'Spare Parts' is a story song about an unwanted pregnancy. A young mother, deserted by the father of her baby, contemplates abandoning the child but finds a way through. The song is in the, for Springsteen, rarely used key of D minor, with an unusual progression through C and A. In the chorus, the music moves from G through D minor to A. Federici, Tallent and Weinberg all feature. The song is underpinned by a strummed rhythmical pattern on the acoustic guitar, with bursts of dirty sound produced by an electric guitar and a harmonica.

'Cautious Man' is solo Springsteen, a sombre character study created from G, C, D, B minor, and B minor 7. 'Walk Like a Man', closing the side, is a compassionate father/son song. Although in F, the melody is coloured by the chords of E minor, D minor 7, and A minor. Springsteen plays the guitars, keyboards and bass; Weinberg is on the drums.

'Tunnel of Love' is the full E Street Band, minus Clemons. The music, in F, is propelled by a four-note phrase on the synthesizer and by Weinberg's percussion. 'Tunnel of Love' and 'Tougher Than the Rest' are the only songs on the album that edge towards arena rock: 'Tunnel of Love' has a Lofgren solo, but it is deliberately understated. The three outstanding songs that follow best express the album's overriding theme. 'Two Faces' is balanced between A major and F♯ minor and features a compelling repeated phrase on the guitar, played percussively. In the bridge, the melody falls to Dmaj7. Near the end of the final verse, F♯ is replaced momentarily by D, a brilliant touch. Bittan, Federici and Weinberg all play on the album's best-known track, 'Brilliant Disguise'. The song's musical structure combines Asus2, Asus4, E, Esus2, F♯ minor, and D. The placing of the woodblock beats is an important element. The song is magnificent, but 'One Step Up' is more original and more beguiling. Tonal ambiguity is maintained throughout, the feeling of moving but never arriving. The excellent pattern Springsteen plays on the acoustic guitar has a root of B♭-A-G-B♭ and utilises B♭add9, Csus4 and G minor 7 chords. In the refrain, a resolution to the tonic, F major, would be the predicable move, but Springsteen ends the sequence by returning to the subdominant, B♭add9. The melody is matched by the imaginative arrangement. The music mirrors the words.

'When You're Alone' is in F, falling to G minor 7 and D minor. Clemons, Lofgren and Scialfa sing backing vocals. The album closes with the valedictory 'Valentine's Day'. An acoustic guitar and mandolin accompany the singer; the bassline sways gently. The song is in waltz time, and the melody travels from E through A, C♯ minor, G♯ minor, and B. As the song comes to an end, a descending syncopated bell-like phrase, played by Springsteen on the synthesizer, slowly fades away.

3 THE 1988 TOURS

After the high-precision rock and roll of *Born in the USA*, *Tunnel of Love* must have disappointed Springsteen's record label; but it sold well enough, and was very well received. Initially, Springsteen decided not to tour the record, but he changed his mind and reassembled the band at the beginning of February 1988. However, he was determined not to repeat the *Born in the USA* tour. For the first time in his career, one sensed that he was ambivalent about the E Street Band. After so many years, grievances and resentments had developed along the way. The band members gave Springsteen their all, but perhaps felt that he didn't quite give them the full recognition they deserved. Springsteen, on his side, felt that the greater burden he carried was underappreciated by the others, and had grown exhausted by constantly having to take care of some of his bandmates' problems, financial or otherwise. To try and establish clear boundaries, for the first time he asked everyone to sign a contract. This was perhaps interpreted by some as a lack of trust.

Rehearsals took place in late January in a theatre in Fort Monmouth, not far from Long Branch. Springsteen made stylistic changes – the stage was white and uncluttered, and the band dressed smartly – and positioned Patti Scialfa at the front of the stage. He added a brass section. Some members of the band, already unhappy because of their reduced role in the studio, were unsure about the changes.

The *Tunnel of Love* songs formed the heart of each show. *The River* era outtakes 'Be True' and 'Roulette', a new song called 'Part Man, Part Monkey', and John Lee Hooker's 'Boom' were frequently performed. Springsteen resurrected the 'Detroit Medley' and Eddie Floyd's 'Raise Your Hand' (last played in 1981) for the encores. The tour was relatively short: three months of arena concerts in the States (February to May), followed by two months of stadium shows in Europe (June to August).

The band kicked off the tour in Worcester, Massachusetts, on 25 February, and then travelled to Chapel Hill (North Carolina), Philadelphia, Richfield (Ohio), Rosemont (Illinois) and Pittsburgh. Next came shows in Atlanta, Lexington (Kentucky), Detroit, Uniondale (New York), Largo (Maryland), Houston and Austin, St Louis (Missouri), and Denver. At the end of April, the band flew to California for five shows at the Memorial Sports Arena in LA, and two in Mountain View. Following two shows in Tacoma (Washington), the band headed back east, stopping off in Bloomington (Minnesota) and Indianapolis. The leg ended with five nights at Madison Square Garden in New York, 13-23 May.

In Europe, the media splashed pictures of Springsteen and Scialfa across their pages, souring the tour and adding to the already building tension. The leg began in Italy with concerts in Turin and Rome. Springsteen was now closing the show with 'Twist and Shout'. In Paris, the band played at the Hippodrome de Vincennes. In England, a two-night stand in Birmingham (Villa Park) was followed by a single show at Wembley Stadium, during which there seemed to be some moments of tension (including a misunderstanding between Springsteen and Bittan at the beginning of 'Backstreets'). From London, the tour took in stops in the Netherlands and Sweden. The first part of the second of the two shows in Stockholm was relayed live to radio stations in Europe and America. At the end of the broadcast Springsteen announced the upcoming Amnesty tour and sang Dylan's 'Chimes of Freedom'.

Following concerts in Dublin, Sheffield (two nights), Frankfurt, Basel and Munich, the band landed in East Berlin for their first appearance behind the Iron Curtain. The concert at the Radrennbahn Weissensee was a significant cultural event for young East Germans: at least 160,000 of them saw the band perform that night. The regime declared that Springsteen was being presented by the Young Communist League and that he was playing in support of Nicaragua. The concert was broadcast on state television. Springsteen hadn't agreed to any of this. He decided to play, but during the show he told the crowd in German: 'I'm not here for or against any government, but to play rock and roll for you East Berliners. I hope that one day, all barriers will be torn down.' The band then launched into 'Chimes of Freedom'. Those watching on TV didn't hear the speech because the censor cut it from the broadcast.

The Berlin concert followed the Amnesty tour announcement in revealing that Springsteen, perhaps influenced by Van Zandt's Artists United Against Apartheid campaign, was prepared to use his influence politically, but in a way that was focused and sensitive to the wider issues. He made his point about the situation in East Germany without referring directly to the Berlin wall.

Next, the band played in West Berlin, Copenhagen, Oslo and Bremen. At the beginning of August, the tour came to an end with shows in Madrid and Barcelona (in the Camp Nou).

The 'Human Rights Now!' tour, in support of Amnesty, proved to be a happy experience. This short tour began at Wembley Stadium on 2 September and took the band to new territories – India, Africa and South America. Springsteen cared deeply about the cause, and enjoyed sharing the stage with Sting (the two became close friends), Peter Gabriel, Tracy Chapman and Youssou N'Dour, and Clemons was overwhelmed by the shows in Zimbabwe and the Ivory Coast.

At tour's end, Springsteen and Scialfa lived for a while in New York. Springsteen, though, couldn't tolerate big city life, so they divided their time between California and New Jersey. On 23 September 1989, all members of the E Street Band (including Van Zandt) came together in New Jersey to celebrate Springsteen's fortieth birthday. Springsteen may have already decided that, after sixteen intense years, he wanted to work independently of the E Street Band. A month later, he told his bandmates that it was over, at least for the foreseeable future. Everyone responded graciously, but it was a shock: the life these musicians had lived, the music they had helped to create, was at a stroke taken away.

PART III
1990-2021

TEN: HIATUS

I   A NEW BAND

When Springsteen announced the breakup of the E Street Band, it was widely assumed that he would take his music in a new direction. Surely, he would work with a new instrumental palate, further exploring the chamber music approach of *Tunnel of Love*?

In fact, Springsteen decided to make a large-scale pop/rock record. In September 1989, Springsteen, who was now living full-time in California with Scialfa, entered a Los Angeles studio with E Streeter Roy Bittan (who, as well as playing, co-wrote several songs and co-produced the album) and several top LA session musicians. Ex-E Streeter David Sancious played keyboards on some of the songs. The sessions lasted throughout 1990 and came to an end in March 1991. Around thirty songs were recorded. Recording with mostly hired hands in Los Angeles smoothed out Springsteen's music to the point that it sounded very slick but somewhat soulless. A few fine songs – including 'I Wish I Were Blind' – became lost in this context. One of the best pieces – 'Sad Eyes' – didn't even make the album.

Springsteen had doubts about the *Human Touch* record and postponed its release for almost a year. In the meantime, between September 1991 and January 1992, he recorded another album, smaller, more personal and possessing a much more authentic tone than *Human Touch*. The songs of *Lucky Town* were influenced by his relationship with Scialfa and the birth of his first child. Springsteen and Scialfa married at their California home in June 1991.

It was probably a mistake to release both records on the same day (31 March 1992). Given that Springsteen was re-launching his career, post-E Street, the sales figures, in both the US and the UK, were disappointing and the reviews mixed. The superb *Lucky Town* would have been better appreciated had it been released on its own. It contained the excoriating Gulf War song 'Souls of the Departed' ('On the road to Basra…') and the tender love song 'If I Should Fall

Behind'. Springsteen went ahead with a year-long world tour, hiring a bunch of musicians who were young and capable, but who never gelled to form a collective identity.

In 1993, Springsteen was asked by Jonathan Demme to write a song for his movie *Philadelphia*. 'Streets of Philadelphia', a solo recording, went on to win the Oscar for Best Song and four Grammy Awards, including Song of the Year.

2 GREATEST HITS

Six years after he made those phone calls, in January 1995, Springsteen asked the members of the band to join him in the studio to record some new songs. The songs would be released as part of a greatest hits package. Nobody knew whether this was the beginning of something real or a one-off reunion, although the latter seemed likely. Springsteen was in something of a career low, unclear about the kind of record he wanted to release, and his fellow musicians knew it. They knew that the records he had recorded and toured without them had underperformed and they would have been forgiven for wondering whether they were now being used somewhat cynically. But everyone – including Van Zandt – turned up at the Hit Factory in New York, where *Born in the USA* had been recorded ten years before. Toby Scott, Chuck Plotkin and Bob Clearmountain were in the booth. Lofgren was recording with the band for the first time.

During ten nights of recording, the band worked on different versions of eight songs, three of which – 'Secret Garden', 'Blood Brothers' and 'This Hard Land' – were released on the *Greatest Hits* album. They had recorded a version of 'This Hard Land' during the *Born in the USA* sessions. The other songs were new to them. Springsteen had recorded versions of these songs with other musicians during the previous year.

The sessions were filmed for a documentary, released under the title *Blood Brothers*. The band can be seen recording 'Back in Your Arms', 'High Hopes' and 'Without You' as well as the released songs. The reunion was successful, with none of the tension or angst of previous E Street Band recording sessions, although the process almost slipped back into old ways with the sixteen separate versions of 'Secret Garden'. In the documentary, Bob Clearmountain, who mixed the songs, summed up a key aspect of the band's quality: 'They just tend to arrange themselves somehow. Like Danny Federici will just play chords or a couple of single notes and not jump out until he feels there's actually a space for him to do something. The same with Roy. It's amazing how you'll hear him playing and suddenly there will be this hole and he'll be playing something there.'[1]

At the time of its release in 1995, the *Blood Brothers* documentary was the only public record of the band working in the studio. The film captured the E Streeters' joy of playing and singing together ('Without You') and their pleasure at finally achieving, after multiple tries, a finished version of 'Blood Brothers'.

A month later, the band assembled at Tramps nightclub in New York to film a live video of the song 'Murder Incorporated', a *Born in the USA* outtake included on the *Greatest Hits* record. The director was Jonathan Demme. Filmed in front of an invited audience, this was the band's first live performance since 1988. After the filming of 'Murder Incorporated', the cameras were switched off and the band played a twelve-song set.

'Secret Garden', 'Blood Brothers' and 'This Hard Land' were Springsteen and the E Street Band at near to their very best, the playing delicate but swinging, the motifs melodic and syncopated. To support the Greatest Hits album, the band appeared on the *Late Show with David Letterman*: they performed 'Tenth Avenue Freeze-Out' and 'Secret Garden'.

3   THE GHOST OF TOM JOAD

The brief but rewarding E Street Band get-together in New York seemed to inspire Springsteen, for immediately afterwards, between March and September 1995, he wrote and recorded the work that is arguably his solo masterpiece, *The Ghost of Tom Joad*. *Joad* was recorded at Springsteen's home studio Thrill Hill West in Los Angeles by Toby Scott and co-produced by Chuck Plotkin, the two collaborators who had provided Springsteen with such important support since *The River*. It was a solo album, but Springsteen called in Federici, Tallent and Scialfa, as well as Soozie Tyrell, to play or sing on a number of the tracks. Of the non-E Street musicians who played on the record, the most prominent were drummer Gary Mallaber and pedal steel guitarist Marty Rifkin. Seven of the twelve songs were performed by Springsteen alone.

Revealingly, Springsteen signed off on the songs as Scott recorded them,

---

[1] Bob Clearmountain, interviewed in Ernie Fritz (director), *Bruce Springsteen and the E Street Band: Blood Brothers* (Columbia Music Video, 1995).

using Scott's on-the-spot mixes rather than handing the tracks to Bob Clearmountain for additional work. He wanted to retain the spontaneity of the moment of creation. It is believed that around another album's worth of material was recorded during the sessions. Of these songs, 'Dead Man Walking' was written for Tim Robbins's movie of the same name (1995), and subsequently included on the *Essential Bruce Springsteen* compilation (2003); the powerful Vietnam War-related 'Brothers Under the Bridge' ('Saigon, all gone'), performed frequently in concert, surfaced on *Tracks* (1998); and 'Tiger Rose' was given to Tallent for inclusion on the Sonny Burgess album he was producing (1996).

In early September, Springsteen and the E Street Band performed at the Hall of Fame's inaugural concert in Cleveland. They also backed Chuck Berry and Jerry Lee Lewis. Everyone now knew that, if Springsteen wanted it, something big could happen. Springsteen's immediate task, though, was to support *The Ghost of Tom Joad* album by embarking on the first solo tour of his career. The album was released on 16 November 1995, and Springsteen hit the road on the 22nd with a concert in Red Bank. His commitment to the project was such that he stayed on the road until the end of May 1997. The first American leg lasted until the end of January 1996. Springsteen then performed in Europe until May, with a brief break in March so that he could attend the Oscars in LA ('Dead Man Walking' was nominated for best song). The UK and Ireland were covered extensively, with shows in Manchester, Birmingham, Newcastle, Edinburgh, Dublin, Belfast, and London (four shows at the iconic Royal Albert Hall and two at the Brixton Academy). After a four-month break, the tour resumed in Pittsburgh and continued until December. The highlights of this leg were the shows Springsteen played back on home turf in New Jersey. During the three shows at the Paramount Theatre in Asbury Park, Springsteen was joined by Scialfa, Soozie Tyrell, Federici, and Van Zandt. During the second show, Vini Lopez came out to guest on 'Spirit in the Night'. These shows featured many songs from Springsteen's first two albums. Federici's accordion and Tyrell's violin were particularly magical on 'Wild Billy's Circus Story', 'Fourth of July, Asbury Park' and 'Shut Out the Light'. Even more memorable, was a single show in Freehold, on 8 November: Springsteen played in the gymnasium of his old school, Saint Rose of Lima, supported by Scialfa and Tyrell. The concert ended with a song Springsteen wrote for the occasion – 'In Freehold'.

In January and February 1997, Springsteen took his show to Australia and Japan. The tour came to an end in Europe, with shows in Austria, Poland, Italy (Florence and Naples) and France (Lyon, Montpellier, Nice, Toulon and Paris). In all, Springsteen gave one hundred and twenty-seven concerts.

The shows offered fans the rare opportunity of seeing Springsteen up-close in theatres; and the chance to hear his songs imaginatively adapted for solo acoustic guitar. He changed melodies by utilising added notes and suspensions, and often muted the strings with his palm. He used the instrument percussively and re-thought his songs in terms of the different tones he could produce, from drum-like beats to an eerie sonic murmur. As a result, a particular atmosphere was created for each song. It was some of the finest acoustic guitar playing of the era.

ELEVEN: WAIT FOR ME

I   TRACKS

The long *Ghost of Tom Joad* tour meant a lot to Springsteen. It left him with nothing left to prove as a solo artist. He could now turn his thoughts to E Street. At heart, he was still a band musician, and he knew that his music was at its most powerful and most influential when played by the E Street Band. At forty-nine, he wasn't ready to give up on the excitement and fulfilment of playing his best music to the biggest crowds. And after more than ten years away, there existed new generations of fans who had never seen the band.

However, while he wanted the shared history and the emotional ties that connected all the members of the band, he didn't want any of the resentments or arguments of old. Everyone, including Springsteen, would need to leave their egos and their grievances at the stage door. Van Zandt wanted to come home and Springsteen wanted him back. The band had never felt complete without him. Springsteen, asked for and obtained Lofgren's agreement.

Springsteen and Scialfa lived, primarily, in California from 1989 to 1996. In the mid-1990s, they decided to raise their young family back home in New Jersey. As well as retaining their Rumson house, they purchased, in August 1994, an old 315-acre farm in Colts Neck.[1] Over time, Springsteen built a new studio (Stone Hill Studio) in one of the buildings on the estate, additional to the studio at Rumson (Thrill Hill East).[2]

In 1998 Springsteen worked on the *Tracks* box set, selecting five CDs worth of unreleased music from his extensive archive, most of it recorded with the E Street Band. It was a glorious set.

---

[1] See *Asbury Park Press* (9 April 1995), p.4.
[2] Springsteen's recording operation is registered as Thrill Hill Recording, and includes home studios in both New Jersey (Thrill Hill East at Rumson; Stone Hill Studio at Colts Neck) and California (Thrill Hill West).

2   THE REUNION TOUR

In March 1999, the members of the E Street Band gathered at the Convention Hall in Asbury Park to begin rehearsals for their reunion tour. The Convention Hall was a special venue for those members of the band who were from New Jersey. It was at the Convention Hall that the young Springsteen had been blown away by the power, musicality and guitar-smashing audacity of the Who. He later saw the Doors there, but missed the Rolling Stones in 1966. During this rehearsal period, Springsteen was inducted into the Rock and Roll Hall of Fame at the Waldorf-Astoria Hotel in New York. His decision to be inducted as a solo artist was a cause of unhappiness on E Street. Springsteen was conflicted on the matter. He didn't disagree when Van Zandt, pressing for a joint induction, told him that Bruce Springsteen *and* the E Street Band was the legend,[1] but still went ahead on his own. The induction ceremony was awkward, with Springsteen bringing all the members of the band onto the stage in what was at best an uneasy compromise.

By the time the band took to the road, though, it became clear that everyone was happy to be back together and filled with hope and ambition. Some of the music was re-thought for the tour, including a full band 'Ghost of Tom Joad' and an extended version of 'The River' with new music. This version began and ended with a new theme played solo by the saxophone. It was Clemons's finest moment since 'Jungleland'. The music was passed from the sax to the harmonica (used classically) and finally, at the song's conclusion, back to the sax, taking the listener full circle. An electric piano and Federici's accordion combined lyrically. It was, for me, some of the finest music created by Springsteen and the band, deeply serious, plaintive and evocative. The song was performed as part of a broodingly powerful central sequence – 'Mansion on the Hill', 'The River', 'Youngstown' (full band, with a dazzling Lofgren solo) and 'Murder Incorporated'. 'Tenth Avenue Freeze-Out', 'Light of Day', and, in the encores, a poignant version of 'If I Should Fall Behind', in which Springsteen, Van Zandt, Lofgren, Scialfa and Clemons shared the verses, and a fine new song called 'Land of Hope and Dreams', would feature in every concert.

The tour (the band's first to start outside of the US) kicked off in Barcelona at the beginning of April with two shows at the Palau Sant Jordi indoor arena, before wild audiences. The band played in Germany (Munich and Cologne)

---

[1] See Springsteen, Speech inducting the E Street Band into the Rock and Roll Hall of Fame, 2014.

and then travelled to Italy for shows in Bologna and Milan. They visited Austria (Vienna) and Switzerland (Zurich) and ended the month in France with a show in Lyon at the Halle Tony Garnier, a building that began life as a slaughterhouse. Bon Jovi joined the band for 'Hungry Heart'.

At the start of May, the band arrived in England. They performed two shows at the Manchester Arena and one at the National Exhibition Centre in Birmingham, the band's first appearance at this venue since the final show of the European leg of *The River* tour in 1981. Edwin Starr guested on a rare performance of 'War'. True to form, in London the first of four nights at the unappealing Earls Court exhibition centre (chosen, presumably, over Wembley Arena because of its higher capacity) was a little tense, with Clemons failing to come in on time during 'Darlington County'. Springsteen laughed this off, humorously saying 'Concentrate, Big Man', but Clemons wasn't happy. The other shows ran smoothly. The third night started with the rarity 'I Wanna Be With You', with each band member entering separately, and included 'Meeting Across the River' and 'Jungleland' played back-to-back. From London, the band played in Ireland (Dublin), Belgium (Ghent), Germany (Berlin, the tour's first open-air gig), and France. During the second of two shows in Paris at the Palais Omnisports de Paris-Bercy the band performed two songs included on the *Tracks* box set – 'Loose End' and 'Lion's Den'. The Paris shows were the last in Europe to take place in indoor arenas. The final phase of the tour consisted of stadium shows in Spain (Zaragoza and Madrid), Italy (Genoa), Germany (Leipzig and Bremen), the Netherlands (Arnhem), Sweden (Stockholm), Denmark (Copenhagen) and Norway (Oslo, on 27 June).

After a short break, back in the States, the band took up a residency at the Meadowlands Arena in East Rutherford that consisted of fifteen concerts (15 July to 12 August). During the stand, Springsteen dropped 'The River' on some nights, replacing it with either 'Point Blank' or 'Independence Day'. Rarities performed included 'In Freehold' (opening night). For the first time during the tour, Springsteen showcased music from *Tracks* – 'Give the Girl a Kiss', 'Back in Your Arms', 'Be True', 'Don't Look Back', 'Janey, Don't You Lose Heart' and 'Frankie' were all played. The penultimate night included performances of 'New York City Serenade' and 'Fourth of July, Asbury Park'. On the final night, 'Jersey Girl' and 'Rosalita' were played.

The tour continued with concerts in Boston (five nights at the Garden Arena), Washington DC (three nights) and the Detroit suburb of Auburn Hills. In Washington, the band started one of the shows with a new introduction that became known as 'Meeting in the Town Tonight', with Clemons saying, 'Brothers and sisters, all rise' before the band launched into 'The Ties

That Bind'. It would be used regularly from then on, sometimes in conjunction with *The River* outtake 'Take 'Em as They Come'. During six nights in Philadelphia (13-25 September), Springsteen programmed a number of songs from his early years, including 'Does This Bus Stop at 82nd Street?', 'Blinded by the Light', 'The Fever', 'Growin' Up' (penultimate show opener) and a majestic full-band 'Incident on 57th Street' (final show opener), as well as Chuck Berry's 'Little Queenie', last played at the Hammersmith Odeon in London in 1975. The final show is regarded as a classic – as well as 'Incident', the band played 'New York City Serenade', the new arrangement of 'Point Blank', with Clemons and Federici taking centre stage during the introduction, and the band's first 'Streets of Philadelphia'.[1]

After three nights in Chicago at the United Centre,[2] the band took a short break. They then headed west, playing in Phoenix, Los Angeles – four nights at the new Staples Centre[3] – and Oakland. Back in the Midwest, there were concerts in Fargo (North Dakota), Milwaukee (Wisconsin), Indianapolis (Indiana), and Cleveland (Ohio). The first leg of the US tour ended with shows in Buffalo (New York) and Minneapolis (on 29 November). There was a long break over Christmas and the New Year.

The band reconvened at the end of February 2000 at Penn State University in Pennsylvania. During March and April, they headed south and west, performing in Florida, Texas, Arizona, Tennessee, Louisiana, Colorado, Oregon, Washington, Missouri, and Kentucky; then, northwards, to North Carolina and Ohio. The tour reached Toronto in Canada in early May. Following a final burst of shows out west in California, Nevada and Utah, the band travelled back to New York via Atlanta, Georgia. During the second of the two Atlanta concerts at the Philips Arena, on 4 June, the band premiered a new song, 'American Skin (41 Shots)', performed between 'Point Blank' and 'Youngstown'. 'American Skin', Springsteen's response to the police shooting of Amadou Diallo in New York, was arguably the greatest protest song of its era. Diallo, a young immigrant from Guinea, was shot dead in the vestibule of his apartment block by four police officers. Springsteen's song embroiled the band in controversy. Despite the unhappiness of the NYPD and some sections of the public, Springsteen and the band played the song during all ten of their Madison Square Garden concerts between 12 June and 1 July. They also debuted a companion piece, 'Code of Silence'.

---

[1] Released as a CD/digital download in 2020.
[2] The 30 September show in Chicago was released as a CD/digital download in 2018.
[3] The 23 October show was released as a CD/digital download in 2019.

The final night of the Madison Square Garden stand, 1 July 2000, was the 132nd and final show of the reunion tour. A setlist that included the early classic 'Lost in the Flood', reinvigorated, and a new song as important as 'American Skin' seemed to sum up the meaning of the E Street Band as one of the great bands, at the height of its power and still relevant. As a postscript to 'If I Should Fall Behind' and 'Land of Hope and Dreams', Springsteen ended the tour with a new version of 'Blood Brothers', gathering his bandmates around him as he sang the final verse. The message was clear. The E Street Band was here to stay.

Previous page: Reunion tour, Fleet Centre,
Boston, 27 August 1999. Springsteen and Bittan.
Photo by Stan Grossfeld/The Boston Globe (Getty Images).

TWELVE: DREAM OF LIFE

I RECORDING SESSIONS 2002

On 9/11, Springsteen drove to Seabright beach near Rumson to gaze across the water at a Manhattan shrouded in a cloud of toxic dust. As he headed home, a fellow motorist rolled down his window and called out 'Bruce, we need you'. Many of the people who died on that day, office workers and members of the emergency services alike, came from Springsteen's local community in Monmouth County.

Springsteen had written and recorded many unreleased songs in the years since *The Ghost of Tom Joad*, but these were mostly solo recordings made at his home studio in New Jersey. In March 2001 he returned to the Hit Factory in New York with the band, Chuck Plotkin and Toby Scott, to work on the album that the reunion tour had promised to deliver. 'Land of Hope and Dreams', 'American Skin (41 Shots)' and around six other songs were recorded. But Springsteen wasn't satisfied with the results.[1]

The tragedy of the attack on New York concentrated Springsteen's mind, leading him to write some fine new material and to speed up the recording process. Instead of continuing with his usual team, Springsteen decided to use one of the leading producers of the time, Brendan O'Brien, producer of records by Pearl Jam and Rage Against the Machine, and to give O'Brien his head. The intention was to achieve a sound that was current and fresh.

In January 2002, the band assembled at O'Brien's Southern Tracks Studios in Atlanta, Georgia. They worked quickly: the marathon sessions of the 70s and 80s would not be repeated. Springsteen brought to Atlanta the songs that he had written post-9/11: 'Lonesome Day', 'Mary's Place', 'You're Missing',

---

[1] Of the songs recorded during the sessions, only 'American Skin (41 Shots)' has been released (on *High Hopes* in 2014).

'The Rising', 'Paradise', 'Empty Sky', 'Into the Fire', 'The Fuse', and 'Worlds Apart'. Alongside these, he selected appropriate material from his notebook of unreleased songs: 'Let's Be Friends' (ca. 2001); 'Nothing Man' (1994); 'Waitin' on a Sunny Day' (1998 – the band rehearsed the song during the reunion tour, but it never made the set); 'Further On (Up the Road)' (premiered during the reunion tour in June 2000); 'My City of Ruins' (2000); and 'Countin' on a Miracle' (2000).

Sixteen songs were recorded: the fifteen that make up *The Rising*, plus 'Down in the Hole', a great song that should have been included. It would be released on *High Hopes* in 2014.

2   THE RISING

Performed by the E Street Band and recorded at Atlanta Southern Tracks Studios, Atlanta, between January and March 2002. Bittan (piano, mellotron, Kurzweil, pump organ, Korg M1, Crumar); Clemons (saxophone, backing vocals); Federici (B3 organ, Vox Continental, Farfisa); Lofgren (electric guitar, dobro, slide guitar, banjo, backing vocals); Scialfa (vocals); Springsteen (lead vocals, electric guitar, acoustic guitar, baritone guitar, harmonica); Tallent (bass); Soozie Tyrell (violin, backing vocals); Van Zandt (electric guitar, mandolin, backing vocals); Weinberg (drums). Additional musicians: Asif Ali Khan and group; Larry Lemaster (cello); Jere Flint (cello); Brendan O'Brien (hurdy-gurdy, glockenspiel); Jane Scarpantoni (cello); Alliance Singers (backing vocals); Mark Pender (trumpet); Mike Spengler (trumpet); Richie Rosenberg (trombone); Jerry Vivino (tenor saxophone); Ed Manion (baritone saxophone); Nashville String Machine (strings). Produced (and mixed) by Brendan O'Brien; recorded by Nick DiDia. Asif Ali Khan and group recorded by Chuck Plotkin at Henson Studios in Hollywood. Released on 29 July 2002.

The album:

   Lonesome Day
   Into the Fire
   Waitin' on a Sunny Day
   Nothing Man
   Countin' on a Miracle
   Empty Sky
   Worlds Apart
   Let's Be Friends (Skin to Skin)

Further On (Up the Road)
The Fuse
Mary's Place
You're Missing
The Rising
Paradise
My City of Ruins

Released outtakes:

High Hopes (2014)
Down in the Hole

With a running time of seventy-three minutes, *The Rising* is Springsteen's second longest work after *The River* (eighty-four minutes). It is, in the old terminology, the E Street Band's second double-album. *The Rising* is not a musical documentary about the tragedy of 9/11. It is one of the strengths of the album that Springsteen's songs of loss and grief rarely refer directly to 9/11 and don't need to be viewed in the context of those events, but, of course, can be.

The key of F (four songs) and its subdominant B♭ (the title track and two more) dominate the work. Three more are in related keys, C or F minor. 'Nothing Man' is in E♭ major.

The Rising begins with the mid-tempo, but melancholy, 'Lonesome Day', a song propelled by an E♭add9 to B♭ riff, played by cellos and Soozie Tyrell's violin. The melody then drops to G minor. Guitars, organ, and cymbals are prominent in the mix. In the short introduction, a harpsichord (emulated by a synthesizer) accompanies a cello. A single beat on the snare introduces the main riff. One of the songs specifically about 9/11 comes next, 'Into the Fire'. A song about courage and sacrifice, it takes the listener into one of the towers as firemen climb the stairs. The music, utilising three chords, F, B♭ and C (Cmaj7/Cadd9), is built on Weinberg's excellent drum pattern. Acoustic guitars and Soozie Tyrell's solo violin give the song an earthy, folk music aesthetic. Part of the vocal line is doubled by one of the acoustic guitars. Scialfa and Tyrell add ghostly vocal harmonies. The violin adds a countermelody.

Having established the overriding tone of the album, Springsteen breaks the tension with the delightful 'Waitin' on a Sunny Day', in C major. The strong melody has a C-A minor-F chord progression. Tyrell's violin leads the music. Stacked acoustic guitars and elaborate vocal harmonies give the mix its depth. Keyboards produce bell-like resonances. There is a modulation to D major before the central instrumental break, and another to E major at the end of the song. Clemons plays a trademark solo during the instrumental fade-out.

One of the album's greatest songs follows, 'Nothing Man'. Written before 9/11, and perhaps initially belonging to Springsteen's body of songs about soldiers returning home, a few telling details were added (pink vapour; the unbelievable blue of the sky) to allow the song to be interpreted in the context of 9/11. Suffering from survivor guilt and post-traumatic stress disorder, the singer feels that he is nothing at all, but is treated as a kind of hero by his local community. At the end of the song, he contemplates suicide. The beautiful melody uses suspensions and major seventh chords. It swings between $E^\flat$-$E^\flat$sus2, C minor-Csus4 and $A^\flat$maj7 (or, to express it differently, after each chord, $E^\flat$, C minor and $A^\flat$, a two-note pattern, G and D, is played). Hauntingly, $B^\flat$ is added in the rise and fall of the refrain. Bittan plays delicate keyboard harmonies. Lofgren's discrete guitar adds imaginative decorations. Springsteen's acoustic guitar and Weinberg's drums provide the rhythm. You can read the words as a poem and 'Nothing Man' is just as devastating, in its pain and sadness and empathy.

The electric guitar driven 'Countin' on a Miracle' opens deceptively with a short introduction for two acoustic guitars. Musically, with its separate sections and powerful juxtaposition of major and minor chords, the song could have sounded like a mid-1970s E Street Band classic. But Bittan's piano is missing here as elsewhere on the album. The melody of the verses moves from A and $F^\sharp$ minor to B minor, D and G. The melody of the chorus swings between D and G and B minor and G. The tempo slows and strings are added in a middle section that introduces E minor.

A theme on the piano introduces 'Empty Sky'. The compelling melody is backed by Weinberg and Tallent's forceful rhythm track. A strummed acoustic plays the progression F-Fsus4-F, followed by G minor-Gsus4-G minor. $E^\flat$ is inserted in the chorus. Bittan's piano re-enters at the start of the second verse, doubling the guitar, and Springsteen's harmonica completes the sparse scoring. During the final repeat of the chorus, Springsteen reverses the G minor-$E^\flat$ progression. The two words 'empty sky' were a powerfully poetic way of conveying the tragedy of 9/11. The song expresses Biblical anger as well as private grief and sets up the extraordinary 'Worlds Apart', a piece that acknowledges the chasm that separates East from West without apportioning blame, and that makes a plea for mutual understanding and tolerance, life over death. Musically, this is achieved by fusing the voices and instruments of the E Street Band with the voices and percussion of Asif Ali Khan's ensemble from Pakistan, recorded by Chuck Plotkin in Los Angeles. It shouldn't fit together but does. Following a quiet introduction, the drums, bass, and guitars kick in hard without drowning out the voices or the subtle parts within the scoring. These include Lofgren's banjo, playing internal riffs, and Springsteen's harmonica. The voices of Asif Ali Khan and his singers combine magically with Scialfa. A solo electric guitar (played by Lofgren or Springsteen) burns into the musical fabric. The song is constructed from a simple two-chord – E minor and D major – phrase, repeated hypnotically. The music dies away, leaving only the two classical instruments of the Indian subcontinent, the harmonium and the tabla and a lone female voice. Springsteen was going against the consensus view of Americans in 2002 by including a song like 'Worlds Apart' in a work inspired by 9/11.

Springsteen lightens the mood with the soulful 'Let's Be Friends (Skin to Skin)', a song dominated by minor 7th chords. The verses swing between C and D minor 7, and the chorus between D minor 7 and E minor 7. There is a switch to G minor 7 and A minor 7 in the bridge at the point when Clemons's sax enters. Scialfa, Tyrell and the Alliance Singers add their voices to Springsteen's. The song's setting is a nightclub. It is unclear whether the man and woman in the song will leave alone or together, for good times have a habit of slipping away.

Electric guitars and Weinberg's driving beat dominate 'Further On (Up the Road)', a brooding rock song in F minor. Keyboards provide a wash of sound, and Scialfa harmonises Springsteen's voice during the chorus. The melody moves between F minor and $A^\flat$, before switching to $E^\flat$ and $D^\flat$. In the chorus, the melody progresses unexpectedly to C before resolving in the home key. Is the song about lawlessness and violence or escape and freedom? Is it about friendship or love? The open road, one of Springsteen's most ambiguous metaphorical obsessions – here its meaning is unresolved.

'The Fuse' explores new sonorities. Lyrically, it focuses on desire and intimacy. A heavy beat on the snare, combined with cymbals and tambourines, sounds heightened and looped, but was – as far as we know – played live by Weinberg. A guitar riff, formed from a suspended D, resolving, plays almost throughout. From D, the music moves moodily and unexpectedly to A minor, and then back to D via G. An echo effect is applied to Springsteen's vocal. After a middle section, in B minor, the percussion stops, and soon afterwards there are several seconds of silence. Two more guitars join the ensemble, and a piano produces fragments of sound. The drum beat re-starts. The lyrics are littered with metaphors and symbolism – the colour red, black dust, (funeral) motorcades, fire. The bedroom is a refuge and sexual intimacy the only balm, for outside the natural world is out of kilter and the familiar has turned sinister. Since 'The Fuse' was written after 9/11, it can be viewed as reflecting the post-9/11 world.

The 9/11 influenced themes of loss and healing connect the album's final five songs. Four of the five are united tonally by the keys of F and its subdominant B♭.

In 'Mary's Place', the singer tries to cope with the death of his girlfriend or wife, possibly in the 9/11 attacks. He looks for spiritual help but only really copes by meeting with her friends and playing her favourite music. Although, this could all be in the grieving man's head. None of it is explicit: it's Springsteen's genius to imply the deeper meanings. The instrumentation includes a cello, played by Jane Scarpantoni, Tyrell's violin, Van Zandt's mandolin, Federici's B3, Bittan's piano, Springsteen and Lofgren's acoustic and electric guitars, and horns. Clemons's sax is more prominent than elsewhere on the album. Tallent's bass dances and Weinberg's drums swing. Backing vocals are provided by members of the band and the Alliance Singers. The music has a lovely feel to it. Founded on a repeated F-Fsus4 progression (played principally by the cello) that rises and falls, it moves through D minor, C, B♭ and C to set up the chorus. In the chorus, G minor and A minor are added. The horns and sax lead an instrumental break that takes in G minor, A minor, D minor and C. The final cadence is unresolved, ending in B♭ and not the tonic. Anyone trying to heal after loss can find consolation in this song.

Tonally related to 'Mary's Place', the beautiful 'You're Missing' is also about loss and grief but is starker and almost unbearable. The elegant melody balances between F and D minor before progressing to B♭ and C. The vocal line is accompanied by a cello, playing a repeated phrase. Part way through the song, the phrase is doubled by Lofgren playing a Dobro(?) guitar. Bittan's piano opens the song and is subdued but significant throughout. In the middle eight, the vocal line is subtly changed, although the chords are D minor, B♭ and C. Keyboard instruments add washes of harmony and suspension, and an organ plays a superb, bitter-sweet, solo in the fade-out.

'The Rising' is aligned to 'Into the Fire' in that it begins with an image of firemen. Musically, the song is quite basic, a two-chord (B♭ and E♭) anthem enriched by cellos and vocal harmonies. 'The Rising' is about the collective will to survive following a tragedy; the dream of life that makes healing possible. The penultimate song, 'Paradise', is one of Springsteen's most mysterious and haunting. The melody moves between C minor and B♭, then rises an octave as C minor changes to A♭. The singer is accompanied by keyboards, an acoustic guitar, and an electric guitar, all playing minimally to create a fragile soundworld. Different ideas of the meaning of paradise connect a suicide bomber and the grieving relative of a victim of terrorism.

The spirituality that connects 'Into the Fire', 'Worlds Apart', 'Mary's Place', 'The Rising', and 'Paradise', is most evident in the song that closes *The Rising*, the gospel music inspired 'My City of Ruins', in B♭ major. Ending the work with the unresolved pain of 'Paradise' would have been more powerful, but Springsteen wanted to stress community and hope. 'My City of Ruins' was written, at the end of the 1990s, as a portrait of Asbury Park, but Springsteen transformed it into something much bigger for *The Rising*. The city becomes Manhattan, but perhaps also Baghdad, Kabul or any place decimated by hatred and war.

The E Street Band at Wembley Arena, London, 27 October 2002.
Photo by Simon Meaker

3 THE RISING TOUR

The Rising was released on 30 July 2002. The album was underrated in America. Keith Harris and Robert Christgau of the *Village Voice*, found little to enjoy. In Europe it was recognised as a masterpiece, one of the most resonant, yet least polemical, works of art inspired by 9/11. David Sinclair, in *The Times*, wrote that the album acts as a 'sounding board' for a nation's grief 'with magisterial dignity and a burning sense of passion which is, at certain points, simply overwhelming.'[1] In *The Telegraph*, Neil McCormick commented: '*The Rising* is the work of a major songwriter grappling with the big issues of the day. [...] Yet, perhaps just as significantly, it is Springsteen's first studio album with the E Street Band since *Born in the USA*. [...] The lyrics are spare and profound, the attention to music detail magnificent (organs, guitars and backing vocals always seem to arrive at exactly the right moment).'[2] Burhan Wazir, writing in *The Observer*, recognised that the work should not be simply categorised as a reaction to 9/11: 'The album is more oblique than that.'[3] *The Rising* reached the number one spot in the charts on both sides of the Atlantic, the first Springsteen album to do so since *Tunnel of Love*.

Rehearsals took place in July 2002, in Fort Monmouth. Later in the month, the band moved to the Convention Hall in Asbury Park to play several concerts before invited audiences. On the 30th, a camera crew from *The Today Show* filmed the band playing 'The Rising' and three other songs. The band had a new member, the violinist Soozie Tyrell. The daughter of a soldier, Tyrell was born in Pisa in 1957. A friend of Patti Scialfa, she had appeared on all of Springsteen's records since 1992's *Lucky Town* and was an essential player on *The Rising*. On the evening of 1 August, the band played 'The Rising' on the *Late Show with David Letterman*; and on the 5th they performed a private dress rehearsal show at the Meadowlands. The opening night of *The Rising* tour took place at the Meadowlands two nights later (7 August).

The first legs of the tour contained no multi-night stands. The concerts were tightly focussed on *The Rising* album; they were relatively short by E Street standards. Throughout the tour, the band played as if on a mission. Bruce Springsteen and the E Street Band may be the only band of their stature and vintage to make a new album the focal point of a tour. An extended 'Mary's

---

[1] David Sinclair, 'Reborn in the USA', in *The Times* (26 July 2002).
[2] Neil McCormick, 'Bruce Rises to the Occasion', in *The Daily Telegraph* (26 July 2002), p.24.
[3] Burhan Wazir, 'CD of the Week', in *The Observer* (28 July 2002).

Place', with The Independent's 'Baby, I've Been Missing You' inserted, was used for the band introductions. 'People Get Ready' was incorporated into 'Land of Hope and Dreams'. 'Waitin' on a Sunny Day' was immediately embraced by audiences. Some of the concerts included solo piano versions of either 'Incident on 57th Street' or 'For You'.

The band played in Washington DC, New York (Madison Square Garden), Cleveland and Detroit, and then travelled west for shows in Las Vegas, Portland, Los Angeles (Inglewood), Phoenix, San Jose, and St Louis. Following a break, the band reconvened on 22 September and continued the tour in Denver, Kansas City, Chicago, Milwaukee, Fargo, St Paul, Boston, Philadelphia and Buffalo. On 5 October, the band guested on *Saturday Night Live*, playing 'Lonesome Day'.

At this point the band halted the US leg to fit in a quick (two-week) visit to Europe. This phase began, on 14 October, with a show in Paris at the Palais Omnisports de Paris-Bercy. Thankfully, for the first time since *The River* tour, all the concerts took place in arenas. The first half of the next show, at the Palau Sant Jordi in Barcelona, was broadcast live on VH1 (the whole concert was later released on DVD). The band then travelled to Bologna, Berlin, Rotterdam and Stockholm before closing the leg at Wembley Arena on a stormy night in London (27 October). 'It's good to be back in this old building,' Springsteen told the audience. 'We love ya,' someone shouted from the back of the hall. 'Too much love can make a man insane,' Springsteen replied. Around key songs from *The Rising*, the band played 'Jackson Cage', a solo piano 'Incident on 57th Street', 'Does This Bus Stop at 82nd Street?', 'The River' (just Springsteen and Soozie Tyrell on violin), 'Born in the USA' and 'Land of Hope and Dreams'.

Back home, the tour swung through the southern States: Dallas (3 November), Houston, Lexington (Kentucky), Greensboro (North Carolina), Birmingham, Orlando, Miami (Bono guesting), Tampa, and Atlanta. On 11 December, the band appeared on *Late Night with Conan O'Brien* and played 'Kitty's Back' and 'Merry Christmas, Baby'. After a concert in Indianapolis on 17 December, the band began a long break over Christmas and the New Year.

The tour recommenced at the end of February 2003 with concerts in Duluth (Georgia), Austin, Jacksonville, Richmond, Atlantic City, Providence, and Rochester. The band spent the rest of March in Australia and New Zealand, playing in Melbourne, Sydney, Brisbane and Auckland. In April, they took the tour to Canada, with stops in Vancouver, Calgary, Edmonton, Ottawa, and Montreal. In June they returned to Europe for stadium shows in the Netherlands, Germany, Belgium, Spain (Estadio de la Comunidad de Madrid), Catalonia (Estadi Olímpic Lluís Companys, Barcelona), France (Stade de

France, Paris), England (two shows at Crystal Palace, London; one at Old Trafford, Manchester), Ireland, Italy (one show at the Stadio Artemio Franchi in Florence; a second at the San Siro in Milan), Denmark, Finland (two shows at the Olympiastadion, Helsinki), Norway, Sweden (two shows at the Ullevi, Gothenburg) and Austria. The first night in Helsinki, 16 June, was the band's debut in Finland.

The final leg of the tour started in July with seven nights at the Giants Stadium in East Rutherford. After visiting Pittsburgh, Philadelphia, Chicago, San Francisco, and Los Angeles, the band gave three further concerts at the Giants Stadium. The tour ended in New York with three nights at Shea Stadium, 1-4 October. On night one the setlist included, 'Souls of the Departed', 'American Skin', 'Tunnel of Love' and 'Brilliant Disguise'; on night two, 'Roulette', 'New York City Serenade' and 'Janey, Don't You Lose Heart'; and on night three, 'I Wish I Were Blind', 'Back in Your Arms', 'Highway 51 Revisited', with Dylan guesting, and, to conclude, 'Blood Brothers'.

THIRTEEN: DEVIL'S ARCADE

I DEVILS AND DUST AND THE SEEGER SESSIONS

Between March and August 2004, Springsteen worked on a solo record at his home studio in New Jersey. He returned to the songs he had written during the *Tom Joad* tour and recorded at his home studio at the tour's end in 1997. It was time, after two big E Street projects, to give some space to this chamber music and to build on the *Tom Joad* experience. Springsteen writes in his autobiography that Brendan O'Brien wanted to re-record the songs, but Springsteen liked the original recordings and simply asked his producer to add some minor embellishments.[1] He wrote only one new song for the record, the title track 'Devils and Dust'.

The record completed, for two weeks in October 2004 the E Street Band headlined the *Vote for Change* tour. Together with REM and Bright Eyes, they gave concerts in the swing states of Pennsylvania, Ohio, Michigan, Minnesota, and Florida, and ended the tour with shows in Washington DC (relayed live on TV) and at the Meadowlands in New Jersey (before an invited audience). Guest artists included John Fogerty, Neil Young, Tracy Chapman, John Mellencamp, Jackson Browne, James Taylor, and Pearl Jam. The objective of the tour was to encourage people to vote in the upcoming presidential election. Although the progressive action group behind the campaign, Move On, declared the tour to be non-partisan, it was known that most of the artists supported John Kerry's bid for the White House. Springsteen would play solo at some of Kerry's rallies.

In March 2005, Springsteen prepared for the *Devils and Dust* solo tour by rehearsing at the Paramount Theatre in Asbury Park. Reports suggested that Lofgren was present for at least one rehearsal, but it is unclear to what purpose.

---

[1] See Springsteen, *Born to Run*, p.444.

The album was released on 25 April, and Springsteen began his tour on the same day with a concert at the Fox Theatre in Detroit. Whereas the solo *Tom Joad* tour had been guitar-orientated, in these shows Springsteen also used several keyboard instruments. Springsteen played in theatres across America until the end of May and then, in June, did the same in Europe, performing in Dublin, London (two shows at the Royal Albert Hall), Brussels, Barcelona, Madrid, Bologna, Rome, Milan, Hamburg, Munich, Frankfurt, Dusseldorf, Rotterdam, Paris (at the Palais-Omnisports de Bercy), Copenhagen, Gothenburg, Stockholm, Hamburg, and Berlin. A second American leg kept Springsteen on the road until 22 November and a final show on home turf in Trenton.

Back in November 1997, following the *Tom Joad* solo tour, the producers of a Pete Seeger tribute album had invited Springsteen to contribute. Springsteen called in Toby Scott and recorded several folk songs, including 'We Shall Overcome', the song chosen, with Scialfa and Soozie Tyrell and some of his favourite local musicians – among them Charles Giordano and other members of the bluegrass band Gotham Playboys. The experience of playing traditional folk music stayed with Springsteen and in March 2005 he reassembled the Seeger musicians to record a new group of songs. Finally, on returning home after the *Devils and Dust* tour, he recorded a number more (January 2006): he now had enough songs for an album.

We Shall Overcome: the Seeger Sessions was released on 24 April 2006. Springsteen took the Seeger Sessions Band on the road in the US and Europe between April and November. This was some of the most relaxed and joyous music-making of Springsteen's career. The sound was wonderful.

2   RECORDING SESSIONS 2007

The rest of the decade would belong to the E Street Band. Recording sessions, produced by O'Brien, took place in Atlanta between February and May 2007. Basic tracks were recorded by Springsteen, Bittan, Tallent and Weinberg. Van Zandt, Lofgren, Federici, Clemons, Scialfa and Soozie Tyrell added their parts later.

3 MAGIC

Performed by the E Street Band and recorded at Atlanta Southern Tracks Studios, Atlanta, between February and May 2007. Bittan (piano, organ); Clemons (saxophone, backing vocals); Federici (organ, keyboards); Lofgren (guitars, backing vocals); Scialfa (backing vocals); Springsteen (lead vocals, guitars, harmonica, pump organ, glockenspiel); Tallent (bass); Soozie Tyrell (violin, backing vocals); Van Zandt (guitars, mandolin, backing vocals); Weinberg (drums). Additional musicians: Jeremy Chatzky (upright bass, 'Magic'); Daniel Laufer (cello, 'Devil's Arcade'); Patrick Warren (Chamberlin, track piano, 'Your Own Worst Enemy', 'Girls in Their Summer Clothes', 'Long Walk Home', 'Devil's Arcade'). Strings arranged by Eddie Horst. Produced (and mixed) by Brendan O'Brien; recorded by Nick DiDia; additional engineering by Billy Bowers. Additional recording at Thrill Hill Recording: engineer Toby Scott. Released on 28 September 2007.

The album:

> Radio Nowhere
> You'll be Comin' Down
> Livin' in the Future
> Your Own Worst Enemy
> Gypsy Biker
> Girls in Their Summer Clothes
> I'll Work for Your Love
> Magic
> Last to Die
> Long Walk Home
> Devil's Arcade
> Terry's Song

If *The Rising* was a reflection on 9/11 and its immediate aftermath, *Magic* was about the America it created. The two albums combined as a commentary on the first decade of the 21st century. *Magic* was, in part, a reaction to the foreign policy decisions of the Bush administration, but it also seemed to predict the bitter mixed-up world of lies and lunacy that, in the United States, formed the conditions that allowed the Trump presidency and the storming of Congress. Dreams and nightmares, dislocation, menace, and the tragedy of war, are ever-present. The album has a brooding power with strong melodies throughout. Despite the hard-rocking aesthetic shared by some of the songs, the tone is melancholic, for the world is out of joint.

The mid-tempo opener, 'Radio Nowhere', uses a four-chord pattern, F♯ minor, D, A and E. The fine melody of 'You'll be Comin' Down' (connecting B, E, and F♯) is undercut by deeply pessimistic lyrics – youth will fade, good moments will end. Layered electric guitars dominate the scoring. There is a modulation to A and C♯ before the central sax solo in F♯.

'Livin' in the Future', in C, also has music that is out of sync with the words, at least until the bridge. The verses move between C and A minor, while the chorus uses the major chords of F, G and C. In the bridge, D minor and A minor dominate. Clemons's sax is prominent. Musically, the song could be a *Darkness* era outtake. The enigmatic lyrics contain apocalyptic imagery and fuse the personal and the political. The theme of dislocation and unease is continued in the next song, 'Your Own Worst Enemy'. The melody is carried on an E, Aadd9, C♯ minor, and Badd9, chord pattern. The descending phrase of the chorus incorporates F♯ minor, E, A, and C♯ minor. Strings, elaborate vocal harmonies, bells and keyboards create a rich tapestry of sound.

The masterly 'Gypsy Biker' is in B♭, but F minor dominates because of the superb B♭ to F minor progression in the opening phrase. The phrase is then underpinned by the chords of A♭, E♭ and B♭. In the bridge, the music moves to C minor. Springsteen's electric guitar and harmonica are prominent. This elegiac rock song packs an emotional punch. Although the meaning is not spelt out, 'Gypsy Biker' connects to Springsteen's Vietnam War themed songs and is a lament for a young soldier killed in the Iraq War. His friends mourn him by riding his bike into the desert and setting it alight. It is the first of the three Iraq War songs on the album, the others being 'Last to Die' and 'Devil's Arcade'.

The next two songs don't have a political dimension. 'Girls in Their Summer Clothes', in C, is a gorgeous pop song marred by over-production; while 'I'll Work for Your Love' is a powerfully Dylanesque love song, intercut with religious imagery. Its music links B♭ with F and E♭.

The album's final sequence of four songs is among Springsteen's finest, as well as his most political. 'Magic' is an allegorical portrait of the mindset of President Bush and his ministers, no less excoriating for being allegorical and no less chilling for being poetic. At the beginning, a trickster pulls a rabbit from a hat; at the end, bodies hang in the trees. From C♯ minor, the music progresses to E and B before returning to its starting point. The chorus is built on a reversal, E to Badd11 to C♯ minor. The middle eight begins with a powerful switch to A major. While the acoustic guitar pattern suggests a folk song, unusual keyboard sonorities take the music in the opposite direction, into the sinister world of the hurdy-gurdy man from Schubert's *Winterreise*.

Van Zandt's mandolin and Soozie Tyrell's violin complete the scoring.

The anti-war song 'Last to Die' is in E minor. The E Street Band combines power with elegance. Each verse is prefaced by a phrase on the electric guitar that connects C with B minor. The musical line of the verses follows the same structure before moving to E minor. In the chorus, E minor connects to C, G and D. The final repeat of the guitar phrase goes to E minor and not B minor.

'Long Walk Home' is arguably the most significant song on the album. The lovely melody connects B♭, G minor, and F. The song was probably written in 2006, not long before Springsteen premiered it, in unfinished form, during the Seeger Sessions tour at Wembley Arena in London that November. Springsteen decided to record the song with E Street's electric guitars, piano, organ, and sax. 'Long Walk Home' unites the personal with the public. A man returns to his hometown and discovers that he is a stranger. 'The singer in 'Long Walk Home', that's his experience,' Springsteen told A.O. Scott of *The New York Times*. 'His world has changed. The things that he thought he knew, the people who he thought he knew, whose ideals he had something in common with, are like strangers. The world that he knew feels totally alien. I think that's what's happened in this country in the past six years.'[1]

At the same time, the song seems to express hope. It is a meditation on the old-fashioned values, such as decency and fellowship, that still permeate American society. It exposes the ruling class's betrayal of these values. And in the album's greatest line, it declares that the flying of the Stars and Stripes is a statement of what America will do but also what it won't do.

If 'Long Walk Home' is *Magic*'s most significant song, 'Devil's Arcade' is its most devastating. A song about the cost and the pity of war, told partly from the point of view of a woman whose husband has been badly injured in Iraq and struggles to recuperate (there are other interpretations, including the death of the soldier), it is among Springsteen's most beautiful compositions. The story is told in images and small fragments that conjure seduction in a bedroom, a military base, a bombing in the desert, a hospital ward beside the sea. The eloquence of the wordplay is matched by the music. The haunting melody, shared by Springsteen's voice, a cello (played by Daniel Laufer) and an electric guitar, is carried by a chord progression of E, B minor, D, F♯ minor, D, F♯ minor, A and E. The song starts with fragments of sound produced by a Chamberlin or pump organ and a distorted guitar chord and ends with Weinberg's drums and cymbals.

---

[1] Quoted in A.O. Scott, 'In Love with Pop, Uneasy with the World', in *The New York Times* (30 September 2007).

4 THE MAGIC TOUR

At the end of September 2007, the band appeared on the *Today* show, performing live in Rockefeller Plaza in New York. That evening, they concluded their rehearsals (held, as usual, in Asbury Park at the Convention Hall) with a benefit concert at the Meadowlands. The tour began at the beginning of October in Hartford. The first phase included two-night stands in Philadelphia, East Rutherford (at the Meadowlands), New York (at Madison Square Garden), Chicago, Oakland, Los Angeles, Washington DC, and ended with two concerts at the Garden in Boston. Of the many *Magic* songs played during this leg, the title track, 'Gypsy Biker', 'Last to Die' and 'Devil's Arcade' were particularly strong. The tour confirmed the brilliance of the *Magic* album.

After the second night in Boston (19 November), Federici began a leave of absence to undergo treatment for cancer. Springsteen programmed three songs from the *Wild, the Innocent and the E Street Shuffle* that showcased Federici's playing of either the organ or the accordion – 'The E Street Shuffle', 'Kitty's Back' and 'Fourth of July, Asbury Park'.[1]

Between 25 November and 19 December, the band was in Europe. Federici was irreplaceable, but a better or more apt substitute than Charles Giordano, a musician who already had a relationship with Springsteen from *The Seeger Sessions* album and tour, and who understood the style of the music and the role of the organ within the ensemble, would have been impossible to find. Patti Scialfa didn't make the trip. They performed in Spain (Madrid and Bilbao), Italy (Milan), the Netherlands (Arnhem), Germany (Cologne), Norway (Oslo), Denmark (Copenhagen), Sweden (Stockholm), the UK (Belfast and London, at the O2), and Paris (at Bercy). 'Santa Claus is Comin' to Town' was played regularly.

The tour continued at the end of February 2008. There were shows in Canada in Montreal, Hamilton and Vancouver, in Buffalo, St Paul, Milwaukee, Indianapolis (on 20 March – Federici returned for a number of songs, his final appearance), Cincinnati and Seattle. Out west, the band played in San Jose, Dallas and Houston. The death of Federici on 17 April, although expected, was a hard blow to take. Concerts were cancelled and rescheduled. The first show after the funeral, on 22 April in Tampa, Florida, began with a montage of clips of Federici accompanied by the recording of 'Blood Brothers'. Listening to the recording of the show, released in 2019, it is impossible not

---

[1] Released as a CD/digital download in 2018.

to sense the presence of Federici in the band's heartfelt playing. As Bittan stepped into Federici's shoes as the accordion player of 'Fourth of July, Asbury Park' Springsteen said, 'Roy, you better get this one right now, somebody's watching'. A poignant 'Growin' Up' followed – 'There we were, way up on the highest hill in Flemington, New Jersey…' At the next show, in Orlando, the band played 'Does This Bus Stop at 82nd Street?', 'Spirit in the Night', and 'Lost in the Flood', and Roger McGuinn guested on 'Mr Tambourine Man'. For some weeks, Springsteen spoke about Federici and selected early songs – 'Wild Billy's Circus Story' was played in Charlotte and 'It's Hard to Be a Saint in the City' in Greensboro. The Greensboro show,[1] at the Coliseum on 28 April, began unexpectedly with two outtakes of the late 1970s, 'Roulette' and 'Don't Look Back'.

During a short break in Jersey in early May, before returning to Europe, the band fitted in a benefit concert at the Count Basie Theatre in Red Bank. The concert was remarkable because the band performed the *Born to Run* and *Darkness on the Edge of Town* albums in their entirety.

Springsteen had started to accept fan requests. During the summer tour of Europe this practice became more prominent. The leg began with concerts in Dublin, Manchester, London (two nights at Arsenal's Emirates Stadium, during which the highlights were rare outings of 'Point Blank' and 'I'm on Fire') and Cardiff (the band's first show in this city), and continued in Dusseldorf, Amsterdam, Hamburg, Antwerp, Milan (at one of the band's favourite venues, the San Siro – the rarity 'None But the Brave' was requested by a fan), Paris (at the Parc des Princes), Copenhagen, Gothenburg (two nights at the Ullevi, the second featuring a rare 'Drive All Night'), Oslo (two nights), and Helsinki. The leg concluded with concerts in San Sebastián, Madrid (at the Bernabéu) and Barcelona (at the Camp Nou).

Returning home, the band gave three concerts at the Giants Stadium in East Rutherford. The final phase of the *Magic* tour took the band to Foxborough (Massachusetts), Jacksonville, Richmond and Nashville, before ending in Missouri with shows in St Louis and Kansas City (23-24 August). The St Louis concert began with the band's cover of 'Then She Kissed Me', last played in 1975 during the *Born to Run* tour. Two other covers from the band's early days, 'Mountain of Love' and Chuck Berry's 'Little Queenie', also made the setlist. In Kansas City, an outtake from *The River* sessions (released on *Tracks*) opened the concert – 'Ricky Wants a Man of Her Own'. The big surprise was Weinberg taking lead vocals on the band's first performance of the old Beatles cover 'Boys', chosen because someone held up a sign reading, 'Let Max Sing'.

---

[1] Released as a CD/digital download in 2020.

5   WORKING ON A DREAM

Performed by the E Street Band and recorded at Atlanta Southern Tracks Studios, Atlanta, with additional recording at Thrill Hill Recording, NJ, Avatar Studios, NY, Clinton Recording Studios, NY, and Henson Recording Studios, CA, between June 2007 and November 2008. Bittan (piano, organ, accordion); Clemons (saxophone, backing vocals); Federici (organ); Lofgren (guitars, backing vocals); Scialfa (backing vocals); Springsteen (lead vocals, guitars, harmonica, keyboards, glockenspiel); Tallent (bass); Soozie Tyrell (violin, backing vocals); Van Zandt (guitars, backing vocals); Weinberg (drums). Additional musicians: Jason Federici (accordion 'The Last Carnival'); Patrick Warren (organ, piano, 'Outlaw Pete', 'This Life', 'Tomorrow Never Knows'). Strings arranged by Eddie Horst. Produced (and mixed) by Brendan O'Brien; recorded by Nick DiDia and Rick Kwan (additional recording by Toby Scott and others). Released on 27 January 2009.

The album:

Outlaw Pete
My Lucky Day
Working on a Dream
Queen of the Supermarket
What Love Can Do
This Life
Good Eye
Tomorrow Never Knows
Life Itself
Kingdom of Days
Surprise, Surprise
The Last Carnival
The Wrestler

The idea of recording back-to-back albums was suggested by Brendan O'Brien as *Magic* was being prepared for release. They had one song in the can, 'What Love Can Do', and Springsteen wrote five more in the space of a week. The band recorded the new songs during the *Magic* tour, between shows, and Springsteen completed the album, *Working on a Dream*, at the end of the tour, during the autumn of 2008. Thom Zimny filmed some of the sessions and his forty-minute film was released on DVD as part of a limited edition of the album. Zimny's camera was the first to film the band in the studio in nearly fifteen years. The new music was lighter, more pop-orientated and less concerned with the zeitgeist than the songs on *Magic*.

While there are some fine songs on *Working on a Dream*, it is, arguably, the weakest of Springsteen's albums with the E Street Band. However, the band members were as committed as ever, the instrumentation constantly arresting.

'Outlaw Pete', in A minor, and 'Queen of the Supermarket', in G, are delightful curiosities with compelling sonorities and internal riffs. In the first, a Western story song, Springsteen doffs his hat to Ennio Morricone. The lyrics would later be turned into an illustrated book for young children (2014). Bittan's piano is dominant in the latter, along with strings and Beatlesque vocal harmonies. 'My Lucky Day' is a fast E Street rocker containing a Clemons sax solo. The somewhat corny 'Working on a Dream' is delicate pop music, propelled by Weinberg and Tallent's imaginative rhythm track. 'What Love Can Do' is a melodic love song in E minor. Acoustic and electric guitars work their magic, along with vocal harmonies and a lone harmonica. In the songs 'This Life' and 'Surprise, Surprise', Springsteen reveals that he can compete with Neil Diamond when it comes to middle of the road pop.

'Good Eye' is a three-chord blues. Springsteen's vocal is distorted and accompanied by an ever-present harmonica. The gentle 'Tomorrow Never Knows' is stylish country music, replete with fiddle and slide guitar. These relatively slight pieces are followed by the album's strongest songs. 'Life Itself' is built on a dark D minor 7 to B^b pattern in the verses and a G minor 7 to B^b pattern in the chorus, and features intertwining electric guitars and another outstanding rhythm track. The imagery is black and wintry. In contrast, the poignant 'Kingdom of Days' is a traditional love song, written for Scialfa. It has an irresistible melody and lush scoring. The song is in F, and has a straightforward structure of F, B^b, and C, until the modulation to D minor in the chorus. The beautiful 'Last Carnival' is an elegy for Federici. His son, Jason, played the accordion.

The song Springsteen wrote and recorded (solo) for the Mickey Rourke movie *The Wrestler*, premiered in August 2008, is included as a bonus track. 'Kingdom of Days' is the album's masterpiece, but 'The Wrestler', in E^b, comes close. This song about male vulnerability, physical and mental, is built on suspended and seventh chords and combines an acoustic guitar with delicate piano.

6 WORKING ON A DREAM TOUR

On 1 February 2009, a few days after the release of *Working on a Dream*, Bruce Springsteen and the E Street Band provided the half-time entertainment at Super Bowl XLIII in Tampa, Florida. In March, the band rehearsed the new material in Asbury Park at the Paramount Theatre and the Convention Hall. The unexpected decision to tour in 2009 meant that some dates clashed with Weinberg's commitments to *The Tonight Show*. The band rehearsed with Weinberg's son Jay so that he could cover for his father. Jay Weinberg was needed for around five shows during the first American leg of the tour, and for the first seven concerts in Europe. Curtis King and Cindy Mizelle joined the band as backup singers.

The band returned to the road at the start of April, only seven months after the end of the *Magic* tour. The tour began out west with arena shows in San Jose, Glendale, Austin, Tulsa, Houston, Denver, and Los Angeles, and continued in Boston, Hartford, Atlanta, Philadelphia, Toronto, St Paul, Chicago, Washington DC, and Pittsburgh. The leg ended at the Meadowlands on 23 May.

In Europe, on 2 June, the band headlined the Pinkpop Festival in the Netherlands. Following three nights in Stockholm and two in Bergen, the band returned to the States to perform at the Bonnaroo Festival in Manchester, Tennessee. They were back in Europe, with Max Weinberg, in time to make their debut at Glastonbury as the Saturday headline act on the Pyramid Stage. Springsteen had always avoided festivals, and there was a definite sense that the Glastonbury audience was not a Springsteen audience. The next night the band headlined the Hard Rock Calling Festival (not a festival in the Glastonbury sense) at Hyde Park in London and fared much better. The show was filmed and later released on DVD. The band then visited the central European cities of Bern, Munich, Frankfurt and Vienna, before playing in Dublin and Glasgow. They headlined the Festival des Vieilles Charrues at Carhaix in Brittany, and then went south to Italy (Rome, Turin and Udine) and Spain (Bilbao, Seville, Benidorm, Valladolid, and Santiago). The European leg ended on 2 August.

The second and final American leg, beginning on 19 August, included both indoor and open-air shows. At the leg's centre was a five-night stand at the soon to be demolished Giants Stadium. Before reaching New Jersey, the band performed in Mansfield (Massachusetts), Saratoga Springs, Tampa, and Chicago (a complete *Born to Run*). Springsteen, Lofgren and Bittan were in New York on 25 September to tape Elvis Costello's *Spectacle* TV show at the

Apollo Theatre. On the opening night of the Giants Stadium residency, Springsteen premiered a new song, 'Wrecking Ball', and during the run the band gave complete performances of *Born to Run*, *Darkness on the Edge of Town*, and *Born in the USA*. Jay Weinberg played the drums on several songs. Now on the home straight, the band travelled to Philadelphia (four nights) and St Louis, and headlined the Rock and Roll Hall of Fame anniversary concert at Madison Square Garden. Following shows in Washington DC and Charlotte, the band returned to Madison Square Garden, where, on night one, they performed *The Wild, the Innocent and the E Street Shuffle*, and, on night two, *The River*. These special shows were equalled by the thirty-four-song tour finale in Buffalo, on 22 November: the band gave a complete performance of *Greetings from Asbury Park, New Jersey*.

FOURTEEN: DARKNESS AND LIGHT

I   WRECKING BALL AND HIGH HOPES

Springsteen turned sixty in September 2009. In the weeks following the end of the *Working on a Dream* tour, the severe depression he had first experienced in 1982 returned. The episode would last for well over a year.

He kept working, writing and recording a group of pop songs connected thematically and mostly set out West. In November 2010, he released the eagerly awaited *Darkness on the Edge of Town* box set under the title *The Promise*. The unreleased material from the *Darkness* recording sessions of 1977-78 was strong enough to be released as a stand-alone album (three LPs or two CDs) consisting of twenty-two tracks. Springsteen and the band added some overdubs and re-recorded one of the songs – 'Save My Love'. The work received universal acclaim. On 16 November 2010, Springsteen appeared on *Late Night With Jimmy Fallon* with Van Zandt and Bittan to promote *The Promise*. They performed 'Because the Night' and 'Save My Love'. On 7 December, the E Street Band, minus Lofgren and Scialfa, gathered at the Carousel House, the Casino, Asbury Park, to perform songs from *The Promise*. The concert was filmed for future release.

Springsteen set aside the Western solo project to record a different set of songs for what began as an intimate solo project. When, at the beginning of January 2011, he brought in the producer Ron Aniello the project rapidly developed into an ensemble recording. Springsteen, though, decided against making an E Street album, preferring to use Aniello and other musicians (Weinberg, Clemons and Scialfa played on two tracks). This would make *The Wrecking Ball* something of an anomaly, for Springsteen asked the band to tour the record.

The album was very well recorded, but one couldn't help but miss the E Street Band – the songs cried out for the band's power and grace. The E Streeters quickly made the songs their own in concert. This was the first tour without the Big Man. Springsteen remembered Clemons during 'Tenth Avenue Freeze-Out' in a simple but moving way. It helped greatly that Clemons's nephew Jake had stepped into his uncle's shoes.

In February 2012, the E Street Band performed 'We Take Care of Our Own' at the Grammy Awards in Los Angeles. They made two appearances on *Late Night with Jimmy Fallon*, playing 'We Take Care of Our Own' and 'Wrecking Ball' on 27 February, and 'Death to My Hometown' and 'Jack of All Trades' (with Tom Morello) on 2 March. Rehearsals took place in Trenton at the Sun National Bank Arena, and in Asbury Park at the Convention Hall.

The *Wrecking Ball* album was released on 6 March to mostly positive reviews. David Fricke, writing in *Rolling Stone*, thought that it was 'the most despairing, confrontational and musically turbulent album Bruce Springsteen has ever made'.[1] For the BBC, *Wrecking Ball* was 'a work of commanding range and masterful execution'.[2] The sceptical Robert Christgau found some things to like. The album reached number one in both the US and the UK charts and *Rolling Stone* selected it as the best album of the year. However, Springsteen would later comment that he had hoped that the album would make a bigger impact than it did.

On 9 March, the band performed at the Apollo Theatre in New York to mark the tenth anniversary of SiriusXM Radio, broadcast live. The tour kicked off on 18 March in Atlanta. Springsteen added a horn section – Jake Clemons and Eddie Manion on saxophones, Curt Ramm and Barry Danielian on trumpets, and Clark Gayton on trombone – and backing singers – Michelle Moore, Cindy Mizelle, Curtis King and Everett Bradley. The first phase of the tour included concerts on home turf in Philadelphia and New York (at the Meadowlands and Madison Square Garden) and in California (San Jose and LA).

In Europe from early May, playing mostly in stadiums, the band kicked off in Seville, and gave marathon concerts lasting three and a half hours or more in Milan (at the San Siro), Florence, and Madrid (at the Bernabéu – Southside Johnny guested on 'Talk to Me', and the band also played another *Darkness* outtake, 'Spanish Eyes'). In England, the first show at the Stadium of Light in Sunderland was typically short because of curfew restrictions, but the band must have started on time at the Etihad in Manchester for they played for three and a quarter hours. On 24 June, the band played the Isle of White festival for the first time. Following a two-week break, the band returned to the stage in Paris on Independence Day. Parisians enjoyed the considerable advantage of

---

[1] David Fricke, 'Wrecking Ball', in *Rolling Stone* (6 March 2012).

[2] Ian Winwood, 'Bruce Springsteen: *Wrecking Ball* Review', *BBC Music* (2 March 2012), at https://www.bbc.co.uk/music/reviews/94m5/ (accessed 13/11/20).

seeing the band indoors, for the two shows took place within the familiar old walls of the Bercy arena. The second night, lasting over three-and-a-half hours, was a classic, with performances of 'Something in the Night', 'Incident on 57th Street', 'Racing in the Street' and a solo piano 'For You'. The band took to the stage to 'Au clair de la lune', played by Bittan and Giordano on their accordions. Patti Scialfa, absent during the first weeks in Europe, was temporarily back with the band. Springsteen danced with his daughter Jessica during 'Dancing in the Dark'.

On 11 July, the band made their debut in Prague. On the 14th, in London, they headlined (for the second time) the Hard Rock Calling Festival in Hyde Park. Tom Morello guested for part of the concert and John Fogerty joined Springsteen on 'Promised Land'. This powerful show was made unique by the presence of Paul McCartney and a conclusion that perhaps reminded the great man of the final live performance of the Beatles on a Saville Row rooftop in 1969. McCartney was watching the show from the wings and Springsteen and Van Zandt wanted him to come out on stage, but it seems he only decided to do so at the last moment (they hadn't rehearsed anything). The band played 'I Saw Her Standing There' and 'Twist and Shout'. This was a moment that would have flabbergasted their fifteen-year-old selves.

An official working for the organiser/promoter pulled the plug at the end of 'Twist and Shout'. The 10.30 curfew had been breached by a few minutes and (presumably) the organiser was legitimately fearful that future licences would not be forthcoming as a result. Springsteen, though, would not have expected an accidental infringement of the 10.30 curfew to provoke such a drastic response, especially given that Sir Paul was on the stage. The sudden loss of sound meant that he couldn't conclude the concert in the normal way.

Everyone involved enjoyed telling the story subsequently, and it was picked up by news outlets in the States. Springsteen began the next show, in Dublin, with the words 'Before we were so rudely interrupted...' The band then played the final bars of 'Twist and Shout' followed by the rarity 'I Fought the Law'.

The 2012 European leg concluded with a run of shows in Scandinavia. The second of two shows in Gothenburg at the Ullevi, in the rain, included rare performances of 'Frankie' and 'Where the Bands Are'. The final show, in Helsinki at the Olympiastadion, was a four-hour marathon.

After only a short break, the band returned to the road in America, performing from August to December in the States, Canada and Mexico (a single show, the band's first south of the border). On 12 December, the band joined Paul McCartney, The Rolling Stones, The Who and others at Madison Square Garden to raise money for the Hurricane Sandy Relief Fund. Three nights later,

Springsteen guested with the Stones at the Prudential Centre in Newark, sharing vocals with Jagger on 'Tumbling Dice'.

In March 2013, the band gave ten concerts in Australia. Van Zandt couldn't make the trip because of filming commitments. Tom Morello was an able substitute. Patti Scialfa was also absent. Springsteen premiered his version of Tim Scott McConnell's 'High Hopes' and The Saints' 'Just Like Fire Would'. There were rare outings of 'Last to Die' and 'Better Days'.

At the end of April, the band, including Van Zandt but minus Scialfa, returned to Europe for three months of mostly stadium shows. Highlights included the first-ever performance of 'Wages of Sin' (Turku, Finland) and an acoustic 'I Wish I Were Blind' (Herning, Denmark). In London, Springsteen performed an acoustic version of 'Promised Land' on the balcony of a studio in Camden (in support of ONE's campaign against extreme poverty). The band played Wembley Stadium for the first time since 1988. The show included a complete performance of *Darkness on the Edge of Town*. Complete performances of *Born in the USA* were given in London (at the Olympic Park) and Paris (at the Stade de France). An impromptu performance of Chuck Berry's 'You Never Can Tell' was a highlight of the show in Leipzig. Arguably, attendees of the concert at the Ippodromo Delle Capannelle in Rome (11 July) witnessed the leg's best moment, a rare and very fine account of 'New York City Serenade' with the strings of the Roma Sinfonietta. The band had rehearsed with the Roma Sinfonietta a day or so before the show. The band played five songs from *Nebraska* in a rare show in Belfast, and performed indoors in the UK for the first time since 2006 at the First Direct Arena in Leeds: rarities included 'Local Hero', 'Secret Garden', 'American Skin' and 'Thundercrack'. In September, the band travelled to Chile, Argentina, and Brazil.

On 14 January 2014, Springsteen unexpectedly released a new album, *High Hopes*, along with a bonus disc of the band's complete *Born in the USA* recorded at the Olympic Park in London. *High Hopes* included E Street Band outtakes from the previous fifteen years (some of them re-worked) along with new recordings made in 2013. The new sessions took place during breaks in the tour, starting with sessions in LA and Australia that March. Ron Aniello and Toby Scott oversaw the project but some of the older material dated from *The Rising* sessions and was produced by Brendan O'Brien and recorded by Nick DiDia. DiDia also engineered the tracks recorded in Sydney, 'High Hopes' and 'Just Like Fire Would'. *High Hopes* was the first E Street record to include cover songs – these two plus 'Dream Baby Dream'.

'Harry's Place' was first considered for *The Rising*. It was recorded during the *Magic* sessions, along with 'Heaven's Wall'. Overdubs (backing singers and

Morello) were added to the basic track of 'Heaven's Wall' in 2013. The recording history of 'American Skin (41 Shots)' is a little confused. The band recorded the song during the sessions at the Hit Factory in New York in March 2001, and *High Hopes* possibly used this master along with a Tom Morello overdub recorded in 2013. The studio version is good but less powerful than the live recording from 2000. A song this significant doesn't need a Morello guitar solo. 'Down in the Hole' was recorded for *The Rising* but left off the album. 'Frankie Fell in Love' was probably recorded in 2013. The poetic and unusual 'Hunter of Invisible Game', in waltz time, was first recorded for *Working on a Dream*. A Morello overdub was added in 2013. 'This is Your Sword' is post-O'Brien, but the date of recording is unconfirmed. The electric 'Ghost of Tom Joad' (in E minor rather than the original key of B minor) was recorded during the break before the band left for Australia in March 2013. 'Dream Baby Dream' also dates from this time.

If the album understandably lacked the cohesion usually achieved by Springsteen, there were some very great songs – 'American Skin', 'Down in the Hole' (in G minor), and 'The Wall' (in E$^\flat$). Springsteen wrote 'The Wall' in the late 1990s, prompted by Joe Grushecky (who also wrote his own song inspired by the Vietnam Veterans Memorial in Washington). The memorial wall lists, in chronological order, the names of the 58,318 Americans who were killed in the Vietnam War. It is unclear when this beautiful performance by the E Street Band (plus Curt Ramm on cornet) was recorded, but it wasn't during the O'Brien era. Overdubs may have been added to an older recording, or it could have been recorded anew in 2013.

The *Wrecking Ball* tour wasn't over. Following the release of *High Hopes*, the band played in South Africa, Australia, New Zealand and the States between January and May 2014. The band opened their final show in Australia in Brisbane with a jazzy and droll cover of the Bee Gees' 'Staying Alive'. In Auckland, pre-show, Springsteen performed a solo version of Lorde's 'Royals' – this long down the road Springsteen could still surprise and amaze.

The *Wrecking Ball* tour was an exhilarating ride for Springsteen and the Band. At its end, Springsteen's depression returned. Coming off a long tour is a challenge for most performers; for those suffering from a mental illness, it can be bleak indeed. On 10 April 2014, in New York, Springsteen inducted the E Street Band into the Hall of Fame. He gave a wonderful speech but looked thin and exhausted. At the time, the public didn't know about Springsteen's battle with depression.

2 THE RIVER REDUX

During 2015 Springsteen worked on a box set to celebrate the thirty-fifth anniversary of *The River*. It contained over fifty tracks, concert footage (part of the show in Tempe in 1980) and a documentary, spread across four CDs and two DVDs. The set contained the album that Springsteen rejected in 1979, *The Ties That Bind*, of interest because the songs were mixed by Bob Clearmountain whereas the versions on *The River*, with the exception of 'Hungry Heart', were re-mixed by Toby Scott and Chuck Plotkin, and eleven previously unreleased outtakes, all of them of the highest standard and at least one – 'Stray Bullet' – a masterpiece.

The set was released on 4 December 2015. Springsteen surprised everyone, including the other members of E Street, when he decided that the band should tour *The River* and that complete performances of the album should be performed at every show. He was revealing the importance of the album within his work by giving it a second tour thirty-five years after its first. His bandmates were delighted, while old-time fans were in second heaven.

The tour began at the start of January 2016. For the whole of the American leg, the band played *The River* in sequence. After the coda of 'Wreck on the Highway' had faded away, the concerts ended with a long section of greatest hits plus the odd rarity. The band played the usual arenas in, among other cities, Pittsburgh, Chicago, New York (Madison Square Garden), Washington, Newark, Toronto, Philadelphia, Sunrise, Atlanta, Louisville, Cleveland, Buffalo, St Paul, Phoenix, LA, Seattle, Denver, Dallas, Kansas City, and Baltimore. The leg came to an end in New York with two shows at the Barclays Centre in Brooklyn on 23 and 25 April. The first show opened with a tribute to Prince, who had died on the 21st – an outstanding version of 'Purple Rain', beautifully arranged and sung and with a majestic guitar solo by Lofgren at its heart.

The European shows, from the middle of May to the end of July, took place, with two exceptions, in stadiums. To the chagrin of some fans, including this author, and Van Zandt, complete performances of *The River* were only given in three cities: Paris (the second of two nights indoors at the Bercy arena), Gothenburg (night three) and Oslo. That night in Paris also included a rare performance of 'The Iceman'. The first of the three nights at the Ullevi in Gothenburg holds the record for the most songs played at an E Street concert – thirty-eight. A long thirty-three song show in splendid weather at Wembley Stadium featured two solo Springsteen performances – 'Does This Bus Stop at 82nd Street?' and 'I'll Work for Your Love' – plus 'Be True' and 'Seeds', a song premiered at Wembley back in 1985. A short second American leg, in August and September, commenced with two shows at the Metlife Stadium in East Rutherford. Both shows began with 'New York City Serenade', complete with strings.

The band took a break for the rest of the year during which Springsteen published *Born to Run*, a candid memoir that amounted to a meditation on his life and times. The sections on his childhood were lyrical and poignant. This was a literary biography that changed perceptions and, by discussing mental illness, offered support to so many others. Springsteen's ability to bring to life people and places, so evident in his songs, was also matched by his desire to find meaning.

There was a down under coda to *The River* tour. In January and February 2017, the band gave fourteen shows in Australia and New Zealand. Opening in Perth on 22 January, two days after Donald Trump's inauguration as President, Springsteen told the audience: 'The E Street Band is so glad to be here in Western Australia. We are a long way from home, but our hearts and spirits are with the hundreds of thousands of women and men who marched yesterday in every city of America and in Melbourne, who rallied against hate and division. […] We stand with you. We are the new American Resistance.'

FIFTEEN: GHOSTS

1 CONFESSIONS

When *The River* tour came to an end, Springsteen began a two-year period of solo work. From October 2017 to December 2018, he performed a one-man show (Scialfa came on stage for two songs) called *Springsteen on Broadway* at the Walter Kerr Theatre in New York. This was a logical extension of his biography, for Springsteen chose songs that enabled him to talk about aspects of his life. The show was written like a play and Springsteen kept to the script for all 238 performances. Then, in early 2019, he completed the album project he had temporarily abandoned at the end of 2010 to make *Wrecking Ball*. *Western Stars* was released to acclaim that June. Springsteen made an accompanying film but didn't tour the record. His thoughts had returned to E Street.

2 RECORDING SESSIONS 2019

Springsteen had written a group of semi-autobiographical songs that referenced his formative years as a member of the Castiles and which addressed themes of loss and mortality. These themes were not new to Springsteen's work. They permeated *The Rising*. But they had become more personal. Springsteen's reflections on his past were deepened by the deaths of a number of people close to him, including Danny, Clarence, Terry Magovern and George Theiss. Despite the sombre nature of the themes, Springsteen wanted the music to rock in the manner of the music of his twenties. He wanted to celebrate friends like Thiess. So, the new songs were written for the E Street Band.

During the previous two years, Van Zandt and Bittan had both suggested to Springsteen that, if they made a new E Street album, they should do so in the manner of the old days, when Springsteen would play his colleagues a song in the studio, they'd discuss it briefly and then start to play it together, finding the arrangement spontaneously and instinctively. 'The E Street Band produces itself,' Van Zandt was fond of saying. They hadn't recorded that way since the brief *Blood Brothers* sessions of 1995. *The Rising* and *Magic* were great records, but they sounded over-produced and lacked the exciting sound and strong E Street personality they could have had.

Van Zandt was perhaps a little surprised, as well as delighted, when Springsteen agreed that the new songs would be recorded live, with few takes and minimal overdubs, returning to the ethos of *Darkness on the Edge of Town*, *The River* and *Born in the USA*, but without the multiple takes. The plan was to record the album in quick time, like the Beatles at Abbey Road. The band assembled at Colts Neck on 11 November 2019. Ron Aniello recorded the music and co-produced with Springsteen. Bob Clearmountain worked on the final mixes. The band members were in their element. 'The E Street Band works extremely well when spontaneity and reaction time is the mandate,' Weinberg explained after the release of the album. The recording process was, in Lofgren's words, 'natural and organic', with improvisation encouraged within the written structure: 'You aren't just trying to place your part on a great track, you are all there together. It's interactive and you have to focus and adapt to what the others are doing.'[1]

Springsteen had what he needed after only five days of work. Of the twelve songs recorded, it is believed that 'Letter to You', 'Last Man Standing', 'The Power of Prayer', 'House of a Thousand Guitars', 'Ghosts' and 'I'll See You in My Dreams' were written in 2018 or 2019. It is not known when Springsteen wrote 'One Minute You're Here', 'Burnin' Train' or 'Rainmaker'. The album was completed by new versions of three songs written (but never released) during the early 1970s. 'Janey Needs a Shooter' was recorded as a piano ballad during *The Wild, the Innocent and the E Street Shuffle* sessions and then by the full band during the *Darkness* sessions (Springsteen allowed Warren Zevon to release his own version, 'Jeannie Needs a Shooter', in 1980). Springsteen played 'If I Was the Priest' to John Hammond during his audition on 3 May 1972 and a demo was recorded the next day at Columbia's studio. Solo performances of 'Song for Orphans' surfaced occasionally during the *Greetings* tour and a version was recorded at 914 Sound during the tour. Springsteen lifted the song from obscurity during the final concert of the *Devils and Dust* tour, at Trenton, NJ, on 22 November 2005. The E Street Band turned these

---

[1] Quoted in Peter Watts, 'The Ties That Bind', in *Uncut* (December 2020).

three folk rarities into 'Like a Rolling Stone' rock and roll classics. 'It's fun to go back and see how wild my lyric writing was, and how uninhibited it was at a certain moment,' Springsteen told *The New York Times*, 'and to be able to take that and bring it into the present with the band, and sing it in my voice right now.'[1]

The initial idea was to release the album in the late spring of 2020 and to tour for most of the rest of the year or even longer, but Springsteen subsequently decided to stay at home during 2020. Then COVID-19 happened. With the future still unclear, Springsteen decided to release the record in October 2020, even though there would be no tour until 2022. Springsteen, serious about civic duty, knew that there were people out there who needed the E Street Band more than ever. *Letter to You* was released on 23 October. A short documentary film about the making of the album was streamed on Apple TV and the band, minus Tallent, who didn't travel to New York because of COVID restrictions, appeared on *Saturday Night Live* on 12 December, playing two of the new songs – 'Ghosts' and 'I'll See You in My Dreams'.

3 LETTER TO YOU

Performed by the E Street Band and recorded at Thrill Hill Recording, Stone Hill Studio, NJ, in November 2019. Bittan (piano); Jake Clemons (saxophone); Giordano (organ); Lofgren (electric guitar, acoustic guitar, backing vocals); Scialfa (backing vocals); Springsteen (lead vocals, electric guitar, acoustic guitar, harmonica); Tallent (bass); Van Zandt (electric guitar, backing vocals); Weinberg (drums). Produced by Springsteen and Ron Aniello; recorded by Ron Aniello; mixed by Bob Clearmountain. Released on 23 October 2020.

The album:

> One Minute You're Here
> Letter to You
> Burnin' Train
> Janey Needs a Shooter
> Last Man Standing
> The Power of Prayer

---

[1] Quoted in Lindsay Zoladz, 'Bruce Springsteen is Living in the Moment', in *The New York Times* (19 October 2020).

House of a Thousand Guitars
Rainmaker
If I Was the Priest
Ghosts
Song for Orphans
I'll See You in My Dreams

Letter to You is book-ended by two songs about the fragility of life, 'One Minute You're Here' and 'I'll See You in My Dreams'. They share a key, B♭, and melodies that incorporate E♭ and F. The first is a folk ballad. Springsteen's acoustic guitar is backed, sweetly, by the keyboards and a tambourine. The bare bleakness of the song haunts the rest of the album. The second is mid-tempo and full-band and features vocal harmonies. It begins with a strummed acoustic and Bittan's piano. The drums and electric guitars kick in after the first verse. In the instrumental break, a guitar solo is completed by the piano and organ. Springsteen performed an acoustic version of the song during the Memorial Ceremony in New York on September 11, 2021.

In-between, there are four songs inspired by Springsteen, Van Zandt and Tallent's formative years as band musicians in New Jersey, 'Last Man Standing', 'The Power of Prayer', 'House of a Thousand Guitars' and 'Ghosts', contextualised by three pieces written by the young Springsteen – 'Janey Needs a Shooter', 'If I Was the Priest' and 'Song for Orphans'.

'Burnin' Train', a love song darkened by sexual and religious imagery, and 'Rainmaker', have no connection to the other songs.

Throughout the album, the band plays with the panache, unity, and sensitivity to the nature of the material, it is famed for. Gathering at Colts Neck, they had no foreknowledge of the songs or the themes of the album. The songs resonated strongly, not least because they connected to the band's history, celebrating the ties that bind. 'It's a celebration of music and the joy of it,' Lofgren told *Uncut*. 'The camaraderie of having a long life together as a team of musicians and sharing it with the audience.' For Bittan, the title track was 'about [Springsteen's] fifty-year career of trying to express the truths he sees and feels, and what that has done for his relationships with his fans, his bands and his family.'

'Letter to You', in A, uses suspended 2 chords (A and D) and F$^\sharp$ minor 7. The chord pattern is reversed for the chorus. Four quick beats on the snare are followed by the descending phrase, doubled by an electric guitar and the piano, that will return during the chorus. Bittan plays a suspended motif behind the vocal. Weinberg's muscular drumming and Tallent's trademark bass pattern drive the music forward and Giordano plays the B3 in the manner of Federici.

The organ duets with a lead guitar during the instrumental break, while the last verse is sung to the accompaniment of the piano and a strummed acoustic guitar (played by Lofgren?). 'Burnin' Train' is a guitar-heavy two-chord (C and G) dirge, lifted by fast drumming and the ringing of a tubular bell.

The words of the enigmatic 'Janey Needs a Shooter', composed in 1971/72, are startling. The verses have a musical structure of A, D, and E. The music falls, powerfully, to F$^\sharp$ minor at the beginning of the chorus. We are back in the heady days of the late 1960s. A 'Like a Rolling Stone' organ riff is prominent and the electric guitars jangle, but Dylan didn't have a drummer like Weinberg. The lyrics are packed with sexual imagery, for the theme is sexual threat and temptation. Vulnerable Janey encounters older men – doctor, priest and neighbourhood cop – poised to abuse their authority, but she is not wholly innocent. The singer, presumably a boy her own age, pursues her too. Is the song a B-movie shocker, a feminist fable or both? Springsteen toned down some of the lyrics. Janey is more culpable in the original. Nevertheless, the song is of its time. It has a wounded majesty.

When George Theiss died in 2018, Springsteen realised that he was the only surviving member of the Castiles. He wrote 'Last Man Standing' for Theiss. In evocative language, Springsteen remembers the pride and the wonder of being in a teen band and the style and charisma of Theiss. He refuses to let the distant past rest in faded photos and yellowed press cuttings. With his E Street colleagues, he brings it alive. The main melody combines A, F$^\sharp$ minor and E. For the chorus, Springsteen uses D and B minor. There is a superb modulation to G before the final sax solo, the melody moving through E minor before returning to D major. This is classical E Street – drums and bass, guitars, piano, organ and saxophone made to sound thrillingly current.

The past remains powerfully present in the next two songs. 'The Power of Prayer', in B, is a memory of first love and an evocation of a long-lost summer. The lilting melody incorporates B, E, and F$^\sharp$. The musical line of the refrain moves through G$^\sharp$ minor and F$^\sharp$ before returning to the tonic. Bittan's piano is prominent. 'House of a Thousand Guitars' is the only song in a minor key, C$^\sharp$ minor. In this song about the healing power of live music, Springsteen refers to a 'criminal clown' who has 'stolen the throne'. The next song, 'Rainmaker', can be read as an allegorical dissection of the Trump phenomenon. The unsettling melody, connecting F$^\sharp$ and C$^\sharp$, uses a two-note suspended motif, played on the piano, later doubled by the guitar, and the atmospheric twangs of an acoustic guitar played, by Lofgren(?), with a slide (think Ry Cooder's score for *Paris, Texas*). 'Rainmaker' is the album's most intriguing piece. The band recorded the song a week after the Presidential Election.

The second of the old songs, 'If I Was the Priest', is a dreamlike parable linking a parody of Western movies with religious iconography. The song eludes interpretation. Its richly expressive language impressed John Hammond but Springsteen didn't go forward with the song, until 2020. Bittan's piano stands out within another terrific live performance. The fine melody connects B♭, F, G minor, and E♭. The music quietens for the final verse, and the last repeat of the chorus is harmonised. Van Zandt plays an impromptu solo in the fade-out.

The second of the songs that directly reference Theiss and the Castiles, 'Ghosts', links B, E, and F♯. The words are poignant, but Springsteen celebrates his ghosts (and prompts us to celebrate ours – the album is called 'letter to you' for a reason) by composing the album's grandest piece of music, a song conceived to open stadium concerts across America and Europe.

'Song for Orphans', in F, moving through D minor and A minor, is the most Dylanesque of Springsteen's early songs. However, Springsteen uses alliteration, internal rhymes and metaphors in his own style, and delights in obscurity and strangeness. Each listener will extract their own meaning from the song's imagery, but the poetic language is a reward in itself.

The album ends tenderly with 'I'll See You in My Dreams'.

APPENDICES

1 KEYS

Songs by Springsteen on E Street Band albums.

C major	Growin' Up / *Greetings from Asbury Park*
	The E Street Shuffle / *The Innocent, the Wild*
	4th of July, Asbury Park / *The Innocent, the Wild*
	Jungleland / *Born to Run*
	Candy's Room / *Darkness*
	Factory / *Darkness*
	The Ties That Bind / *The River*
	Two Hearts / *The River*
	You Can Look / *The River*
	Working on the Highway / *Born in the USA*
	Waitin' on a Sunny Day / *The Rising*
	Let's Be Friends (Skin to Skin) / *The Rising*
	Living in the Future / *Magic*
	Girls in Their Summer Clothes / *Magic*
	Working on a Dream / *Working on a Dream*
	Burnin' Train / *Letter to You*
C♯ major	Hungry Heart / *The River*
C♯ minor	Jackson Cage / *The River*
	Paradise / *The Rising*
	Magic / *Magic*
	House of a Thousand Guitars / *Letter to You*
D major	Mary Queen of Arkansas / *Greetings from Asbury Park*
	I Wanna Marry You / *The River*
	Fade Away / *The River*
	Nebraska / *Nebraska*
	Mansion on the Hill / *Nebraska*
	Highway Patrolman / *Nebraska*
	Used Cars / *Nebraska*
	My Father's House / *Nebraska*

	The Fuse / *The Rising*
	My Lucky Day / *Working on a Dream*
D minor	Spare Parts / *Tunnel of Love*
	Life Itself / *Working on a Dream*
E♭ major	Meeting Across the River / *Born to Run*
	Nothing Man / *The Rising*
	This Life / *Working on a Dream*
	The Wrestler / *Working on a Dream*
	Harry's Place / *High Hopes*
	The Wall / *High Hopes*
E major	Blinded by the Light / *Greetings from Asbury Park*
	Born to Run / *Born to Run*
	She's the One / *Born to Run*
	Badlands / *Darkness*
	Crush on You / *The River*
	I'm on Fire / *Born in the USA*
	Valentine's Day / *Tunnel of Love*
	Your Own Worst Enemy / *Magic*
	Devil's Arcade / *Magic*
	Hunter of Invisible Game / *High Hopes*
E minor	Spirit in the Night / *Greetings from Asbury Park*
	Lost in the Flood / *Greetings from Asbury Park*
	Adam Raised a Cain / *Darkness*
	The River / *The River*
	Worlds Apart / *The Rising*
	Last to Die / *Magic*
	What Love Can Do / *Working on a Dream*
	Ghost of Tom Joad / *High Hopes*
F major	For You / *Greetings from Asbury Park*
	Rosalita / *The Wild, the Innocent*
	Thunder Road / *Born to Run*
	Tenth Avenue Freeze-Out / *Born to Run*
	Night / *Born to Run*
	Racing in the Street / *Darkness*
	Sherry Darling / *The River*
	Independence Day / *The River*
	Drive All Night / *The River*
	No Surrender / *Born in the USA*
	Tougher Than the Rest / *Tunnel of Love*

	Walk Like a Man / *Tunnel of Love*
	Tunnel of Love / *Tunnel of Love*
	One Step Up / *Tunnel of Love*
	When You're Alone / *Tunnel of Love*
	Into the Fire / *The Rising*
	Empty Sky / *The Rising*
	Mary's Place / *The Rising*
	You're Missing / *The Rising*
	Kingdom of Days / *Working on a Dream*
	This is Your Sword / *High Hopes*
	Song for Orphans / *Letter to You*
F minor	Further On (Up the Road) / *The Rising*
F♯ major	Ramrod / *The River*
	Open All Night / *Nebraska*
	Reason to Believe / *Nebraska*
	Tomorrow Never Knows / *Working on a Dream*
	Rainmaker / *Letter to You*
F♯ minor	Streets of Fire / *Darkness*
G major	Does This Bus Stop / *Greetings from Asbury Park*
	The Angel / *Greetings from Asbury Park*
	Wild Billy's Circus Story / *The Wild, the Innocent*
	Backstreets / *Born to Run*
	Something in the Night / *Darkness*
	Promised Land / *Darkness*
	Darkness on the Edge of Town / *Darkness*
	Cadillac Ranch / *The River*
	Stolen Car / *The River*
	The Price You Pay / *The River*
	Darlington County / *Born in the USA*
	Ain't Got You / *Tunnel of Love*
	All That Heaven Will Allow / *Tunnel of Love*
	Cautious Man / *Tunnel of Love*
	Terry's Song / *Magic*
	Queen of the Supermarket / *Working on a Dream*
	Good Eye / *Working on a Dream*
G minor	Downbound Train / *Born in the USA*
	Down in the Hole / *High Hopes*
A major	It's Hard to Be a Saint / *Greetings from Asbury Park*

	New York City Serenade / *The Wild, the Innocent*
	Prove It All Night / *Darkness*
	Out in the Street / *The River*
	Wreck on the Highway / *The River*
	Atlantic City / *Nebraska*
	Bobby Jean / *Born in the USA*
	I'm Goin' Down / *Born in the USA*
	Glory Days / *Born in the USA*
	My Hometown / *Born in the USA*
	Two Faces / *Tunnel of Love*
	Brilliant Disguise / *Tunnel of Love*
	Countin' on a Miracle / *The Rising*
	Radio Nowhere / *Magic*
	Surprise, Surprise / *Working on a Dream*
	American Skin (41 Shots) / *High Hopes*
	Letter to You / *Letter to You*
	Janey Needs a Shooter / *Letter to You*
	Last Man Standing / *Letter to You*
A minor	Kitty's Back in Town / *The Wild, the Innocent*
	State Trooper / *Nebraska*
	Outlaw Pete / *Working on a Dream*
B♭ major	Incident on 57th Street / *The Wild, the Innocent*
	Lonesome Day / *The Rising*
	The Rising / *The Rising*
	My City of Ruins / *The Rising*
	Gypsy Biker / *Magic*
	I'll Work for Your Love / *Magic*
	Long Walk Home / *Magic*
	The Last Carnival / *Working on a Dream*
	Frankie Fell in Love / *High Hopes*
	One Minute You're Here / *Letter to You*
	If I Was the Priest / *Letter to You*
	I'll See You in My Dreams / *Letter to You*
B major	Johnny 99 / *Nebraska*
	Born in the USA / *Born in the USA*
	Dancing in the Dark / *Born in the USA*
	You'll Be Coming Down / *Magic*
	The Power of Prayer / *Letter to You*
	Ghosts / *Letter to You*
B minor	Point Blank / *The River*

Cover Me / *Born in the USA*
Heaven's Wall / *High Hopes*

II   CHRONOLOGY 1942-1985

1942
Birth of Clarence Clemons on 11 January.

1949
Birth of Vini Lopez on 22 January.
Birth of Roy Bittan on 2 July.
Birth of Bruce Springsteen in Long Branch, NJ, on 23 September.
Birth of Garry Tallent on 27 October.
During his childhood, Springsteen lives with his family in rented houses in Freehold. He attends St Rose of Lima Catholic School.

1950
Birth of Danny Federici on 23 January.
Birth of Steven Van Zandt on 22 November.

1951
Birth of Max Weinberg on 13 April.
Birth of Nils Lofgren on 21 June.
Birth of Suki Lahav on 16 July.

1953
Birth of Patti Scialfa on 29 July.
Birth of David Sancious on 30 November.

1956
Elvis Presley appears on CBS's Ed Sullivan Show on 9 September.

1957
Birth of Soozie Tyrell on 4 May.

1961
President Kennedy escalates US involvement in the Vietnam War by sending thousands of military advisers.

1963

Springsteen attends Freehold High School.

Assassination of President Kennedy on 23 November.

Release of The Beatles' 'I Want to Hold Your Hand' in America on 26 December.

1964

Release of the Beatles' first Capitol Records album *Meet the Beatles!* on 20 January.

The Beatles perform on the Ed Sullivan Show on 9 February, watched by 73 million people, among them Springsteen and Van Zandt.

1965

Springsteen joins the Castiles, a band led by George Thiess and managed by Tex Vineyard.

Springsteen and Van Zandt meet when the Castiles and Van Zandt's band, the Shadows, share the bill at a teen dance.

In March, President Johnson sends the first American ground troops to Vietnam. In July, he signs off on the drafting of over 30,000 men per month and passes a law criminalising the burning of draft cards.

1966

The Castiles record two songs written by Springsteen and Thiess at a local studio.

1967

Springsteen graduates from Freehold High School. He briefly attends Ocean County College.

1968

Martin Luther King is assassinated on 4 April.

Robert Kennedy is assassinated on 6 June.

Springsteen is called to the draft board. Because of a recent concussion he fails the medical and isn't drafted.

Springsteen leaves the Castiles and, in August, forms Earth with bassist John Graham and drummer Michael Burke.

1969

Springsteen's parents and younger sister move to California.

Springsteen begins to attend the Upstage Club in Asbury Park (the club opened in February 1968). Here he meets the future E Streeters Vini Lopez, Danny Federici, Garry Tallent and David Sancious.

Springsteen disbands Earth and forms Child with Federici, Lopez and bass player Vinnie Roslin. The name changes to Steel Mill in November.

1970

Van Zandt joins Steel Mill in February to play bass following the departure of

Roslin.

1971

Springsteen disbands Steel Mill in January. In May, Springsteen and Van Zandt form the short-lived Dr Zoom and the Sonic Boom.

In July, Springsteen forms the band that will eventually be named the E Street Band. It begins life as the Bruce Springsteen Band. The initial members are Springsteen, Van Zandt, Lopez, Sancious and Tallent. Federici and Clemons will soon join.

The Upstage closes for good in October.

In November, Tinker arranges for Springsteen to meet Mike Appel of the Wes Farrel Organisation in NYC. Appel tells Springsteen to come back after he has written more songs.

1972

In February, a song-rich Springsteen returns to see Appel and in March he signs a management, publishing and recording contract with Appel's company Laurel Canyon.

Appel gets him an audition with John Hammond at Columbia Records. The audition takes place on 2 May. Columbia signs him as a singer-songwriter.

Recording of *Greetings from Asbury Park, NJ*, takes place at 914 Sound, Blauvelt, NY, between June and October. Appel produces. Van Zandt is evicted from the band at the start of the sessions because Columbia, not wanting a band record, vetoes the use of electric guitars. Springsteen records either solo or with Clemons, Lopez, Sancious, and Tallent.

The *Greetings from Asbury Park* tour starts at the end of October. The tour will continue until the autumn of 1973 and merge into the *Wild, the Innocent and the E Street Shuffle* tour.

1973

President Nixon ends the draft in January.

Release of *Greetings from Asbury Park, NJ*, on 5 January.

The Wild, the Innocent and the E Street Shuffle is recorded at 914 Sound between May and September. It is released on 5 November.

The Wild, the Innocent and the E Street Shuffle tour begins. The tour will continue until March 1975.

1974

Lopez is sacked mid-tour in February. Ernest Carter replaces him.

In May, the name E Street Band is used officially for the first time.

Jon Landau's review of the 9 May late-night show at the Harvard Theatre in Cambridge is published in *The Real Paper*.

The recording of *Born to Run* begins at 914 Sound in May. Sessions continue there until October.

In July, Marc Brickman joins the touring team as lighting designer.

In August, Sancious and Carter leave the band. They are replaced by Roy Bittan and Max Weinberg, who make their first appearances in September.
Suki Lahav joins the band in October.

1975

The *Born to Run* sessions resume at the Record Plant in NYC in March.
Jon Landau joins Appel as co-producer; Jimmy Iovine replaces Louis Lahav as engineer.
Suki and Louis Lahav return to Israel.
The Vietnam War ends with the fall of Saigon on 30 April.
The *Born to Run* sessions last until July.
Van Zandt returns to the band.
The *Born to Run* tour starts on 20 July. The tour will continue, with breaks, until May 1976.
In August, the band play the Bottom Line in NYC.
Born to Run is released on 25 August.
In October, the band play the Roxy Theatre in LA.
On 18 November, the band makes its European debut at the Hammersmith Odeon in London.

1976

The *Born to Run* tour ends in May. Appel prevents Springsteen from recording his next album with Landau. In July, Springsteen takes Appel to court to gain control of his work. The case will last until May 1977.
Unable to record, the band returns to the road in August, and, with a break over the New Year, continues to tour until March 1977.

1977

In January, the E Street Band records 'Say Goodbye to Hollywood' with Ronnie Spector at Columbia Recording Studios in NYC.
The lawsuit is settled in May.
At the beginning of June, Springsteen and the band begin recording a new album at Atlantic Studios in NYC.
In September, recording is moved to the Record Plant.

1978

The recording of *Darkness on the Edge of Town* ends in March.
The *Darkness on the Edge of Town* tour begins on 23 May. It will last until 1 January 1979.
Darkness on the Edge of Town is released on 2 June.
In August, the band play Madison Square Garden in NYC.

1979

The *Darkness* tour ends on 1 January.

The recording of a new album starts at the Power Station in NYC in March.
In September, Springsteen signs off on an album called *The Ties That Bind*, but then changes his mind. The band continues to record.
In September, the band headlines two *No Nukes* concerts at Madison Square Garden.

1980

Recording ends in May with completion of *The River*.
The River tour begins on 3 October. It will last until September 1981.
The River is released on 17 October.
The band perform at the Spectrum in Philadelphia on 8 December. John Lennon is murdered in NYC.

1981

The European leg of *The River* tour begins on 7 April with a show in Hamburg. The band makes its debut in Germany, Switzerland, France, Catalonia, Belgium, Denmark and Norway and returns to the UK, the Netherlands and Sweden.
A two-night stand at the Palais des Sports de Saint-Ouen in Paris begins on 18 April.
A six-night stand at Wembley Arena in London begins on 29 May.
The European leg ends at the NEC in Birmingham on 8 June.
A six-night stand at the Meadowlands in NJ begins on 2 July.
The River tour ends on 14 September.
In December, Springsteen makes a demo recording of some of his new songs at his home in Colts Neck, NJ.

1982

The recording of a new album starts at the Power Station in January. Sessions continue until the summer. Springsteen decides to pause the sessions and to release the Colts Neck demo as his new album. *Nebraska* is released on 20 September.
Springsteen spends the winter of 1982/83 in Los Angeles. He records new material at his LA home studio.

1983

In the spring, Springsteen returns to New Jersey.
Van Zandt decides to leave the band.
The E Street Band sessions resume in May, at the Hit Factory. With a break in the summer, the sessions will continue until February 1984.

1984

The recording of *Born in the USA* ends in February.
Nils Lofgren joins the band in May.
'Dancing in the Dark' is released as a single on 9 May.
Patti Scialfa joins the band in June.
Born in the USA is released on 4 June.

The *Born in the USA* tour starts on 29 June. It will last until October 1985.
In August, the band gives ten concerts at the Meadowlands in East Rutherford, NJ.
In October, the band gives seven concerts at the Los Angeles Memorial Sports Arena.

1985
In March, the band tours Australia and Japan for the first time.
At the end of May, the European leg of the tour begins.
In July, the band gives three concerts at Wembley Stadium in London.
The *Born in the USA* tour ends in LA on 2 October.

III EVOLUTION OF THE E STREET BAND

CHILD / STEEL MILL

Formed as Child in early 1969. Renamed Steel Mill in November 1969. Disbanded January 1971.

Springsteen (lead vocals, guitar), Federici (keyboards), Lopez (drums), Vinnie Roslin (bass, until February 1970), Van Zandt (bass, from February 1970), Robbin Thompson (vocals, from August 1970).

DR ZOOM AND THE SONIC BOOM

Formed and disbanded in May 1971.

Springsteen (guitar), Lopez (drums, backing vocals), David Sancious (keyboards), Southside Johnny (vocals, harmonica), Tallent (bass), Van Zandt (guitar), Bobby Williams (drums), Albee Tellone (saxophone), Bobby Feigenbaum (saxophone), and others.

BRUCE SPRINGSTEEN BAND / E STREET BAND

Formed in July 1971. The name Bruce Springsteen Band stopped being used when Springsteen recorded his first album. The band remained unnamed until 1974.

July 1971-July 1972: Springsteen, Lopez, Sancious, Tallent, Van Zandt.

June-October 1972 (*Greetings from Asbury Park* recording sessions): Springsteen, Clemons, Lopez, Sancious, Tallent.

October 1972-June 1973: Springsteen, Clemons, Federici, Lopez, Tallent.

June 1973-February 1974: Springsteen, Clemons, Federici, Lopez, Sancious, Tallent.

February 1974-August 1974: Springsteen, Ernest Carter (drums), Clemons, Federici, Sancious, Tallent.

September 1974 to March 1975: Springsteen, Bittan, Clemons, Federici, Suki Lahav (violin), Tallent, Weinberg.

July 1975-1984: Springsteen, Bittan, Clemons, Federici, Tallent, Van Zandt,

Weinberg.

1984- : Springsteen, Bittan, Clemons (d. 2011), Federici (d. 2008), Lofgren, Scialfa, Tallent, Van Zandt (from 1999), Weinberg.

IV E STREET BAND RECORDING HISTORY

June to October 1972
Studio: 914 Sound, Blauvelt, New York
Producers: Mike Appel, Jimmy Cretecos
Engineer: Louis Lahav
Album: *Greetings from Asbury Park, New Jersey* (released 5 January 1973)

May to September 1973
Studio: 914 Sound, Blauvelt, New York
Producers: Mike Appel, Jimmy Cretecos
Engineer: Louis Lahav
Album: *The Wild, the Innocent and the E Street Shuffle* (released 5 November 1973)
Outtakes: *Tracks* (1998)

May 1974 to July 1975
Studios: 914 Sound, Blauvelt, New York; Record Plant, New York City
Producers (914 Sound Studios): Springsteen, Mike Appel
Producers (Record Plant): Springsteen, Mike Appel, Jon Landau
Engineer (914 Sound): Louis Lahav
Engineer (Record Plant): Jimmy Iovine
Mixed by: Jimmy Iovine; 'Born to Run' mixed by Louis Lahav
Album: *Born to Run* (released 1 September 1975)
Outtakes: *Tracks* (1998)

June 1977 to March 1978
Studios: Atlantic Studios, New York City; Record Plant, New York City
Producers: Springsteen, Jon Landau; production assistance, Van Zandt
Engineer: Jimmy Iovine
Mixed by: Jimmy Iovine, Chuck Plotkin
Album: *Darkness on the Edge of Town* (released 2 June 1978)
Outtakes: *Tracks* (1998); *The Promise* (2010)

March 1979 to May 1980
Studio: Power Station, New York City
Producers: Springsteen, Jon Landau, Van Zandt
Engineers: Neil Dorfsman, Bob Clearmountain, (Jimmy Iovine)

Mixed by: Bob Clearmountain, Chuck Plotkin, Toby Scott
Album: *The River* (released 17 October 1980)
Outtakes: *Tracks* (1998); *The Ties That Bind: The River Collection* (2015)

January 1982 to February 1984
Studios: Power Station, New York City; Hit Factory, New York City
Producers: Springsteen, Van Zandt, Jon Landau, Charles Plotkin
Engineer: Toby Scott
Mixed by: Bob Clearmountain
Album: *Born in the USA* (released on 4 June 1984)
Outtakes: *Tracks* (1998); *Greatest Hits* (1995); *The Essential Bruce Springsteen* (2003)

January to July 1987
Studios: Thrill Hill East, New Jersey; Hit Factory, New York City; A&M Studios, Los Angeles
Producers: Springsteen, Jon Landau, Charles Plotkin
Engineer: Toby Scott
Mixed by: Bob Clearmountain
Album: *Tunnel of Love* (released on 6 October 1987)
Outtakes: *Tracks* (1998)

January 1995
Studio: Hit Factory, New York City
Producers: Springsteen, Jon Landau, Chuck Plotkin
Engineer: Toby Scott
Mixed by: Bob Clearmountain
Album: *Greatest Hits* (released 27 February 1995)
Outtakes: *Blood Brothers* EP (1996); *Tracks* (1998)

March 2001
Studio: Hit Factory, New York City
Producers: Springsteen, Chuck Plotkin
Engineer: Toby Scott
Recordings unreleased

January to March 2002
Studio: Atlanta Southern Tracks Studios, Atlanta
Producer: Brendan O'Brien
Engineer: Nick DiDia
Mixed by: Brendan O'Brien
Album: *The Rising* (released 29 July 2002)
Outtakes: *High Hopes* (2014)

February to May 2007
Studio: Atlanta Southern Tracks Studios, Atlanta; additional recording at Thrill

Hill Recording
Producer: Brendan O'Brien
Engineer: Nick DiDia (Toby Scott)
Mixed by: Brendan O'Brien
Album: *Magic* (released 28 September 2007)
Outtakes: *High Hopes* (2014)

June 2007 to November 2008
Studio: Atlanta Southern Tracks Studios, Atlanta; additional recording at Thrill Hill Recording, NJ, Avatar Studios, NY, Clinton Recording Studios, NY, Henson Recording Studios, CA
Producer: Brendan O'Brien
Engineers: Nick DiDia and Rick Kwan (and Toby Scott and others)
Mixed by: Brendan O'Brien
Album: *Working on a Dream* (released 27 January 2009)
Outtakes: *High Hopes* (2014)

2013
Studios: Various, including Studios 301, Sydney, Australia (March 2013)
Producers: Springsteen, Ron Aniello
Engineers: Toby Scott, Nick DiDia
Mixed by: Bob Clearmountain
Album: *High Hopes* (released 14 January 2014)
Outtakes: *American Beauty* EP (2014)

November 2019
Studio: Thrill Hill Recording, Stone Hill Studio, Colts Neck, NJ
Producers: Springsteen, Ron Aniello
Engineer: Ron Aniello
Mixed by: Bob Clearmountain
Album: *Letter to You* (released 23 October 2020)

V   E STREET DISCOGRAPHY

[i] BRUCE SPRINGSTEEN AND THE E STREET BAND

[a] Albums

1973	Greetings from Asbury Park, New Jersey
1973	The Wild, the Innocent and the E Street Shuffle
1975	Born to Run
1978	Darkness on the Edge of Town
1979	No Nukes [2 songs]
1980	The River [double LP]
1984	Born in the USA
1986	Live 1975-85 [box set]
1987	Tunnel of Love
1995	Greatest Hits
1998	Tracks [box set]
2001	Live in New York City [2 CDs]
2002	The Rising
2003	The Essential Bruce Springsteen
2006	Hammersmith Odeon, London '75
2007	Magic
2009	Working on a Dream
2009	Springsteen and the E Street Band Greatest Hits
2010	The Promise
2013	Get Up, Stand Up! Concert Highlights [2 CDs]
2013	12/12/12: Concert for Sandy Relief [2 songs]
2014	High Hopes
2015	The Ties That Bind: The River Collection [box set]
2020	Letter to You
2021	Legendary 1979 No Nukes Concerts

[b] Singles and EPs (incomplete for the digital era)

1973	Blinded by the Light - B side: The Angel Spirit in the Night

	- B side: For You
1975	Fourth of July, Asbury Park (Sandy)
	- B side: The E Street Shuffle
	Born to Run
	- B side: Meeting Across the River
	Tenth Avenue Freeze-Out
	- B side: She's the One
1978	Prove it All Night
	- B side: Factory
	Badlands
	- B side: Streets of Fire
	The Promised Land
	- B side: Streets of Fire
1979	Rosalita (Come Out Tonight)
	- B side: Night
1980	Hungry Heart
	- B side: Held Up Without a Gun
	Point Blank
	- B side: Ramrod
1981	Fade Away
	- B side: Be True
	Sherry Darling
	- B side: Be True
	The River
	- B side: Independence Day
	Cadillac Ranch
	- B side: Wreck on the Highway
1982	Atlantic City
	- B side: Mansion on the Hill
	Open All Night
	- B side: The Big Payback
1984	Dancing in the Dark
	- B side: Pink Cadillac
	Cover Me
	- B side: Jersey Girl (live)
	Born in the USA
	- B side: Shut Out the Light
1985	I'm on Fire
	- B side: Johnny Bye
	Glory Days
	- B side: Stand on It
	I'm Goin' Down
	- B side: Janey, Don't You Lose Heart
	My Hometown

	- B side: Santa Claus Is Comin' To Town
1986	War (live)
	- B side: Merry Christmas Baby (live)
1987	Fire
	- B side: Incident on 57th Street (live)
	Born to Run (live)
	- B side: Johnny 99 (live)
	Brilliant Disguise
	- B side: Lucky Man
	Tunnel of Love
	- B side: Two for the Road
1988	One Step Up
	- B side: Roulette
	Tougher Than the Rest
	- B side: Tougher Than the Rest (live)
	Spare Parts
	- B side: Spare Parts (live)
	Chimes of Freedom [EP]
	- Tougher Than the Rest (live)
	- Be True (live)
	- Chimes of Freedom (live)
	- Born to Run (live)
1995	Murder Incorporated
	- B side: Because the Night (live)
	Secret Garden
	- B side: Thunder Road (live)
1996	Blood Brothers [EP]
	- Blood Brothers (alternative version)
	- High Hopes
	- Murder Incorporated (live)
	- Secret Garden (strings version)
	- Without You
1999	I Wanna Be with You
	- B side: Where the Bands Are
2008	Magic Tour Highlights [Digital EP]
2014	American Beauty [EP]
	- Only 'Hey Blue Eyes' is by the E Street Band

[c] Backing Ronnie Spector

1977	Say Goodbye to Hollywood
	- B side: Baby Please Don't Go

[d] Producing and backing Gary US Bonds

1981	Dedication
1982	On the Line

[ii] BRUCE SPRINGSTEEN SOLO

1982	Nebraska
1992	Human Touch
1992	Lucky Town
1995	The Ghost of Tom Joad
1998	Tracks
2005	Devils and Dust
2006	We Shall Overcome
2012	Wrecking Ball
2018	Springsteen on Broadway
2019	Western Stars

[iii] ROY BITTAN

2015	Out of the Box

[iv] CLARENCE CLEMONS

1993	Rescue
1985	Hero
1989	A Night with Mr C
1995	Peacemaker
1995	Get It On
2002	Live in Asbury Park
2004	Live in Asbury Park, Vol. 2
2008	Brothers in Arms

[v] NILS LOFGREN

Grin

1970	Grin
1971	1+1
1972	All Out
1973	Gone Crazy

Solo

1975		Nils Lofgren
1976		Cry Tough
1977		I Came to Dance
1978		Night After Night
1979		Nils
1981		Night Fades Away
1981		Best of Nils Lofgren
1982		Rhythm Romance (UK)
1983		Wonderland
1985		Flip
1986		Code of the Road: Live '85 (Europe)
1990		Walk Don't Run (UK)
1991		Silver Lining
1992		Crooked Line
1992		Rare Track Collection
1993		Every Breath Soundtrack
1993		Live on the Test (UK)
1995		Damaged Goods
1997		Acoustic Live
1997		Archive Live, Stone Pony 1985
1998		New Lives, BBC (UK)
1999		Ultimate Collection
2001		Breakaway Angel
2003		Nils Lofgren Band Live
2006		Sacred Weapon
2008		The Loner, Nils Sings Neil
2011		Old School
2014		Face the Music [box set]
2015		UK 2015
2019		Blue with Lou
2020		Weathered

[vi] PATTI SCIALFA

1993		Rumble Doll
2004		23rd Street Lullaby
2007		Play It as It Lays

[vii] GARRY TALLENT

| 2019 | More Like Me |

[viii] STEVEN VAN ZANDT

Southside Johnny and the Asbury Dukes

1976	I Don't Want to Go Home
1976	Live at the Bottom Line
1977	This Time It's for Real
1978	Hearts of Stone
1979	Havin' a Party
1991	Better Days
2007	Jukebox

Solo (Disciples of Soul)

1982	Men Without Women
1983	Voice of America
1985	Sun City
1987	Freedom, No Compromise
1989	Revolution
1999	Born Again Savage
2017	Soulfire
2018	Soulfire Live [box set]
2019	Summer of Sorcery
2019	Lilyhammer: The Score
2020	Rock n Roll Rebel [box set]
2021	Macca to Mecca! Live at the Cavern Club
2021	Summer of Sorcery Live! At the Beacon Theatre

VI OFFICIAL CONCERT RECORDINGS

Note: Sound recording unless marked with * (DVD) or ** (Sound and DVD). European shows in bold.

1975	Oct 18	West Hollywood, CA: The Roxy
	Nov 18	**London, England: Hammersmith Odeon** **
	Nov 24	**London, England: Hammersmith Odeon**
	Dec 31	Upper Darby, PA: Tower Theatre
1977	Feb 7	Albany, NY: Palace Theatre
	Feb 8	Rochester, NY: Auditorium Theatre
1978	Jul 1	Berkeley, CA: Berkeley Community Theatre
	Jul 7	West Hollywood, CA: The Roxy
	Aug 9	Cleveland, OH: The Agora
	Sep 19	Passaic, NJ: Capitol Theatre
	Sep 20	Passaic, NJ: Capitol Theatre
	Sep 30	Atlanta, GA: Fox Theatre
	Dec 8	Houston, TX: The Summit **
	Dec 15	San Francisco, CA: Winterland Arena
	Dec 16	San Francisco, CA: Winterland Arena
1979	Sep 21	New York, NY: Madison Square Garden (*No Nukes*) * [Combined with Sep 22]
	Sep 22	New York, NY: Madison Square Garden (*No Nukes*) * [Combined with Sep 21]
1980	Nov 5	Tempe, AZ: ASU Centre ** [DVD incomplete]
	Dec 28	Uniondale, NY: Nassau Memorial Coliseum
	Dec 29	Uniondale, NY: Nassau Memorial Coliseum
	Dec 31	Uniondale, NY: Nassau Memorial Coliseum
1981	Jun 5	**London, England: Wembley Arena**
	Jul 9	East Rutherford, NJ: Brendan Byrne Arena

1984	Aug 5	East Rutherford, NJ: Brendan Byrne Arena
	Aug 6	East Rutherford, NJ: Brendan Byrne Arena
	Aug 20	East Rutherford, NJ: Brendan Byrne Arena
1985	Aug 22	East Rutherford, NJ: Giants Stadium
	Sep 27	Los Angeles, CA: Memorial Coliseum
1988	Mar 28	Detroit, MI: Joe Louis Arena
	Apr 23	Los Angeles, CA: LA Sports Arena
	Apr 28	Los Angeles, CA: LA Sports Arena
	May 23	New York, NY: Madison Square Garden
	Jul 3	**Stockholm, Sweden: Stockholms Stadion**
1999	Sep 25	Philadelphia, PA: First Union Centre
	Sep 30	Chicago, IL: United Centre
	Oct 23	Los Angeles, CA: Staples Centre
2000	Jun 27	New York, NY: Madison Square Garden
	Jul 1	New York, NY: Madison Square Garden
2002	Oct 16	**Barcelona, Catalonia: Palau Sant Jordi** *
2003	Jun 16	**Helsinki, Finland: Olympiastadion**
2007	Nov 19	Boston, MA: TD Banknorth Garden
2008	Apr 22	Tampa, FL: St Pete Times Forum
	Aug 23	St Louis, MO: Scottrade Centre
	Mar 20	Indianapolis, IN: Conseco Fieldhouse
	Apr 28	Greensboro, NC: Greensboro Coliseum
2009	May 4	Uniondale, NY: Nassau Memorial Coliseum
	Jun 28	**London, England: Hyde Park** *
	Oct 20	Philadelphia, PA: Wachovia Spectrum
	Nov 7	New York, NY: Madison Square Garden
	Nov 8	New York, NY: Madison Square Garden
	Nov 22	Buffalo, NY: HSBC Arena
2012	Mar 9	New York, NY: Apollo Theatre
	Jul 28	**Gothenburg, Sweden: Ullevi**
	Jul 31	**Helsinki, Finland: Olympiastadion**
	Aug 15	Boston, MA: Fenway Park
	Sep 22	East Rutherford, NJ: MetLife Stadium
	Nov 12	St Paul, MN: Xcel Energy Centre

2013	Jun 30	**London, England: Olympic Park**
		* [*Born in the USA* sequence only]
	Jul 24	**Leeds, England: First Direct Arena**
	Jul 11	**Rome, Italy: Ippodromo delle Capannelle**
2014		All shows
2016		All shows
2017		All shows

VII E STREET BAND TOURS

TOUR 1
Greetings from Asbury Park Tour of the US
October 1972 to September 1973, 11 months (including breaks)

TOUR 2
Wild, the Innocent and the E Street Shuffle Tour of the US
September 1973 to March 1975, 19 months (including breaks)

TOUR 3
Born to Run Tour of the US, Canada, England, the Netherlands, and Sweden
July 1975 to May 1976, 11 months (including breaks)

TOUR 4
The 'Lawsuit' Tour of the US and Canada
September 1976 to March 1977, 7 months (including breaks)

TOUR 5
Darkness on the Edge of Town Tour of the US and Canada
May to December 1978, 8 months (including breaks)

TOUR 6
The River Tour of the US, Canada, and Europe
October 1980 to September 1981, 12 months (including breaks)
1 US/Canada, Oct 80-Mar 81
2 Europe, Apr-Jun 81
3 US, Jul-Sep 81

TOUR 7
Born in the USA Tour of the US, Canada, Australia, Japan, and Europe
June 1984 to October 1985, 16 months (including breaks)
1 US/Canada, Jun 84-Jan 85
2 Australia/Japan, Mar-Apr 85
3 Europe, Jun-Jul 85
4 US/Canada, Aug-Oct 85

TOUR 8
Tunnel of Love Express Tour of the US, Canada, and Europe
February to August 1988, 7 months (including breaks)
1 US, Feb-May 88
2 Europe, Jun-Aug 88

TOUR 9 (with other acts)
Amnesty Human Rights Now Tour of Europe, Canada, the US, Japan, India, Africa, and South America
September to October 1988

TOUR 10
The Reunion Tour of Europe, the US and Canada
April 1999 to July 2000, 15 months (including breaks)
1 Europe, Apr-Jun 99
2 US/Canada, Jul 99-Jul 00

TOUR 11
The Rising Tour of the US, Canada, Europe, Australia, and New Zealand
August 2002 to October 2003, 15 months (including breaks)
1 US, Aug-Oct 02
2 Europe, Oct 02
3 US/Canada, Nov 02-Mar 03
4 Australia, Mar 03
5 Canada/US, Apr 03
6 Europe, May-Jun 03
7 US/Canada, Jul-Oct 03

TOUR 12 (with other acts)
Vote for Change Tour of the US
October to November 2004

TOUR 13
Magic Tour of the US, Canada, and Europe
September 2007 to August 2008, 12 months (including breaks)
1 US/Canada, Sep-Nov 07
2 Europe, Nov-Dec 07
3 US/Canada, Feb-May 08
4 Europe, May-Jul 08
5 US, Jul-Aug 08

TOUR 14
Working on a Dream Tour of the US, Canada, and Europe
April to November 2009
1 US/Canada, Apr-May 09

2 Europe, May-Aug 09
3 US, Aug-Nov 09

TOUR 15
Wrecking Ball / High Hopes Tour of the US, Canada, Europe, Australia, New Zealand, South America, and South Africa
March 2012 to May 2014, 27 months (including breaks)
1 US, Mar-May 12
2 Europe, May-Jul 12
3 US/Canada, Aug-Dec 12
4 Australia, Mar 13
5 Europe, Apr-Jul 13
6 South America, Sep 13
7 South Africa, Jan-Feb 14
8 Australia/New Zealand, Feb-Mar 14
9 US, Apr-May 14

TOUR 16
The River Tour of the US, Canada, Europe, Australia, and New Zealand
January 2016 to February 2017, 14 months (including breaks)
1 US/Canada, Jan-Apr 16
2 Europe, May-Jul 16
3 US, Aug-Sep 16
4 Australia/New Zealand, Jan-Feb 17

VIII E STREET BAND CONCERTS IN EUROPE

Chronological by country.

United Kingdom
1975 Born to Run tour
      Nov 18   London: Hammersmith Odeon
      Nov 24   London: Hammersmith Odeon
1981 The River tour
      May 11   Newcastle: City Hall
      May 13   Manchester: Apollo Theatre
      May 14   Manchester: Apollo Theatre
      May 16   Edinburgh: Playhouse
      May 17   Edinburgh: Playhouse
      May 20   Stafford: Bingley Hall
      May 26   Brighton: The Brighton Centre
      May 27   Brighton: The Brighton Centre
      May 29   London: Wembley Arena
      May 30   London: Wembley Arena
      Jun 1   London: Wembley Arena
      Jun 2   London: Wembley Arena
      Jun 4   London: Wembley Arena
      Jun 5   London: Wembley Arena
      Jun 7   Birmingham: NEC
      Jun 8   Birmingham: NEC
1985 Born in the USA tour
      Jun 4   Newcastle: St James's Park
      Jun 5   Newcastle: St James's Park
      Jul 3   London: Wembley Stadium
      Jul 4   London: Wembley Stadium
      Jul 6   London: Wembley Stadium
      Jul 7   Leeds: Roundhay Park
1988 Tunnel of Love tour
      Jun 21   Birmingham: Villa Park
      Jun 22   Birmingham: Villa Park
      Jun 25   London: Wembley Stadium
      Jul 9   Sheffield: Bramall Lane

	Jul 10	Sheffield: Bramall Lane
1988	Amnesty tour	
	Sep 2	London: Wembley Stadium
1999	Reunion tour	
	May 1	Manchester: Evening News Arena
	May 2	Manchester: Evening News Arena
	May 16	Birmingham: NEC
	May 18	London: Earls Court
	May 19	London: Earls Court
	May 21	London: Earls Court
	May 23	London: Earls Court
2002	The Rising tour	
	Oct 27	London: Wembley Arena
2003	The Rising tour	
	May 26	London: Crystal Palace Stadium
	May 27	London: Crystal Palace Stadium
	May 29	Manchester: Old Trafford Cricket Ground
2007	Magic tour	
	Dec 15	Belfast: Odyssey Arena
	Dec 19	London: O2 Arena
2008	Magic tour	
	May 28	Manchester: Old Trafford
	May 30	London: Emirates Stadium
	May 31	London: Emirates Stadium
	Jun 14	Cardiff: Millennium Stadium
2009	Working on a Dream tour	
	Jun 27	Pilton: Glastonbury Festival
	Jun 28	London: Hyde Park (Hard Rock Calling Festival)
	Jul 14	Glasgow: Hampden Park
2012	Wrecking Ball tour	
	Jun 21	Sunderland: Stadium of Light
	Jun 22	Manchester: Etihad Stadium
	Jun 24	Seaclose Park: Isle of Wight Festival
	Jul 14	London: Hyde Park (Hard Rock Calling Festival)
2013	Wrecking Ball tour	
	Jun 15	London: Wembley Stadium
	Jun 18	Glasgow: Hampden Park
	Jun 20	Coventry: Ricoh Stadium
	Jun 30	London: Olympic Park (Hard Rock Calling)
	Jul 20	Belfast: King's Hall complex (outdoors)
	Jul 23	Cardiff: Millennium Stadium
	Jul 24	Leeds: First Direct Arena
2016	The River tour	
	May 25	Manchester: Etihad Stadium

Jun 1 Glasgow: Hampden Park
  Jun 3 Coventry: Ricoh Stadium
  Jun 5 London: Wembley Stadium

Sweden
1975 Born to Run tour
  Nov 21 Stockholm: Konserthuset
1981 The River tour
  May 3 Gothenburg: Scandinavium
  May 7 Stockholm: Johanneshovs Isstadion
  May 8 Stockholm: Johanneshovs Isstadion
1985 Born in the USA tour
  Jun 8 Gothenburg: Ullevi
  Jun 9 Gothenburg: Ullevi
1988 Tunnel of Love tour
  Jul 2 Stockholm: Stockholms Stadion
  Jul 3 Stockholm: Stockholms Stadion
1999 Reunion tour
  Jun 23 Stockholm: Stockholms Stadion
  Jun 24 Stockholm: Stockholms Stadion
2002 The Rising tour
  Oct 24 Stockholm: Globe Arena
2003 The Rising tour
  Jun 21 Gothenburg: Ullevi
  Jun 22 Gothenburg: Ullevi
2007 Magic tour
  Dec 12 Stockholm: Globe Arena
2008 Magic tour
  Jul 4 Gothenburg: Ullevi
  Jul 5 Gothenburg: Ullevi
2009 Working on a Dream tour
  Jun 4 Stockholm: Stockholms Stadion
  Jun 5 Stockholm: Stockholms Stadion
  Jun 7 Stockholm: Stockholms Stadion
2012 Wrecking Ball tour
  Jul 27 Gothenburg: Ullevi
  Jul 28 Gothenburg: Ullevi
2013 Wrecking Ball tour
  May 3 Solna: Friends Arena
  May 4 Solna: Friends Arena
  May 11 Solna: Friends Arena
2016 The River tour
  Jun 25 Gothenburg: Ullevi
  Jun 27 Gothenburg: Ullevi

Jun 23 Gothenburg: Ullevi

Netherlands
1975 Born to Run tour
    Nov 23 Amsterdam: RAI
1981 The River tour
    Apr 28 Rotterdam: Sportpaleis Ahoy
    Apr 29 Rotterdam: Sportpaleis Ahoy
1985 Born in the USA tour
    Jun 12 Rotterdam: Stadion Feyenoord
    Jun 13 Rotterdam: Stadion Feyenoord
1988 Tunnel of Love tour
    Jun 28 Rotterdam: Stadion Feyenoord
    Jun 29 Rotterdam: Stadion Feyenoord
1999 Reunion tour
    Jun 19 Arnhem: Gelredome
    Jun 20 Arnhem: Gelredome
2002 The Rising tour
    Oct 22 Rotterdam: Sportpaleis Ahoy
2003 The Rising tour
    May 6 Rotterdam: Stadion Feyenoord
    May 8 Rotterdam: Stadion Feyenoord
2007 Magic tour
    Dec 1 Arnhem: Gelredome
    Dec 12 Antwerp: Sportpaleis
2008 Magic tour
    Jun 18 Amsterdam: Amsterdam Arena
2009 Working on a Dream tour
    May 30 Landgraaf: Megaland (Pinkpop Festival)
2012 Wrecking Ball tour
    May 28 Landgraaf: Megaland (Pinkpop Festival)
2013 Wrecking Ball tour
    Jun 22 Nijmegen: Goffertpark
2016 The River tour
    Jun 14 The Hague: Malieveld

Germany
1981 The River tour
    Apr 7 Hamburg: Congress Centrum
    Apr 9 Berlin: ICC Berlin
    Apr 14 Frankfurt: Festhalle
    Apr 16 Munich: Olympiahalle
1985 Born in the USA tour
    Jun 15 Frankfurt: Waldstadion

	Jun 18	Munich: Olympiastadion
1988	Tunnel of Love tour	
	Jul 12	Frankfurt: Waldstadion, Frankfurt
	Jul 17	Munich: Olympia Reitstadion Riem
	Jul 19	Berlin: Radrennbahn Weissensee
	Jul 22	Berlin: Waldbühne
	Jul 30	Bremen: Weserstadion
1999	Reunion tour	
	Apr 13	Munich: Olympiahalle
	Apr 15	Cologne: Kölnarena
	Apr 23	Regensburg: Donau Arena
	May 29	Berlin: Parkbühne Wuhlheide
	May 30	Berlin: Parkbühne Wuhlheide
	Jun 13	Leipzig: Bruno-Plache-Stadion
	Jun 15	Offenbach: Stadion Am Bieberer Berg
	Jun 17	Bremen: Weserstadion
2002	The Rising tour	
	Oct 20	Berlin: Velodrom
2003	The Rising tour	
	May 10	Ludwigshafen: Südweststadion
	May 22	Gelsenkirchen: Arena Aufschalke
	Jun 10	Munich: Olympiastadion
	Jun 12	Hamburg: Aol Arena
2007	Magic tour	
	Dec 2	Mannheim: Sap Arena
	Dec 13	Cologne: Kölnarena
2008	Magic tour	
	Jun 16	Dusseldorf: LTU Arena
	Jun 21	Hamburg: Hsh Nordbank Arena
2009	Working on a Dream tour	
	Jul 2	Munich: Olympiastadion
	Jul 3	Frankfurt: Commerzbank-Arena
2012	Wrecking Ball tour	
	May 25	Frankfurt: Commerzbank-Arena
	May 27	Cologne: Rheinenergiestadion
	May 30	Berlin: Olympiastadion
2013	Wrecking Ball tour	
	May 26	Munich: Olympiastadion
	May 28	Hannover: AWD-Arena
	Jul 5	Mönchengladbach: Borussia-Park
	Jul 7	Leipzig: Red Bull Arena
2016	The River tour	
	Jun 17	Munich: Olympiastadion
	Jun 19	Berlin: Olympiastadion

Switzerland
1981　The River tour
　　　　Apr 11　　　Zurich: Hallenstadion
1988　Tunnel of Love tour
　　　　14 Jul　　　Basel: St Jakob Stadion
1999　Reunion tour
　　　　Apr 26　　　Zurich: Hallenstadion
2009　Working on a Dream tour
　　　　Jun 30　　　Bern: Stade de Suisse
2012　Wrecking Ball tour
　　　　Jul 9　　　　Zurich: Letzigrund
2013　Wrecking Ball tour
　　　　Jul 3　　　　Geneve: Stade de Geneve
2016　The River tour
　　　　Jul 31　　　Zurich: Letzigrund

France
1981　The River tour
　　　　Apr 18　　　Paris: Palais des Sports (Saint-Ouen)
　　　　Apr 19　　　Paris: Palais des Sports (Saint-Ouen)
　　　　Apr 24　　　Lyon: Palais des Sports de Gerland
1985　Born in the USA tour
　　　　Jun 23　　　Montpellier: Stade Richter
　　　　Jun 25　　　Saint-Étienne: Stade Geoffroy-Guichard
　　　　Jun 29　　　Paris: Parc de la Courneuve
　　　　Jun 30　　　Paris: Parc de la Courneuve
1988　Tunnel of Love tour
　　　　Jun 19　　　Paris: Hippodrome de Vincennes
1988　Amnesty tour
　　　　Sep 4　　　Paris: Palais Omnisports de Paris-Bercy
　　　　Sep 5　　　Paris: Palais Omnisports de Paris-Bercy
1999　Reunion tour
　　　　Apr 28　　　Lyon: Halle Tony Garnier
　　　　Jun 2　　　Paris: Palais Omnisports de Paris-Bercy
　　　　Jun 3　　　Paris: Palais Omnisports de Paris-Bercy
2002　The Rising tour
　　　　Oct 14　　　Paris: Palais Omnisports de Paris-Bercy
2003　The Rising tour
　　　　May 24　　　Paris: Stade de France
2007　Magic tour
　　　　Dec 17　　　Paris: Palais Omnisports de Paris-Bercy
2008　Magic tour
　　　　Jun 27　　　Paris: Parc des Princes
2009　Working on a Dream tour

	Jul 16	Carhaix: Les Vieilles Charrues Festival
2012	Wrecking Ball tour	
	Jun 19	Montpellier: Park and Suites Arena
	Jul 4	Paris: Palais Omnisports de Paris-Bercy
	Jul 5	Paris: Palais Omnisports de Paris-Bercy
2013	Wrecking Ball tour	
	Jun 29	Paris: Stade de France
2016	The River tour	
	Jul 11	Paris: Palais Omnisports de Paris-Bercy
	Jul 13	Paris: Palais Omnisports de Paris-Bercy

Spain

1981	The River tour	
	Apr 21	Barcelona: Palau Municipal d'Esports
1988	Tunnel of Love tour	
	Aug 2	Madrid: Estadio Vicente Calderón
	Aug 3	Barcelona: Camp Nou
1988	Amnesty tour	
	Sep 10	Barcelona: Camp Nou
1999	Reunion tour	
	Apr 9	Barcelona: Palau Sant Jordi
	Apr 11	Barcelona: Palau Sant Jordi
	Jun 5	Zaragoza: Estadio la Romareda
	Jun 7	Madrid: Estadio de la Comunidad
2002	The Rising tour	
	Oct 16	Barcelona: Palau Sant Jordi
2003	The Rising tour	
	May 15	Gijón: Estadio Municipal El Molinón
	May 17	Barcelona: Estadi Olímpic Lluís Companys
	May 19	Madrid: Estadio de la Comunidad
2007	Magic tour	
	Nov 25	Madrid: Palacio de Deportes de la Comunidad
	Nov 26	Bilbao: Bizkaia Arena
2008	Magic Tour	
	Jul 15	San Sebastián: Estadio Anoeta
	Jul 17	Madrid: Bernabéu
	Jul 19	Barcelona: Camp Nou
	Jul 20	Barcelona: Camp Nou
2009	Working on a Dream tour	
	Jul 26	Bilbao: Estadio San Mamés
	Jul 28	Seville: Estadio Olimpico de la Cartuja
	Jul 30	Benidorm: Estadio Municipal de Foietes
	Aug 1	Valladolid: Estadio José Zorrilla
	Aug 2	Santiago de Compostela: Auditorio Monte do Gozo

2012 Wrecking Ball tour
    May 13   Seville: Estadio Olimpico de La Cartuja
    May 15   Las Palmas: Estadio de Gran Canaria
    May 17   Barcelona: Estadi Olimpic Lluis Companys
    May 18   Barcelona: Estadi Olimpic Lluis Companys
    Jun 2   San Sebastian: Estadio Anoeta
    Jun 17   Madrid: Bernabeu
2013 Wrecking Ball tour
    Jun 26   Gijón: Estadio Municipal El Molinón
2016 The River tour
    May 14   Barcelona: Camp Nou
    May 17   San Sebastian: Estadio Anoeta
    May 21   Madrid: Bernabeu

Belgium
1981 The River tour
    Apr 26   Brussels: Forest National
1999 Reunion tour
    May 27   Ghent: Flanders Expo
2003 The Rising tour
    May 12   Brussels: Koning Boudewijnstadion
2008 Magic tour
    Jun 23   Antwerp: Sportpaleis
2013 Wrecking Ball tour
    Jul 13   Werchter: Festivalpark (TW Classic Festival)
2016 The River tour
    Jul 9   Werchter: Festivalpark (TW Classic Festival)

Denmark
1981 The River tour
    May 2   Copenhagen: Brondby-Hallen
1988 Tunnel of Love tour
    Jul 25   Copenhagen: Idraetsparken
1999 Reunion tour
    Jun 26   Copenhagen: Parken Stadium
2003 The Rising tour
    Jun 14   Copenhagen: Parken Stadium
2007 Magic tour
    Dec 8   Copenhagen: Forum København
2008 Magic tour
    Jun 29   Copenhagen: Parken Stadium
2009 Working on a Dream tour
    Jul 8   Herning: MCH Arena
2012 Wrecking Ball tour

	Jul 7	Roskilde: Festivalpladsen (Roskilde Festival)
2013	Wrecking Ball tour	
	May 14	Copenhagen: Parken Stadium
	May 16	Herning: Jyske Bank Boxen
2016	The River tour	
	Jun 22	Copenhagen: Telia Parken
	Jul 20	Horsens: Casa Arena

Norway

1981	The River tour	
	May 5	Drammen: Drammenshallen
1988	Tunnel of Love tour	
	Jul 27	Oslo: Valle Hovin Stadion
1999	Reunion tour	
	Jun 27	Oslo: Valle Hovin Stadion
2003	The Rising tour	
	Jun 19	Oslo: Valle Hovin Stadion
2007	Magic tour	
	Dec 4	Oslo: Oslo Spektrum
2008	Magic tour	
	Jul 7	Oslo: Valle Hovin Stadion
	Jul 8	Oslo: Valle Hovin Stadion
2009	Working on a Dream tour	
	Jun 9	Bergen: Koengen
	Jun 10	Bergen: Koengen
2012	Wrecking Ball tour	
	Jul 21	Oslo: Valle Hovin Stadion
	Jul 23	Bergen: Koengen
	Jul 24	Bergen: Koengen
2013	Wrecking Ball tour	
	Apr 29	Oslo: Telenor Arena
	Apr 30	Oslo: Telenor Arena
2016	The River tour	
	Jun 29	Oslo: Ullevaal Stadion
	Jul 26	Trondheim: Granasen Arena
	Jul 28	Oslo: Frognerparken

Republic of Ireland

1985	Born in the USA tour	
	Jun 1	Slane Castle
1988	Tunnel of Love tour	
	Jul 7	Dublin: RDS Arena
1999	Reunion tour	
	May 25	Dublin: RDS Arena

2003	The Rising tour	
	May 31	Dublin: RDS Arena
2008	Magic tour	
	May 22	Dublin: RDS Arena
	May 23	Dublin: RDS Arena
	May 25	Dublin: RDS Arena
2009	Working on a Dream tour	
	Jul 11	Dublin: RDS Arena
	Jul 12	Dublin: RDS Arena
2012	Wrecking Ball tour	
	Jul 17	Dublin: RDS Arena
	Jul 18	Dublin: RDS Arena
2013	Wrecking Ball tour	
	Jul 16	Limerick: Thomond Park
	Jul 18	Cork: Pairc Ui Chaoimh
	Jul 27	Kilkenny: Nowlan Park
	Jul 28	Kilkenny: Nowlan Park
2016	The River tour	
	May 27	Dublin: Croke Park
	May 29	Dublin: Croke Park

Italy

1985	Born in the USA tour	
	Jun 21	Milan: San Siro
1988	Tunnel of Love tour	
	Jun 11	Turin: Stadio Comunale
	Jun 15	Rome: Stadio Flaminio
	Jun 16	Rome: Stadio Flaminio
1988	Amnesty tour	
	Sep 8	Turin: Stadio Comunale
1999	Reunion tour	
	Apr 17	Bologna: alamalaguti
	Apr 19	Milan: Fila Forum
	Apr 20	Milan: Fila Forum
	Jun 11	Genoa: Stadio Luigi Ferraris
2002	The Rising tour	
	Oct 18	Bologna: Palamalaguti
2003	The Rising tour	
	Jun 8	Florence: Stadio Artemio Franchi
	Jun 28	Milan: San Siro
2007	Magic tour	
	Nov 28	Milan: Datch Forum
2008	Magic tour	
	Jun 25	Milan: San Siro

2009　Working on a Dream tour
    Jul 19　　　　Rome: Stadio Olimpico
    Jul 21　　　　Turin: Stadio Olimpico di Torino
    Jul 23　　　　Udine: Stadio Friuli
2012　Wrecking Ball tour
    Jun 7　　　　Milan: San Siro
    Jun 10　　　Florence: Stadio Artemio Franchi
    Jun 11　　　Trieste: Stadio Nereo Rocco
2013　Wrecking Ball tour
    May 23　　　Naples: Piazza del Plebiscito
    May 31　　　Padua: Stadio Euganeo
    Jun 3　　　　Milan: San Siro
    Jul 11　　　　Rome: Ippodromo delle Capannelle
2016　The River tour
    Jul 3　　　　Milan: San Siro
    Jul 5　　　　Milan: San Siro
    Jul 16　　　Rome: Circus Maximus

Hungary

1988　Amnesty tour
    Sep 6　　　　Budapest: Nepstadion

Greece

1988　Amnesty tour
    Oct 3　　　　Athens: Olympic Stadium

Austria

1999　Reunion tour
    Apr 24　　　Vienna: Wiener Stadthalle
2003　The Rising tour
    Jun 25　　　Vienna: Ernst-Happel-Stadion
2009　Working on a Dream tour
    Jul 5　　　　Vienna: Ernst-Happel-Stadion
2012　Wrecking Ball tour
    Jul 12　　　Vienna: Ernst-Happel-Stadion

Finland

2003　The Rising tour
    Jun 16　　　Helsinki: Olympiastadion
    Jun 17　　　Helsinki: Olympiastadion
2008　Magic tour
    Jul 11　　　　Helsinki: Olympiastadion
2009　Working on a Dream tour
    Jun 2　　　　Tampere: Ratinan Stadion
2012　Wrecking Ball tour

  Jul 31   Helsinki: Olympiastadion
2013 Wrecking Ball tour
  May 7   Turku: HK Areena
  May 8   Turku: HK Areena

Czech Republic
2012 Wrecking Ball tour
  Jul 11   Prague: Synot Tip Arena

Portugal
2012 Wrecking Ball tour
  Jun 3   Lisbon: Bela Vista Park (Rock in Rio Festival)
2016 The River tour
  May 19 Lisbon: Bela Vista Park (Rock in Rio Festival)

INDEX

(I Love) Everything About You, 80
914 Sound Studios
   (Blauvelt, NY), 36, 38, 44, 45, 54, 58,
     61, 63, 64, 173, 194
A Love So Fine, 64
A Night Like This, 64
Abbey Road Studios
   (London), 90, 173
Adam Raised a Cain, 79, 81, 84
Africa, 132, 169
After Dinner, 80
After the Goldrush, 121
Agora, The
   (Cleveland), 53, 85
Ahmanson Theatre
   (Los Angeles), 42
Ain't Good Enough for You, 79
Ain't Got You, 127, 129
Albany, 45, 75, 203
All That Heaven Will Allow, 127, 129
Alliance Singers, 145, 148, 149
American Skin (41 Shots), 142, 143, 144, 153, 168, 169
Amsterdam, 72, 212
Andre, Wayne, 63
Angel, The, 37, 38, 40
Angel's Blues, 47
Aniello, Ron, 168, 173, 174
Animals, The, 24, 75
Ann Arbor, 99
Annapolis, 72
Apollo Theatre
   (Manchester), 102, 209
   (NYC), 164, 166, 204
Appel, Mike, 33, 34, 36, 38, 40, 44, 45, 50, 51, 52, 53, 54, 57, 58, 59, 60, 63, 68, 71, 74, 76, 83, 194
Appel, Steve, 51

Appleton, Mike, 71
Arabian Nights, 37, 39
Arizona, 85, 142
Arizona State University, 99
Arizona Veterans Memorial Coliseum
   (Phoenix), 85
Arnhem, 141, 159, 212
Artists United Against Apartheid, 109, 132
As I Lay Dying
   (Faulkner), 94
Asbury Park, 17, 20, 26, 27, 28, 31, 32, 48, 60, 75, 85, 121, 137, 139, 140, 151, 154, 159, 163, 165, 166
Asbury Park High School, 121
Asif Ali Khan Group, 145, 147, 148
Atlanta, 85, 101, 124, 131, 142, 144, 145, 152, 155, 156, 161, 163, 166, 170, 195, 196, 203
Atlantic City, 110, 111, 112, 116, 123, 152
Atlantic Studios
   (NYC), 76, 78, 194
Auburn Hills, 141
Austin, 100, 131, 152, 163
Australia, 124, 137, 152, 168, 169, 171, 196
Austria, 137, 141, 153, 219
Baby I, 24
Baby I'm So Cold, 116
Baby, I've Been Missing You, 152
Bach, J.S., 99
Back in Your Arms, 135, 141, 153
Backstreets, 51, 54, 59, 61, 63, 66, 72, 75, 131
Backstreets Magazine, 59
Bad Boy, 116
Badlands, 79, 80, 84, 99, 122

(Film), 106, 112
Baker, Ginger, 55
Ballad of Easy Rider, 104
Ballad of Jesse James, The, 31
Baltimore, 170
Barcelona, 101, 132, 140, 152, 155, 160, 204, 215, 216
Barsalona, Frank, 75
Basel, 132, 214
Batlan, Mike, 110, 115
Baton Rouge, 100
Battle of Monmouth, 20
BBC Radio 3, 16, 96
BBC2, 17
Be True, 88, 91, 92, 131, 141, 170
Beatles, The, 16, 23, 24, 31, 41, 44, 68, 72, 87, 88, 93, 95, 102, 129, 160, 162, 167, 173
Because the Night, 79, 83, 165
Beck, Jeff, 25
Belfast, 137, 210
Belgium, 101, 141, 152, 216
Bells of San Salvador, 116
Berg, John, 68
Berkeley, 85, 203
Berlin, 101, 132, 141, 152, 155, 212, 213
Berry, Chuck, 24, 41, 42, 72, 114, 137, 142, 160, 168
Betty Jean, 116
Big Payback, The, 110
Billboard, 42, 43, 120, 122
Bingley Hall
  (Stafford), 102, 209
Birmingham
  (England), 17, 103, 131, 137, 141, 209, 210
  (USA), 85
Bittan, Roy, 14, 54, 55, 56, 57, 63, 64, 65, 66, 67, 68, 71, 76, 78, 81, 82, 83, 90, 93, 94, 95, 96, 99, 110, 114, 117, 118, 119, 126, 130, 131, 134, 136, 145, 147, 149, 155, 156, 160, 161, 162, 163, 165, 167, 172, 174, 175, 176, 177
Blackwell, Richard, 46
Blinded by the Light, 37, 38, 39, 40, 142
Blood Brothers, 135, 136, 143, 153, 159, 173, 195

(Documentary), 135
Bloomington, 85, 131
Blue Moon, 80
Bob Marley and the Wailers, 43
Bobby Jean, 109, 115, 118, 119
Body and Soul, 116
Bologna, 141, 152, 155, 218
Bon Jovi, 141
Boom Boom, 131
Born in the USA, 18, 76, 108, 109, 110, 114, 117, 118, 119, 120, 121, 122, 123, 125, 126, 130, 135, 136, 151, 164, 168
Born in the USA (Song), 106, 107, 111, 114, 117, 118, 120, 123, 152
Born to Run, 16, 49, 54, 55, 59, 60, 61, 63, 64, 68, 69, 72, 74, 76, 77, 80, 82, 84, 105, 106, 112, 121, 160, 163
Born to Run (Autobiography), 20, 55, 88, 107, 154, 171
Born to Run (Song), 53, 55, 56, 59, 63, 66, 103, 119
Born to Run 30th Anniversary Edition (box set), 42, 50, 71
Born to Run, the Bruce Springsteen Story (Dave Marsh), 58
Boston, 24, 72, 76, 85, 141, 152, 159, 163, 204
Bottom Line
  (NYC), 68, 69
Bowie, David, 16, 42, 56, 99
Boys, 160
Bramall Lane
  (Sheffield), 209, 210
Break Out, 80
Breakaway, 80, 83
Brecker, Michael, 63
Brecker, Randy, 63, 64, 67
Bremen, 132, 141, 213
Brickman, Marc, 53, 72, 88
Bright Eyes, 154
Brighton, 101, 102, 209
Brighton Centre, 102, 209
Brilliant Disguise, 128, 130, 153
Bring on the Night, 91
Brisbane, 124, 152
Brixton
  (London), 101
Brixton Academy

(London), 137
Broadway, 55
Brokenhearted, The, 79
Brooklyn, 20
Brothers Under the Bridge, 137
Brothers Under the Bridges, 22, 109, 115
Browne, Jackson, 89, 154
Bruce Springsteen Band, 27, 31, 121
Brussels, 101, 155, 216
Bryn Mawr, 50, 57
Buffalo, 85, 100, 142, 152, 159, 164, 170, 204
Burgess, Sonny, 137
Burnin' Train, 173, 174, 175
Cadillac Ranch, 91, 93, 96, 103
Cain, James M., 106
Calello, Charles, 64
California, 28, 29, 32, 85, 99, 107, 126, 131, 132, 134, 139, 142, 166
Cambridge, 52
Can't Help Falling in Love, 125
Canada, 101, 123, 142, 152, 159, 167
Candy's Boy, 79
Candy's Room, 79, 81
Capitol Theatre
 (Passaic), 85
Car Wash, 109, 115
Cardiff, 210
Carlson, Pete, 85
Carol, 72
Carter, Ernest, 14, 52, 55, 63, 64
Cash, Johnny, 113
Castaway, 80
Castiles, The, 23, 24, 25, 26, 27, 172, 176, 177
Catalonia, 101, 132, 140, 152, 160
Cautious Man, 127, 129
Cavern Club
 (Liverpool), 26
Chain Lightning, 92
Chapel Hill, 131
Chapman, Tracy, 132, 154
Chapter and Verse, 29, 31
Charlie's Place
 (Cambridge), 53
Cheap Thrills, 80
Chicago, 43, 85, 99, 121, 142, 152, 153, 159, 163, 170, 204
Chicago (Band), 43

Child, 27, 28, 29, 51
Child Bride, 107, 111
Chimes of Freedom, 132
Chosen, The, 37, 39
Christgau, Robert, 84, 151, 166
Cincinnati, 99, 104
Cindy, 88, 92, 163, 166
City at Night, 80
City Hall
 (Newcastle), 102, 209
Civic Arena
 (Pittsburgh), 124
Civic Centre Arena
 (St Paul), 122
Clapton, Eric, 25
Clearmountain, Bob, 87, 88, 90, 100, 109, 135, 136, 137, 170, 173, 174, 194
Clemons, Clarence, 14, 17, 31, 32, 37, 38, 39, 41, 42, 44, 45, 46, 47, 49, 50, 51, 52, 57, 58, 61, 63, 64, 65, 67, 68, 71, 72, 78, 82, 83, 90, 93, 94, 95, 97, 114, 118, 119, 121, 124, 130, 132, 140, 141, 142, 145, 147, 148, 149, 155, 156, 161, 162, 165, 166, 172
Clemons, Jake, 14, 166, 174
Cleveland, 53, 85, 137, 142, 152, 170, 203
Cliff, Jimmy, 103
Club Soul City, 116
Code of Silence, 142
Cologne, 140, 159, 213
Colorado, 85, 142
Colts Neck, 106, 107, 110, 117, 139, 196
Columbia Recording Studios
 (NYC), 75, 173
Columbia Records, 33, 34, 36, 50, 59, 69
Come On (Let's Go Tonight), 79
Common Ground, 116
Convention Hall
 (Asbury Park), 140, 151, 159, 163, 166
Cooder, Ry, 176
Cooke, Sam, 57
Copenhagen, 101, 132, 141, 155, 159, 160, 216, 217
Costello, Elvis, 102, 163
Count Basie Theatre
 (Red Bank), 160

Countin' on a Miracle, 145, 147
Cover Me, 106, 114, 117, 118
Cowboys of the Sea, 39
Cox, Courteney, 122
Crazy Rocker, 80
Creedence Clearwater Revival, 100, 101
Cretecos, Jimmy, 36, 38, 40, 45, 194
Crisler Arena
 (Ann Arbor), 99
Crosby, Stills and Nash, 89
Crush on You, 91, 95
Crystal Palace Stadium
 (London), 210
Cupid, 57
Cynthia, 109, 115
Dallas, 52, 85, 100, 152, 159, 170
Dancing in the Dark, 109, 115, 117, 118, 119, 122, 167
DAR Constitution Hall
 (Washington DC), 58
Darkness on the Edge of Town, 76, 78, 80, 83, 84, 87, 92, 106, 120, 157, 160, 164, 165
Darkness on the Edge of Town (Song), 79, 83
Darlington County, 106, 107, 110, 115, 117, 118, 141
Davis, Clive, 34, 37, 44, 68
Davis, Richard, 38, 64
Days of Heaven, 106
De Palma, Brian, 122
Dead Man Walking, 137
Delivery Man, 116
Demme, Jonathan, 135, 136
Denmark, 101, 132, 141, 160
Denselow, Robin, 99, 122
Denver, 99, 131, 152, 163, 170
Detroit, 31, 99, 104, 131, 141, 152, 155, 204
Detroit Medley, 131
Devil's Arcade, 22, 156, 157, 158, 159
Devils and Dust, 67, 154, 155, 173
Devils and Dust (Song), 154
Diallo, Amadou, 142
Diamond, Neil, 162
Diddley, Bo, 66
DiDia, Nick, 145, 156, 161, 168, 195, 196
Dire Straits, 88

Does This Bus Stop at 82nd Street?, 37, 38, 40, 142, 152, 160, 170
Dollhouse, 91, 92
Don't Back Down, 116
Don't Look Back, 79, 141, 160
Don't Say No, 80
Doors, The, 140
Dorfsman, Neil, 87, 88, 90, 115, 194
Dovells, The, 37
Down by the River, 80
Down in the Hole, 145, 146, 169
Downbound Train, 106, 107, 109, 115, 117, 118
Dr Zoom and the Sonic Boom, 30
Drammen, 101, 217
Dream Baby Dream, 169
Drifters, The, 93
Drive All Night, 76, 80, 90, 91, 96, 97, 160
Dublin, 132, 137, 141, 155, 160, 163, 167, 217, 218
Dusseldorf, 155, 160, 213
Dylan, Bob, 16, 24, 33, 34, 39, 41, 42, 43, 44, 57, 70, 88, 102, 132, 153, 176, 177
E Street Band, 14, 16, 17, 18, 24, 26, 27, 29, 31, 34, 42, 48, 49, 52, 55, 60, 61, 63, 64, 67, 69, 76, 78, 84, 89, 90, 93, 94, 103, 106, 107, 108, 109, 110, 112, 113, 114, 118, 120, 121, 125, 126, 130, 132, 134, 135, 136, 137, 139, 140, 143, 145, 146, 151, 154, 155, 156, 159, 161, 163, 165, 166, 169, 170, 171, 172, 173, 174, 175
E Street Shuffle, The, 45, 48, 72, 159
Earls Court
 (London), 16, 141, 210
Earth, 25
East Orange, 103
East Rutherford, 103, 123, 125, 141, 153, 159, 160, 171, 203, 204
Ed Sullivan Show, 23
Edinburgh, 102, 137, 209
Eight Days a Week, 129
Emerick, Geoff, 90
Empty Sky, 145, 147
England, 84, 101, 102, 125, 131, 141, 152, 153, 160, 166, 203, 204, 205
Essential Bruce Springsteen, The, 115,

137
Etihad Stadium
 (Manchester), 210
Europe, 84, 85, 99, 124, 131, 137, 141, 152, 155, 159, 160, 163, 166, 168, 170
Evacuation of the West, 47
Evening News Arena
 (Manchester), 210
Factory, 79, 83, 101, 103, 106
Fade Away, 91, 96
Fade to Black, 116
Fargo, 142
Faulkner, William, 93, 94
Federici, Danny, 14, 26, 27, 28, 30, 36, 41, 42, 44, 45, 46, 47, 49, 51, 57, 68, 76, 78, 82, 83, 90, 94, 97, 100, 114, 117, 118, 120, 126, 129, 130, 135, 136, 137, 140, 142, 145, 149, 155, 156, 159, 160, 161, 162, 172, 175
Federici, Jason, 161, 162
Fever, The, 31, 47, 86, 109, 142
Fillmore West
 (San Francisco), 29
Finland, 160
Fire, 79
Fire on the Wing, 47
First Direct Arena
 (Leeds), 210
Flannigan, Erik, 125
Flemington, 28, 160
Flint, Jere, 145
Florence, 137, 153, 166, 218, 219
Florida, 101, 142, 154, 159, 163
Floyd, Eddie, 131
Fogerty, John, 101, 154, 167
Follow That Dream, 101, 103, 109, 116
For You, 37, 39, 40, 72, 152, 167
Ford, John, 93
Fort Dix, 52
Fort Monmouth, 131, 151
Forum, The
 (Inglewood), 85
Fourth of July, Asbury Park (Sandy), 21, 44, 45, 48, 137, 141, 159, 160
Fox Theatre
 (Atlanta), 85
France, 101, 125, 131, 137, 141, 152, 160, 168, 214, 215

Frankfurt, 132, 155, 163, 212, 213
Frankie, 76, 80, 107, 110, 115, 120, 141, 167
Frankie Fell in Love, 169
Franklin, Aretha, 33
Freehold, 20, 21, 23, 24, 28, 48, 94, 105, 118, 119, 137
Freehold High School, 23
From Small Things (Big Things One Day Come), 92
Fugitive's Dream, 116
Further On (Up the Road), 145, 146, 148
Fuse, The, 145, 146, 148
Gabriel, Peter, 132
Galveston Bay, 22
Garbarini, Vic, 99
Garden Arena
 (Boston), 141
Garden City, 50
Garden State Parkway Blues, 29
Genoa, 141, 218
Georgia, 142
Gerde's Folk City
 (NYC), 34
Germany, 101, 125, 132, 140, 141, 152, 159, 160, 212
Ghent, 141, 216
Ghost of Tom Joad, The, 136, 137, 139, 144
Ghost of Tom Joad, The (Song), 140, 169
Ghosts, 173, 174, 175, 177
Giants Stadium
 (East Rutherford), 125, 153, 160, 163, 164, 204
Giordano, Charles, 14, 155, 159, 167, 174, 175
Girls in Their Summer Clothes, 156, 157
Give the Girl a Kiss, 79, 141
Glasgow, 210, 211
Glastonbury Festival, 210
Glory Days, 106, 110, 115, 118, 119
Glory of Love, 116
Godspell, 55
Goin' Back, 29, 69, 80
Goin' Back to Georgia, 29
Goldsmith, Lynn, 89
Gone (Seeds), 116

Good Eye, 161, 162
Gotham Playboys, 155
Gothenburg, 101, 153, 155, 160, 167, 170, 204, 211, 212
Gotta Get That Feeling, 79
Graham, Bill, 29
Greatest Hits, 135, 136
Greensboro, 101, 160
Greensleeves, 23
Greenwich Village (NYC), 24, 121
Greetings from Asbury Park, New Jersey, 37, 39, 40, 164, 194
Grin, 29, 121
Growin' Up, 34, 37, 38, 40, 42, 72, 142, 160
Grushecky, Joe, 169
Guardian, The, 99, 122
Gulf War, 22, 134
Gun in Every Home, A, 116
Guthrie, Woody, 101, 112
Gypsy Biker, 156, 157, 159
Hall, John, 89
Halle Tony Garnier (Lyon), 141, 214
Hamburg, 101, 155, 160, 212, 213
Hammersmith Odeon (London), 16, 69, 70, 72, 102, 142, 203, 209
Hammond, John, 33, 34, 36, 41, 44, 68, 173, 177
Hampden Park (Glasgow), 210, 211
Hard Rock Calling Festival, 210
Harry's Place, 168
Harvard Square Theatre (Cambridge), 52
Haynes, Bart, 27
Heartbreak Hotel, 86
Hearts of Stone, 79, 109
Heaven's Wall, 168
Held Up Without a Gun, 92
Hendrix, Jimi, 25
High Hopes, 145, 146, 168
High Hopes (Song), 135, 168
Highlands, 31
Highway 51 Revisited, 153
Highway Patrolman, 106, 110, 111, 113, 116, 123, 125

Hippodrome de Vincennes (Paris), 131, 214
Hit Factory (NYC), 107, 114, 126, 135, 144, 169, 195
Hold On, 116
Holiday, Billie, 33
Hollinger Field House (West Chester College), 56
Holmdel, 75, 87
Honeymooners, The, 128
Hooker, John Lee, 112, 131
Horst, Eddie, 161
House of a Thousand Guitars, 173, 175, 176
Houston, 52, 85, 100, 131, 152, 159, 163, 203
Houston Chronicle, 52
Human Rights Now Tour, 132
Human Touch, 134
Hungry Heart, 88, 90, 91, 92, 95, 119, 141, 170
Hunter of Invisible Game, 169
Hyde Park (London), 204, 210
I Don't Care, 116
I Don't Want to Go Home, 108
I Got My Eye on You, 80
I Wanna Be With You, 80, 92, 141
I Wanna Marry You, 88, 91, 92, 95
I Want to Hold Your Hand, 23
I Want You, 57
I Wish I Were Blind, 134, 153, 168
I'll See You in My Dreams, 173, 174, 175, 177
I'll Work for Your Love, 156, 157, 170
I'm a Rocker, 90, 91, 96
I'm Goin' Down, 106, 110, 115, 118, 119, 122
I'm on Fire, 106, 107, 109, 115, 117, 118, 125, 160
Ian, Janis, 45
Iceman, 79, 83, 170
Ida Rose, 116
If I Should Fall Behind, 135, 140, 143
If I Was the Priest, 34, 173, 175, 176
In Freehold, 137, 141
In the Midnight Hour, 101
Incident on 57th Street, 44, 46, 48, 57,

100, 142, 152, 167
Independence Day, 21, 76, 80, 91, 93, 94, 101, 103, 125, 141, 166
India, 132
Indiana, 142
Indianapolis, 85, 101, 131, 142, 152, 159
Into the Fire, 145, 146
Invitation to Your Party, 116
Iovine, Jimmy, 59, 61, 63, 72, 76, 77, 78, 85, 90, 194
Iowa City, 85
Iraq War, 157
Ireland, 20, 124, 132, 137, 141, 153, 160, 217
It's a Shame, 79
It's All Over Now, 23
It's Hard to Be a Saint in the City, 21, 34, 37, 39, 40, 42, 160
It's My Life, 24, 75
Italy, 20, 125, 131, 137, 141, 152, 153, 159, 160, 163, 205, 218
Ivory Coast, 132
Jackson Cage, 91, 94, 95, 103, 152
Jackson, Ruth, 114
James Lincoln, 116
Janey Needs a Shooter, 64, 173, 174, 175, 176
Janey, Don't You Lose Heart, 109, 110, 115, 125, 141, 153
Japan, 124, 137
Jazz Musician, 37, 39
Jersey Girl, 123, 141
Jewell, Derek, 16, 70, 71, 102, 103
Joel, Billy, 45, 75
Johnny 99, 110, 111, 112, 116, 124
Johnny Bye Bye, 102, 103, 107, 109, 115
Johnny Go Down, 116
Johnson, Lyndon B., 22
Johnson, Robert, 112
Jolé Blon, 103
Judge Song, The, 29
Jungleland, 49, 54, 57, 61, 64, 67, 103, 140, 141
Just Like Fire Would, 168
Kansas City, 85, 101, 152, 160, 170
Keats, John, 66
Kennedy, John F., 22
Kentucky, 131, 142, 152
Kerouac, Jack, 93

King, Carole, 69
King's Big Chance, 80
King's Hall (Belfast), 210
King's Highway, 116
Kingdom of Days, 161, 162
Kitty's Back in Town, 46, 48
Klansman, The, 116
Klein, Joe, 112
KLOL-FM Houston, 52
KMET-FM, 85
Koppelman, Charles, 45, 50
Kovac, Ron, 104
KSAN-FM, 85
Kwan, Rick, 161
Kyoto, 124
La Bamba, 114
Lady and the Doctor, 39
Lahav, Louis, 36, 38, 40, 45, 54, 59, 63, 66, 194
Lahav, Suki, 14, 44, 45, 46, 47, 54, 56, 57, 59, 61, 64, 67, 121
Lake Oswego, 124
Land of Hope and Dreams, 140, 143, 144, 152
Landau, Jon, 52, 53, 58, 59, 60, 61, 63, 68, 71, 74, 78, 87, 89, 90, 114, 194, 195
Largo, 100, 104, 131
Last Carnival, The, 161, 162
Last Man Standing, 173, 174, 175, 176
Last Time, The, 86
Last to Die, 156, 157, 158, 159, 168
Late Show with David Letterman, 136, 151
Laufer, Daniel, 158
Laurel Canyon Productions, 33
Lawsuit Tour, The, 76
Led Zeppelin, 16, 29
Leeds, 125, 168, 205, 209, 210
Leibovitz, Annie, 122
Leipzig, 141, 168, 213
Lemaster, Larry, 145
Lennon, John, 17, 59, 100
Let's Be Friends, 145, 148
Letter to You, 174, 175
Letter to You (Song), 173, 174, 175
Levine, Arnold, 85
Lewis, Jerry Lee, 42, 55, 137

Lexington, 131
Liberty Hall
   (Houston), 52
Life Itself, 161, 162
Light of Day, 116, 140
Like a Rolling Stone, 176
Lincoln Centre
   (NYC), 56
Linda Let Me Be the One, 64
Lion's Den, 107, 115, 141
Lititz, 99, 121
Little Girl Like You, 116
Little Melvin and the Invaders, 32
Little Queenie, 72, 142, 160
Little Richard, 24
Little Steven and the Disciples of Soul, 109
Little Things (My Baby Does), The, 79
Little White Lies, 92
Live 1975-85, 69, 85, 123, 125, 126
Livin' in the Future, 156, 157
Living on the Edge of the World, 91, 92
Lofgren, Nils, 14, 29, 31, 69, 115, 118, 120, 121, 123, 125, 126, 130, 135, 139, 140, 145, 147, 148, 149, 154, 155, 156, 161, 163, 165, 170, 173, 174, 175, 176
London, 16, 26, 39, 55, 66, 69, 71, 72, 101, 102, 103, 125, 131, 137, 141, 142, 152, 153, 155, 159, 160, 163, 167, 168, 203, 204, 205, 209, 210, 211
Lonely Night in the Park, 64
Lonesome Day, 144, 145, 146, 152
Long Branch, 20, 131
Long Walk Home, 156, 158
Loose End, 88, 90, 91, 92, 141
Lopez, Vini, 14, 27, 28, 29, 30, 31, 37, 38, 39, 40, 42, 44, 45, 46, 47, 48, 49, 51, 55, 137
Los Angeles, 18, 26, 28, 42, 69, 85, 88, 90, 99, 104, 107, 124, 125, 126, 131, 134, 136, 142, 152, 153, 159, 163, 166, 204
Losin' Kind, The, 111, 116
Lost in the Flood, 22, 37, 38, 39, 40, 72, 143, 160
Louisiana, 142
Louisville, 85, 170
Love's on the Line, 116
Lowell, Lisa, 121
Lucky Man, 128
Lucky Town, 134
Lyon, 101, 137, 141
Madison Square Garden
   (NYC), 43, 85, 89, 100, 131, 142, 143, 152, 159, 164, 166, 167, 170, 203, 204
Madrid, 132, 141, 152, 155, 159, 160, 166, 215, 216
Magic, 156, 161, 173
Magic (Song), 156, 157
Magovern, Terry, 172
Main Point Coffeehouse
   (Bryn Mawr), 50, 57
Malick, Terrence, 106, 112
Mallaber, Gary, 136
Man at the Top, 109, 115
Man Who Got Away, The, 90, 92
Manchester, 102, 137, 141, 153, 160, 163, 166, 209, 210
Manchester Arena
   (Manchester), 141
Manfred Mann, 72
Manion, Ed, 145
Mansion on the Hill, 106, 110, 111, 112, 116, 140
Marcus, Greil, 68
Margaret and the Distractions, 26
Marley, Bob, 43
Marsh, Dave, 58
Martin, George, 90
Mary Lou, 92
Mary Queen of Arkansas, 37, 38, 40
Mary's Place, 144, 146, 149, 152
Maryland, 32, 72, 121, 131
Maryland State College, 32
Max's Kansas City
   (NYC), 42, 43, 50, 56
MC5, 58
McCartney, Paul, 31, 53, 88, 167
McCormick, Neil, 151
McGuinn, Roger, 160
McMillan, Ian, 96
Meadowlands Arena
   (East Rutherford), 103, 123, 141, 151, 154, 159, 163, 166
Meet Me in the City, 92

Meeting Across the River, 64, 66, 67, 86, 106, 112, 141
Melbourne, 124, 152, 171
Mellencamp, John, 154
Memorial Coliseum (Los Angeles), 125
Memorial Sports Arena (Los Angeles), 99, 104, 124, 131
Memphis, 72, 85, 101
Men Without Women, 109
Meola, Eric, 68
Miami, 17, 85, 152
Miami Horns, 123
Middletown Township, 24
Milan, 125, 141, 153, 155, 159, 160, 166, 218, 219
Millennium Stadium (Cardiff), 210
Miller, Debby, 122
Milwaukee, 99, 142, 152, 159
Minneapolis, 142
Minnesota, 122, 131, 154
Missouri, 131, 142, 160
Mondale, Walter, 124
Monde, Le, 102
Money We Didn't Make, The, 116
Monmouth Arts Centre (Red Bank), 68, 75
Monmouth County (NJ), 106, 121, 144
Montpellier, 137, 214, 215
Montreal, 85, 101, 152, 159
Moondance, 72
Morello, Tom, 169
Morricone, Ennio, 99, 162
Morrison, 104
Morrison, Van, 16, 42, 72
Mountain of Love, 160
Mountain View, 131
Mr Tambourine Man, 160
Munich, 101, 132, 140, 155, 163, 212, 213
Murder Incorporated, 107, 115, 136, 140
MUSE, 89
Music Hall (Boston), 85
Muther's Music Emporium, 50
My City of Ruins, 145, 146, 149
My Father's House, 21, 106, 110, 111, 114, 116
My Hometown, 109, 114, 115, 119, 120, 166
My Love Will Not Let You Down, 107, 109, 115
My Lucky Day, 161, 162
N'Dour, Youssou, 132
Naples, 137, 219
Nash, Graham, 89
Nashville, 50, 85, 101, 160
Nashville String Machine, 145
Nassau Coliseum (Uniondale), 100
Nassau Community College, 50
National Exhibition Centre (Birmingham), 17, 103, 141, 209, 210
Nebraska, 18, 105, 106, 107, 109, 110, 111, 117, 122, 123, 124, 168
Nebraska (Song), 106, 110, 111, 112, 116, 123
Nebraska (State), 112
Neptune Township, 27
Netherlands, The, 20, 72, 101, 125, 131, 141, 152, 160, 163, 212
Nevada, 142
New Jersey, 17, 20, 21, 25, 26, 28, 29, 30, 32, 36, 37, 40, 51, 67, 68, 70, 71, 80, 94, 103, 110, 113, 114, 120, 123, 126, 132, 137, 139, 140, 144, 154, 160, 163, 194
New Musical Express, 84
New Orleans, 85
New York, 17, 18, 20, 21, 24, 25, 32, 33, 36, 37, 40, 42, 43, 48, 49, 50, 55, 56, 63, 65, 68, 76, 78, 80, 84, 87, 89, 90, 100, 102, 103, 105, 107, 114, 131, 132, 135, 136, 140, 142, 144, 152, 153, 159, 163, 166, 169, 170, 172, 174, 203, 204
New York (State), 36, 38, 45, 63
New York City Serenade, 21, 46, 47, 49, 53, 57, 141, 142, 153, 168, 171
New York Song, 47
New York University, 121
New Zealand, 171
Newark, 22, 27, 55, 168, 170
Newcastle, 102, 125, 137, 209
Newsweek, 23, 34, 71
Nice, 137

Night, 63, 65
Night Fire, 92
No Nukes, 89, 96, 101, 203
No Surrender, 109, 114, 115, 117, 118, 119, 123
None But the Brave, 109, 115, 160
Norman, Philip, 68, 70
North Carolina, 131, 142, 152
North Dakota, 142
Norway, 101, 132, 141, 153, 159, 160, 217
Nothing Man, 145, 146, 147
O'Brien, Brendan, 144, 145, 161, 168
O'Connor, Flannery, 105
Oakland, 99, 142, 159
Ocean County College
 (NJ), 25
Odyssey Arena
 (Belfast), 210
Ohio, 86, 123, 131, 142, 154
Old Grey Whistle Test, 17, 71, 85
Old Trafford Cricket Ground
 (Manchester), 210
Olympic Park
 (London), 168
On the Prowl, 116
Once Upon a Time in the West, 99
One Hundred Miles from Jackson, 117
One Love, 117
One Minute You're Here, 173, 174, 175
One Step Up, 127, 128, 130
One Way Street, 79
Open All Night, 110, 111, 114, 116
Orbison, Roy, 24, 65
Oregon, 124, 142
Osaka, 124
Oscars, The, 137
Oslo, 132, 141, 159, 160, 170, 217
Ottawa, 101, 152
Our Love Will Last Forever, 80
Out in the Street, 91, 95
Out of Work, 117
Outlaw Pete, 161, 162
Outside Looking In, 79
Pacific Recording Studio
 (San Mateo), 29
Palace Concert Theatre
 (Providence), 68
Palais des Sports
 (Paris), 101, 214
Palais Omnisports de Paris-Bercy
 (Paris), 141, 152, 214, 215
Palau Sant Jordi
 (Barcelona), 140, 152, 204, 215
Palladium, The
 (NYC), 85
Paradise, 145, 146, 149
Paradise by the C, 57, 92
Paramount Theatre
 (Asbury Park), 85, 137
Parc de la Courneuve
 (Paris), 125, 214
Paris, 101, 125, 131, 137, 141, 152, 153, 155, 159, 160, 166, 168, 170, 214, 215
Paris, Texas, 176
Parsons, Tony, 84
Part Man, Part Monkey, 131
Party Lights, 92
Passaic, 85, 203
Pearl Jam, 144, 154
Pender, Mark, 145
Penn State University, 142
Pennsylvania, 41, 50, 56, 57, 99, 142, 154
People Get Ready, 152
Phantoms, 47
Philadelphia, 50, 53, 56, 72, 85, 104, 123, 131, 142, 152, 153, 159, 163, 164, 166, 170, 204
 (Film), 135
Philips Arena
 (Atlanta), 142
Phillips, Julianne, 124
Phoenix, 85, 142, 152, 170
Pink Cadillac, 109, 111, 115, 123
Pink Floyd, 16, 53
Pittsburgh, 85, 100, 124, 131, 137, 153, 163
Playhouse, The
 (Edinburgh), 102, 209
Plotkin, Chuck, 77, 78, 90, 106, 114, 126, 135, 136, 144, 145, 147, 170, 195
Point Blank, 91, 94, 95, 96, 103, 106, 141, 142, 160
Point Pleasant, 41
Poland, 137

Portland, 85, 99, 152
Potter, Margaret, 26, 27, 31
Potter, Tom, 26, 31
Power of Prayer, The, 173, 174, 175, 176
Power Station
  (NYC), 87, 88, 90, 106, 114, 194, 195
Preacher's Daughter, 80
Premier Talent, 75
Presley, Elvis, 23, 24, 72, 101, 102, 125
Pretty Baby, Will You Be Mine, 128
Pretty Flamingo, 72
Price You Pay, The, 88, 91, 92, 97
Prince, 170
Promise, The, 76, 79, 165, 194
Promise, The - The Darkness on the Edge of Town Story
  (box set), 85, 165
Promise, The (Song), 75, 80, 82, 83
Promised Land, 79, 81, 82, 83, 84, 167, 168
Protection, 117
Prove It All Night, 79, 83
Providence, 61, 68, 152
Purple Rain, 170
Pyle, Barbara, 61
Quad Angles
  (West Chester College paper), 56
Queen of the Supermarket, 161, 162
Racing in the Street, 16, 76, 77, 79, 82, 83, 167
Radio Nowhere, 156, 157
Radrennbahn Weissensee
  (Berlin), 132, 213
Rage Against the Machine, 144
Rainmaker, 173, 175, 176
Raise Your Hand, 131
Raitt, Bonnie, 52, 89
Ramm, Curt, 169
Ramrod, 76, 80, 91
Reagan, Ronald, 99, 101, 123, 124
Real Paper, The, 52, 58
Reason to Believe, 110, 111, 114, 116, 123
Record Plant
  (NYC), 54, 55, 58, 59, 63, 64, 76, 78, 85, 87, 194
Red Bank, 68, 75, 121, 137, 160
Red Rocks Amphitheatre
  (Morrison), 85, 104

Refrigerator Blues, 117
REM, 154
Rendezvous, 79
Restless Nights, 90, 91, 92
Richfield, 86, 131
Richfield Whistle, 117
Richmond, 152, 160
Ricky Wants a Man of Her Own, 91, 92, 160
Ricoh Stadium
  (Coventry), 211
Rifkin, Marty, 136
Rising, The, 145, 146, 150, 151, 152, 156, 168, 169, 172, 173
Rising, The (Song), 145, 146, 149, 151
River, The, 76, 82, 90, 92, 93, 94, 95, 99, 101, 105, 106, 108, 110, 112, 113, 131, 136, 141, 142, 146, 152, 160, 164, 170, 171, 172, 173
River, The (Song), 21, 88, 89, 90, 91, 92, 95, 96, 99, 103, 106, 125, 140, 141, 152
Robbins, Tim, 137
Robert Ford, 117
Rochester, 75, 100, 152, 203
Rock and Roll Hall of Fame, 137, 140, 164, 169
Rock Creek Park
  (Washington DC), 68
Rockaway the Days, 109, 115
Rockin' All Over the World, 103
Roll Away the Stone, 117
Rolling Stone, 23, 58, 68, 100, 109, 122
Rolling Stones, The, 16, 24, 86, 140
Rome, 131, 155, 163, 168, 205, 218, 219
Rosalita, 17, 46, 49, 65, 85, 141
Rose, Biff, 42
Rosemont, 104, 131
Rosenberg, Richie, 145
Roslin, Vinnie, 27, 29
Rotterdam, 101, 152, 155, 212
Roulette, 90, 91, 92, 131, 153, 160
Roundhay Park
  (Leeds), 125, 209
Roxy
  (Philadelphia), 50
Roxy Theatre
  (Los Angeles), 69, 71, 85, 125, 203
Royal Albert Hall

(London), 137, 155
Rumson, 126, 139, 144
Run Through the Jungle, 101
Sad Eyes, 134
Saint Rose of Lima School, 21, 137
San Antonio, 85
San Diego, 85, 104
San Francisco, 27, 29, 30, 85, 153, 203
San Jose, 85, 152, 159, 163, 166
San Mateo, 29
San Siro
   (Milan), 125, 160, 166, 218, 219
Sanborn, David, 63
Sancious, David, 14, 27, 31, 37, 38, 39, 40, 41, 43, 44, 45, 46, 47, 48, 49, 52, 55, 56, 63, 64, 134
Santa Ana, 44, 47
Satellite Lounge
   (Cookson), 52
Saturday Night Live, 174
Save My Love, 79, 165
Savin' Up, 117
Say Goodbye to Hollywood, 75
Scarpantoni, Jane, 145, 149
Scheniman, Bill, 114
Schruers, Fred, 21, 93, 100
Sciaky, Ed, 56
Scialfa, Patti, 14, 121, 130, 131, 132, 134, 136, 137, 139, 140, 145, 146, 148, 151, 155, 156, 159, 161, 162, 165, 167, 168, 172, 174
Scorsese, Martin, 67, 102
Scott, Toby, 90, 101, 106, 114, 123, 125, 126, 135, 136, 144, 155, 156, 161, 168, 170, 195, 196
Searchers, The, 69, 72
   (Film), 80
Seaside Bar Song, 47
Seattle, 85, 99, 159, 170
Secret Garden, 135, 136, 168
Secret to the Blues, 47
Seeds, 116, 125, 170
Seeger Sessions Band, 155
Seeger, Pete, 33, 155
Seven Tears, 117
Sha-La-La, 72
She's the One, 57, 61, 64, 66
Sheffield, 132, 209, 210
Shepard, Sam, 122

Sherry Darling, 76, 80, 91, 94
Shut Down, 117
Shut Out the Light, 22, 107, 109, 110, 115, 124, 137
Sigma Sound Studios
   (Philadelphia), 56
Sinclair, David, 151
Sir Lord Baltimore, 32
Slane Castle, 124, 217
Smith, Bessie, 33
So Young and in Love, 32, 64
Someday (We'll Be Together), 79
Something in the Night, 75, 79, 81, 82, 167
Song for Orphans, 173, 175, 177
Souls of the Departed, 134, 153
South America, 132
Southern Tracks Studios
   (Atlanta), 144, 145, 156, 161, 195, 196
Southside Johnny, 31, 108, 166
Southside Johnny and the Asbury Jukes, 37, 108
Spain, 101, 132, 141, 152, 159, 160, 163, 215
Spanish Eyes, 79, 166
Spanish Harlem, 57
Spare Parts, 127, 129
Spector, Phil, 24, 55
Spector, Ronnie, 75
Spectrum, The
   (Philadelphia), 56, 85, 100, 104, 123, 204
Speed Limit 25, 27
Spengler, Mike, 145
Spirit in the Night, 21, 32, 37, 39, 40, 41, 137, 160
Springsteen on Broadway, 172
Springsteen, Adele, 20, 28
Springsteen, Bruce, 14-196
Springsteen, Douglas, 20, 21, 25, 28, 83, 93
Springsteen, Jessica, 167
Springsteen, Pamela, 28
Springsteen, Virginia, 21, 23, 96
St James's Park
   (Newcastle), 125, 209
St Louis, 85, 99, 101, 131, 152, 160, 164, 204
St Paul, 99, 101, 122, 152, 159, 163, 204

Stade de Colombes
  (Paris), 125
Stafford, 102
Stand On It, 109, 115
Staples Centre
  (Los Angeles), 142, 204
Starr, Edwin, 125, 141
Starr, Ringo, 55
State Trooper, 110, 111, 113, 114
Steel Mill, 27, 28, 29, 30, 31, 41, 42
Steinbeck, John, 80, 93
Sting, 88, 132
Stockholm, 72, 101, 131, 141, 152, 155, 159, 163, 204, 211
Stolen Car, 88, 91, 92, 96, 97, 101, 103, 106, 107, 113
Stone Pony
  (Asbury Park), 121
Stop the War, 117
Stray Bullet, 90, 92, 170
Street Fighting Man, 123, 125
Street Legal
  (Dylan), 16
Street Queen, 39
Streets of Fire, 79, 83
Streets of Philadelphia, 135, 142
Student Prince
  (Asbury Park), 31
Sugarland, 109, 117
Summer on Signal Hill, 117
Summit Theatre
  (Houston), 85
Sun City, 109
Sundance Blues Band, 31
Sunday Times, The, 70, 71, 102, 103
Surprise, Surprise, 161, 162
Sweden, 72, 101, 125, 131, 141, 152, 153, 160, 204, 211
Sweet Melinda, 29
Switzerland, 101, 141, 214
Swoop Man, 117
Sydney, 124, 152, 168, 196
Syracuse, 124
Tacoma, 131
Take 'Em as They Come, 91, 92, 142
Talk to Me, 79, 109, 166
Tallent, Garry, 14, 26, 31, 32, 37, 38, 39, 40, 42, 44, 45, 46, 47, 48, 49, 52, 57, 63, 64, 65, 66, 78, 81, 82, 90, 93, 94, 95, 96, 97, 114, 117, 118, 119, 129, 136, 137, 145, 149, 155, 156, 161, 174, 175
Taylor, James, 154
Taylor, Livingston, 58
Tellone, Albany, 45
Tempe, 99, 170, 203
Tennessee, 124, 142, 163
Tenth Avenue Freeze-Out, 32, 60, 63, 65, 72, 123, 136, 140, 166
Terry's Song, 156
Texas, 52, 85, 107, 142
That's What You Get, 24
The Losin' Kind, 107
The Time That Never Was, 92
Theiss, George, 23, 24, 172, 176
Then She Kissed Me, 160
Things Ain't That Way, 128
This Hard Land, 107, 115, 135, 136
This is Your Sword, 169
This Land Is Your Land, 101, 102, 112
This Life, 161, 162
This Time It's for Real, 109
Thomas, Rufus, 52
Thompson, Ray, 69
Thrill Hill Recording, 139, 156, 161, 174, 196
Thrill Hill Recording - Stone Hill Studio
  (Colts Neck, NJ), 139, 174, 196
Thrill Hill Recording - Thrill Hill East
  (Rumson, NJ), 126, 139, 154
Thrill Hill Recording - Thrill Hill West
  (Los Angeles), 126, 136, 139
Thunder Road, 57, 61, 63, 65, 66, 69, 71
Thundercrack, 42, 46, 51, 168
Ties That Bind - The River Collection
  (box set), 90, 92, 99, 195
Ties That Bind, The
  (1979 album), 87, 88, 92, 170
Ties That Bind, The (Song), 88, 90, 91, 93, 94, 142
Tiger Rose, 137
Time, 71
Times, The, 66
Tinker West, Carl, 28, 29, 30, 31, 32
Tokyo, 124
Tokyo (Song), 44, 53
Tomorrow Never Knows, 161, 162
Toronto, 85, 101, 142, 163, 170

Tougher Than the Rest, 127, 129
Toulon, 137
Tower Theatre
  (Philadelphia), 72
Townshend, Pete, 102, 103
Tracks, 46, 47, 64, 79, 91, 111, 115, 120, 128, 137, 139, 141, 160
Tramps Nightclub
  (NYC), 136
Trapped, 103
Trenton, 173
Triangle Song, 80
True Love is Hard to Come By, 117
Trump, Donald, 171, 176
Tucker, George, 56
Tunnel of Love, 126, 127, 129, 130, 131, 134, 151, 209, 211, 212, 213, 214, 215, 216, 217, 218
Tunnel of Love (Song), 126, 153
Turin, 131, 163, 218, 219
TV Movie, 109, 115
Twist and Shout, 72, 100, 101, 131, 167
Two Faces, 128, 130
Two For the Road, 128
Two Hearts, 39, 91, 94, 95, 123
Two Hearts in True Waltz Time, 39
Tyrell, Soozie, 14, 115, 121, 136, 137, 145, 146, 148, 149, 151, 152, 155, 156, 158, 161
U2, 102
Under the Big Sky, 117
Under the Boardwalk, 93
Uniondale, 100, 131, 203, 204
United Centre
  (Chicago), 142
United Kingdom, 41, 85, 101, 102, 122, 137, 159, 160, 166, 168
University of Kentucky, 51
University of Maryland, 42
University of Michigan, 99
University of Princeton, 85
University of Richmond, 29
Unsatisfied Heart, 117
Upstage Club
  (Asbury Park), 26, 27, 30, 31
Used Cars, 106, 110, 111, 113, 116
Utah, 142
Valentine's Day, 128, 130
Van Zandt, Steven, 14, 17, 24, 27, 29, 30, 31, 36, 40, 41, 60, 63, 67, 69, 71, 72, 75, 77, 78, 80, 87, 88, 90, 93, 94, 96, 97, 100, 107, 108, 109, 114, 118, 119, 120, 123, 124, 125, 132, 137, 139, 140, 145, 149, 155, 156, 158, 161, 165, 167, 168, 170, 172, 174, 175, 177, 194, 195
Vancouver, 85, 152, 159
Verb, The
  (BBC Radio 3), 96
Vico Equense (Naples), 20
Vienna, 141, 163, 219
Vietnam Veterans of America
  Foundation, 104
Vietnam War, 17, 21, 22, 27, 39, 104, 107, 113, 137, 169
Villa Park
  (Birmingham), 131, 209
Village Voice, The, 55, 84, 151
Vineyard, Tex, 23
Virginia, 29, 32
Visitation at Fort Horn, 37, 39
Vivino, Jerry, 145
Voice of America, 109
Vote for Change, 154
Wages of Sin, 107, 110, 115, 120, 168
Waitin' on a Sunny Day, 145, 146, 152
Waldorf-Astoria Hotel
  (NYC), 140
Walk Like a Man, 21, 127, 129
Walking in the Street, 64
Walking the Dog, 52
Walking Through Midnight, 129
Wall, The, 22, 169
Walter Kerr Theatre
  (NYC), 172
War, 125, 141
Warren, Patrick, 161
Washington, 142
Washington DC, 58, 68, 104, 141, 152, 154, 159, 163, 164
Way, The, 80
We Shall Overcome, 155
We Shall Overcome: the Seeger Sessions, 155
Wear My Ring Around Your Neck, 72
Weinberg, Jay, 163
Weinberg, Max, 14, 55, 63, 64, 65, 78, 81, 82, 83, 90, 94, 95, 97, 103, 114,

117, 118, 119, 120, 126, 129, 130,
145, 146, 147, 148, 149, 155, 156,
158, 160, 161, 163, 164, 165, 173,
174, 175
Wembley Arena
   (London), 16, 102, 141, 152, 158, 203,
   209, 210
Wembley Stadium
   (London), 125, 131, 132, 168, 170,
   209, 210, 211
Wes Farrell Organisation, 32
West Chester College, 41, 56
West Long Branch, 60
West Side Story, 48
Western Stars, 172
What Love Can Do, 161, 162
Wheeler, Harold, 37, 38
When You Need Me, 128
When You Walk in the Room, 69, 72
When You're Alone, 128, 130
Where the Bands Are, 91, 92, 167
Whisky a Go Go Club
   (Los Angeles), 88
Whitetown, 92
Who, The, 16, 24, 140
Who'll Stop the Rain, 100, 101, 103, 104
Wild Billy's Circus Story, 42, 46, 48,
   137, 160
Wild, the Innocent and the E Street
   Shuffle, The, 43, 45, 47, 50, 53, 54,
   55, 56, 57, 159, 164, 173, 194
William Davis, 117
Williams, Hank, 96, 112
Williams, Richard, 41, 42, 122
Wind and the Rain, The, 29
Wings for Wheels, 50
Winterland Arena
   (San Francisco), 85, 203
Winterreise, 157
Wisconsin, 142
Wish, The, 128
Without You, 135
WNEW-FM, 68, 85
Worcester
   (MA), 131
Workin' On It, 117
Working on a Dream, 161
Working on a Dream (Song), 161, 162
Working on the Highway, 106, 107, 115,
   117, 118
Worlds Apart, 145, 147
Wreck on the Highway, 91, 93, 96, 97,
   99, 101, 106, 170
Wrecking Ball, 172
Wrestler, The, 161, 162
Wrong Side of the Street, 79
Wyoming, 112
You Can Look (But You Better Not
   Touch), 88, 91, 92, 95
You Mean So Much to Me, 109
You'll be Comin' Down, 156, 157
You're Missing, 144, 146, 149
Young Americans, 42
Young, Neil, 121, 154
Youngstown, 140, 142
Your Love is All Around Me, 117
Your Own Worst Enemy, 156, 157
Zaragoza, 141, 215
Zero and Blind Terry, 44, 46, 47
Zevon, Warren, 173
Zimbabwe, 132
Zimny, Thom, 71, 161
Zurich, 101, 141, 214

www.ingramcontent.com/pod-product-compliance
Lightning Source LLC
Chambersburg PA
CBHW030257100526
44590CB00012B/431